Lightning & Thunder
A Miracle Love Story

ALBERT LYNN CLARK

DEDICATION

To my wife, Carolyn Clark who humored me when I spent hours at the computer working from home for the US Air Force, writing, searching the internet, reading my email, and sharing her life and family with me.

This book details our life together, God's miracles we saw every day. Our adventures and experiences around the world. Unfortunately, I spend most of the time describing what I did while she stayed home making the best wife, companion, friend, and mother anyone could. It is very unusual to find such a good woman. I wish I could write this book from her perspective, but she never complained or bragged about what she did while I was off working for most of our life together. I cannot begin to know all her thoughts and desires, but I know she truly loved me and would sacrifice anything for her family and me.

Carolyn was dedicated to me and the kids with very little consideration for herself. She always made us feel that her happiness was in direct proportion to our happiness.

I don't believe that any couple had a better marriage. We were married for 45 years before God took her away.

ACKNOWLEDGMENTS

Thank you to the education I received. Thank you to all the science fiction, mystery and thriller authors out there. Thank you for my 33 first cousins who spent days and weeks discussing strange things about science, possible futures, and sharing their books.

First Published for Print February 2017

ISBN-13: 978-1541151994
ISBN-10: 1541151992

CONTENTS

1 It Began with Lightning

I had just gotten back from the Vietnam War. I had applied for a Date of Separation (DOS) just over a year earlier and received orders to go to Southeast Asia dated 4 hours earlier than the date time stamp on my request. Let me explain. When an officer enters the United States Air Force he signs up for twenty years of active duty and a reserve recall commitment until age sixty. Technically, after four years of active duty an officer can request a Date of Separation to get out of active duty at the end of the four years or any year thereafter. However, they can also be recalled to active duty until their sixtieth birthday. Since the only reason I had signed up for the Air Force was to not be known as a draft dodger I never planned on more than the minimum four years of active duty. I actually had a federal civil service job that was being held for me during that four years. My intent was to get out and return to my civil service job in Oklahoma.

However, the Air Force had magically beat me to the punch with the orders for Southeast Asia which locked me in for another year. When I reapplied for a Date of Separation, they locked me in for another year because I just had a "cushy" overseas assignment. That was within the standard rules. This also meant they would no longer hold the civilian job beyond the four years that had already passed.

Anyway, I now found myself stationed as a Nuclear Ordnance Supply Officer (NOSO) at Blytheville Air Force Base in far north eastern Arkansas. I knew nothing about being a Nuclear Ordnance Supply Officer other than I had learned the manual inventory record keeping for conventional munitions while a Munitions Accountable Supply Officer in Southeast Asia. I had never attended the Air Force school for either job, but here I was. I knew no one. I had planned on being back in Oklahoma at my civil service job working with people I already knew. Also, since I had hired into a civil service job with automatic promotions to GS-11, I could forget that too, because I only had automatic re-hiring for four years and it had been five.

After having been shot at, routinely going out with our Explosive Ordnance Disposal team to destroy faulty bombs and fuses off base into the jungle in Southeast Asia, going on Temporary Duty (TDY) to several bases in South Vietnam and traveling by cargo plane to Saigon, Okinawa, other bases in Thailand, and walked the streets unarmed by myself in those places, I had no fear of anything. No, I would not say no fear, just pretending to have no fear and never having anything bad happen to me. The only time I was truly scared was when I was expecting many truckloads of munitions being delivered one day and there were none when I got to the bomb dump. I called the US Army guard post outside the gate and was told there was a serious problem.

I went to the guard post and saw a couple of hundred foreign national trucks loaded with munitions and the gate closed with no sign of the Army guards. I drove up to the guard shack, parked, walked down the row of sandbags to the door to their sandbagged bunker and was apprised of the situation. "Captain Clark, glad you are here, we are in trouble."

"How's that?"

"When we went to open the gates all the trucks started jockeying to rush the gate at once. We have a limit of 6 trucks at a time. We were lucky to get the gates closed again. Then they started pulling guns out of their trucks and we took shelter here in our bunker. We phoned for assistance but you are the only one to show up."

"Have you tried talking to them?"

"We're not leaving the bunker until we get some re-enforcements."

"Let me see what I can do." I started toward the door.

"Sir, you can't go out there, there are about a hundred guns trained on us and no one wants to be first to start shooting."

"Somebody has to do something, we need those munitions for today's aircraft missions." I went on out the door, stopped just outside the sandbagged entry and made a show of propping my M-16 automatic rifle against the outside of the sandbags then took off my gun belt and laid it on top of the sandbag wall that was only about 4 feet high at this point.

I walked to the gate, signaled the Army to remotely release the gate, walked through to the outside of the fence, closed the gate, signaled for it to be locked again, and walked toward the wall of trucks. "Who here speaks English?" Silence. I could feel and see the guns being pointed at me instead of the Army bunker. "We aren't going anywhere until someone speaks up. You can see I am not armed as I left my guns back there on the sandbags. Let me know what the problem is."

"I speak English. We have no one in charge, but your Army people in the bunker locked the gate and started pointing guns at us so we got our guns and pointed at them."

"So you want to get unloaded and be on your way."

"Yes, will you open the gates and let us in?

The Army guys were doing their job. We can only allow in six trucks at a time. When they are unloaded, they can leave and we let in another six trucks. They said everyone was trying to go at once."

"We all want to get unloaded and everyone wanted to be first."

"Well, we will only let in six trucks at a time. I will choose the first six. Tell everyone what we are doing and then I will select who goes first, but everyone has to put their guns back in their trucks."

"Not going to happen. No one wants to put their guns back."

"Tell everyone, to look at what their trucks are carrying. I don't think anyone wants to shoot and maybe hit what you are carrying. Those are bombs, fuses for bombs, ammunition, grenades. The first shot that hits the wrong place and this whole area from the bunker to the highway will be one smoking hole in the ground. Tell the rest what I said, have them put those guns away, line up in an orderly line so the first six trucks can get back out when they are empty and I will start the unloading process."

I could tell he translated correctly as a number of the armed drivers looked at their loads and quickly put their guns up and started their engines with some trucks backing up, other turning around and heading back toward the highway to join the line of trucks.

I pointed at the English speaker and said, "You are the first truck because you talked with me. I know a lot of you drivers can speak English well enough but you did speak with me and translated, so you are first, then you and you, and you. I picked out the six trucks and they started pulling up in the line at the gate in the order I chose, then as I picked out the second six trucks they started jockeying behind the first six. I turned and headed back to the gate.

The Army team chief came out of the bunker, met me, and opened the gate wide. When the gate was fully open I made the motion for the trucks to start coming. When the first six were inside the gate, I held up my hand and the rest of the trucks stopped. The line behind them was now shifting into an orderly line back toward the highway leaving one side of the road open for departing trucks when they were unloaded.

"Captain Clark, I can't believe that you got everything under control like that. How did you do it?"

"I convinced them they did not want bullets hitting their loads of munitions and killing everyone. I then picked the ones that seemed to be the worst cases to be the first six and the second six trucks by how menacing they looked. As you can see, once that impasse was broken, and word passed down the line everyone got with the program. I will leave behind the second six trucks if everything looks okay."

"That had to take a lot of nerve to go out there in front of a hundred guns."

"I figured when they saw a different uniform from yours they might figure out I was an officer and no one really wanted to start shooting anyway. I think everything is under control."

I walked back to the sandbags, strapped on my handgun, slung the M-16 over my shoulder and watched the first six trucks turn in their paperwork to the Army troops and proceed on to the Air Force gate slowly and orderly. Because of a slight hill we could not see the Air Force munitions gate, but by radio, all was orderly. Shortly after, the six trucks returned, the Army gate was opened and as soon as those six trucks were headed for the highway, I motioned for the next six trucks to proceed. I could tell the Army was nervous about the next six, but when the sixth truck in the second group entered and I held up my hand the line of trucks stopped to wait for that second six to be unloaded. I followed that second six back to my office inside the Air Force munitions area.

Apparently, my deed was well known among the Air Force people. I didn't get any medals and didn't deserve any for doing something stupid and really scary. But I was single.

Now I was back in the states and that past year was behind me. My civil service return rights had disappeared and here I was rudderless in the world.

There I was feeling very put down and lonely watching a severe lightning storm holding onto the metal balcony rail on the second floor of the apartment building where I rented. It was after midnight and I thought I was the only one outside watching all the lightning, smelling the ozone in the air, and feeling the thunder. Then I looked to my left and the lightning flashed very brightly and I saw a small young woman outside her apartment holding onto that same balcony rail wa

tching the lightning. Magnetism made me want to meet her. I don't know why, but I was instantly drawn to her. God's little miracles that happen everyday that we may not recognize at the time. Sort of like seeing a ball bouncing out in the street and hitting the brakes before the unseen kid runs out in front of you. If you had not reacted ahead of time you might have hit the kid. Getting run off a highway into the ditch to avoid an accident and not hitting anything while driving through a ditch and back onto the road with nothing except a racing heart. Those and many more have happened to me and I gave a little thanks to God that he protected me.

Now I am not that spontaneous and really at that time of my life, shy. I never dated much in high school or college. In high school my goal was college so I dated very little because back in the fifties and early sixties many girls were looking for potential husbands to marry as soon as they finished high school with bonus points if they got married before finishing high school and being pregnant when they got their diploma.

I guess that was okay for those guys that were going to become common labor in the town where they went to school and for the girls that never wanted to leave their hometown but continue living with their family and friends around them. Most of my friends were destined to be that manual labor. They were good friends, but back in the early sixties before the Vietnam War, guys did not think that much about going on to college.

However, in my family, college was an extension of high school. Not graduating from college in my family was as stigmatized as dropping out of school in junior high. Matter of fact, my thirty-three first cousins and their children now have over forty-five degrees from the University of Oklahoma, seventeen from Oklahoma State and another dozen from Texas Tech. So college came before marriage.

It was okay for those guys that were going to take over their father's business, be it a farm or gas station. Again their girls would be satisfied being a farmer's wife or gas station owner's wife and wanted to stay at home.

I did not want to get saddled with a homebody. I had not planned on joining the military when in high school, but I did plan on getting my college degree before I got serious about a girl. The pill had been invented, but in my day, if the girl got pregnant you were expected to get married.

I had met two of the three single young women in my apartment. Both were college graduates and attractive. One was a long haired blond that worked for the local bank and the other was a slender brunette that was a primary school teacher. The day after I moved into my apartment I was working on my two seater sports car with a roll bar to extract a better tune and more speed. It had been in storage for the year I was in Southeast Asia. These two girls had come out to talk with me as I worked. I had not seen this third single woman of the apartment building. Story of my life, I just don't walk up and talk to girls or women, they come to me. Here I was going to introduce myself without her coming to me. Different from the start, but something drove me down the balcony to talk with her.

I walked on down by her. "Hello, I am your new neighbor a couple of apartments down."

"Oh! Hello. I didn't see you walk up. How long have you been standing there?"

"Here, just a couple of seconds, but I was down in front of my apartment watching the storm for the last thirty minutes or so."

"I'm, Carolyn. What's your name?"

"Al Clark."

"I just love the lightning."

"I always have, we have something in common already, let's get married." Why did I say something crazy like that? What made me say that. She was very short whereas the few girls I had dated were five six or so. She was not as attractive as the other two girls I met and almost ignored. I thought to myself, what if she took me serious?

"What did you say?"

"I said, 'Let's get married and we can watch lightning together for years."

"Yeah, sure. The lightning is about over and I have to get to bed since I have to get up and go to work in the morning. So, if you will excuse me."

"What kind of work do you do?"

"I'm a social worker for Arkansas social services."

"And?"

"When people ask for welfare, I help them fill out the paperwork and do a little background investigation then make my recommendation and turn it over to my boss for approval of food stamps or whatever. I heard that a single Air Force officer had just moved in, so you must be him."

"I guess I am. I just arrived from Southeast Asia."

"That's nice, but I really have to get some rest so if you will excuse me?"

"I'll be watching for you during the next storm."

2 Getting to Know Her

She went into her apartment and closed the door. That was my first meeting with the love of my life. She was far from the normal strikingly pretty girls I had dated in the past. Don't get me wrong, I had never dated that much in my life, but I usually went for the pretty ones that every other guy did.

I went to work and wondered why I had asked this girl to marry me, even as a joke. I arranged for some old junk furniture be delivered from the air base to my apartment. It was junk furniture and none too clean. It was furniture that was left behind in base housing when the military families had been reassigned and just left it behind for people like me without any furniture to use. I had a chrome and Formica kitchen table and three chrome chairs, one of which had to have bolts tightened so it would stand on its own. A brown really old sofa with cushions that had pretty much seen some heavy people that had mashed the cushions, but at least it had no tears in it. (Have you ever considered how hard English is. "She had tears in her eyes. The cloth had tears in it." My sofa was not crying.)

The brunette school teacher came by to see my furniture and offered to let me borrow her vacuum cleaner to clean up the sofa. I cleaned out under the cushions finding candy wrappers and coins and a lot of dirt that I vacuumed up with my borrowed vacuum cleaner. I kept the bed frame and credenza and bed end table brought by the base, but rejected the mattress and box springs as unhealthy to sleep on. When I came back from downtown buying a new box springs and mattress (cheap but new), the two attractive girls were in my apartment cleaning the credenza and end table for me. I had not locked the door and they let themselves in. They had also washed the plates, glasses, and cups loaned from the air base.

They had finished their cleaning, but wanted to stay and talk. "I'm sorry, all I have is tap water to offer you a drink. How can I repay you for cleaning everything for me?"

The blond said, "I'll go get some beer." I don't remember her name, but will call her Jane. The brunette was slender but very busty and named Kelly.

Kelly asked, "So what do you do at the base?"

"I'm a supply officer."

"You mean airplane parts and office paper?"

"Yeah, something like that." I did not want to tell them I was accountable for a couple of hundred nuclear weapons and would be working around them every day."

"So did you carry a gun in Southeast Asia?"

Jane came in with three bottles of Budwiser, set them on the table and sat on the rickety chair that I had put back together. "Nice furniture. Is it safe?"

"It is on loan from the base. The only thing I own is the stereo that I had in college and my car. Is the furniture safe? I think so, I tightened the bolts on that chair you are sitting on so I don't think it will collapse, but I wouldn't try leaning back too hard."

"I interrupted your answer to Kelly's question. Did you carry a gun over there?"

I may talk around the truth, but I will not lie. "Yes, I carried a handgun and an M-16, but never had to use either one."

Jane said, "I have met a lot of military working at the bank and most of them did not carry guns over there. Why did you?"

Kelly interjected, "Were you just a supply officer over there too, or did you do something else?"

I did not want to tell them that I controlled all the bombs and bullets for the air base over there so I avoided the whole truth. "My supply station was six miles off base so

I had to commute to my supply office daily. We had security at the gates, but we never had any attacks. Everyone that worked off base had to carry guns, just in case."

"Do you carry a gun here?"

I still wanted the subject to stay away from nuclear weapons so I moved past the question. "Before I went over there I got specialized training on handling weapons, just in case. I had to take the full security police gun firing test getting marksman in both handgun and long gun, but I never shot at anything alive. I don't think I have to worry about anyone breaking into my supply office here which is on base." Again, almost a lie. My storage area was miles from the main base closer to the B-52 alert pad than the rest of the air base. I did not tell them that I shared the gate shack to the storage area with security police whose main job was to guard the nuclear weapons storage area and send roving patrols twenty-four hours a day around the square mile of storage area. Every building had an alarm back to that security office. Part of my job was to tell security to disarm a building every time I authorized someone to enter or leave a building. Not every building had nuclear weapons. Some had plastic explosives and convention ammunition including a few million rounds of twenty millimeter shells for the tail guns of the B-52s there. By sharing the gate shack anyone coming or going had to have my permission to go through the double gates. Every vehicle was checked underneath for someone or some thing trying to sneak in. Just getting into my office required security police to remotely unlock a personnel gate to get into a fenced area between that gate and security where people had to either work there or have my permission to enter either the security or my office.

"What do you do Jane, besides work at the bank?"

Jane said, "My job is a loan officer at the bank. People come to me to borrow money. I help them fill out the loan request papers, check their credentials, review their request and collateral they have for the loans and then pass the paperwork to a vice-president to approve or disapprove. I keep them talking while they wait or give them a time to check back if it is a bigger loan and then escort them to the door. A car loan on a new car may take thirty minutes, but a house loan takes days or sometimes weeks."

"So Kelly, how is teaching the little kids?"

"Oh, I love the kids. It is the parents that sometimes cause stress. Sometimes when a kid is not doing well, I have to call in the parents to try to find out why or explain to them that little Johnny needs some special help at home to keep up. The parents usually don't like hearing that little Johnny is not keeping up and blame me. Not all parents, some take on the responsibility of helping their child and I get to see that child turn around and excel."

"That sounds stressful and rewarding. I guess I should tell you that my father has been both a teacher and a school superintendent all of his life. I grew up as a teacher's kid."

"And how was that?"

"Every time we moved to a new school the local bully had to take my measure and the other kids distrusted me as a potential tattle-tail. It usually meant a fight. I didn't always win, but garnered some respect."

"Didn't you tell your father?"

"No, and that is what gained me some respect from the other students. In fact, usually that bully ended up being a good friend or at least mutual respect. What do you do around here for fun?"

"Not much. There is no movie theater except at the base and you have to go on base with a military member to see a show or you drive down to Memphis. You do not want to go into a bar around here. Again, go to Memphis. It has everything you need. All we have here is a grocery store and a pharmacy. "

3 The Invitation

About that time, Carolyn came in the open door. "I just bought myself a color television set so we have something to do Saturday night. Miss America will be broadcast live in color so everyone is invited down to my apartment to watch. That is at 7PM. Bring snacks and your own drinks."

Jane said, "I'll bake some cookies."

Kelly said, "I'll bring some chips and dip."

"I'll bring some cokes and seven-up or whatever soft drinks you think would be good. What about alcohol? I can go by the class six store on base and buy it cheap."

Carolyn said, "Vodka for me."

Jane said, "I'll bring beer."

Kelly said, "School teachers can't get caught drinking so I will just have soft drinks."

I said, "Rum and Vodka then. Who all is invited?"

"Pass it around, I am inviting only those single people that live here in the apartments. You might bring your own chairs as I don't have much to sit on."

The little meeting broke up then as an ambulance came to one of the one story two bedroom apartments on the street. Everyone went out to the balcony. Jane said, "I think that is the Lobowinces' place. Maybe its time for her baby?"

"Let's go over there and see."

Carolyn stayed behind putting a delicate hand on my forearm. "You will come won't you?"

"Absolutely!" Her touch was electrifying. She was not attractive like Jane and Kelly, but I had to fight not embracing her and kissing her right then and there."

Carolyn followed the other two girls down the stairs and across the parking lot to see if a new baby was coming. I watched her go stupefied by my reaction to her touch. I have dated a number of girls, but none that I was so attracted to. There was never any electricity there before.

4 Experienced?

In high school I was the date for the May Queen, the Homecoming Queen and just about every other high school Queen. One girl I remember well, Cynthia. She was the homecoming queen and one of the most attractive girls in the two thousand kids in my high school. She had to dance with the homecoming king and his court and we only got to dance a couple of times. We had to leave to get her home by 10PM even though the party would go on until midnight. As she explained to me on the way to her parents mansion. "This is the first time I have been alone with a guy. My parents are very strict. I'm sorry I didn't get to spend more time with you at the dance, but I was obligated to do my thing as Queen."

"Don't worry about it. I enjoyed watching you and I danced with a few other girls too."

"I saw you, but you didn't look too happy about it."

"Who wouldn't want to spend the evening with the prettiest girl in the school?"

"Thank you. I don't consider myself pretty. I'm not even sure why I was voted Queen. I was surprised my parents let me attend the dance at all. I have never been to a dance and they only let me go because you agreed to be my date. Apparently, my parents really like your dad or they would not have approved of letting you take me home. I'm also sorry we have to go straight home. It's not like I am a prisoner, its just that they have big plans for me going to college and taking over the business after graduation. They don't want me side tracked by some guy out after money."

I walked her to her door, which opened before we got there. Her father said, "Thank you for escorting my daughter, maybe you will see each other in college next year. No dating though. She is not allowed until she has taken on the responsibility of my company."

"No problem, Sir. I was honored to be her escort tonight, and yes, I will also be getting my degree."

I drove back for the last two hours of the dance to dance with some of the girls that had no dates for the evening. I was thinking that I didn't really know Cynthia. I had no idea that she lived in a mansion and had never dated. I had always thought of her as one of the girls that dated all the jocks in school. Come to think of it. I had never seen her at any of the school dances so maybe she had dated college boys, but no, apparently, she just was not allowed to date. What a waste. Maybe I would see her at college next year and I could ask her out in return for her asking me to be her escort tonight. How would her parents keep her from dating next year?

When in Southeast Asia, more specifically Thailand and Vietnam it was common for the GIs and even many of the officers to sleep with the local girls for a small amount of money. When the average local male is lucky to make twenty-five dollars a month, a young girl could turn several hundred a month for renting out their bodies. Mostly they relied on abortions for birth control. Morning after pills or whatever. I would never pay for sex. Just a thing with me. Besides various forms of venereal disease was common and I usually knew several people I worked with taking tetracycline for it. No thanks. That is not to say that I was not roped into strip shows from time to time.

One time in Saigon some co-workers invited me to go down for dinner in downtown. We went to a nice upscale restaurant and the next thing I know girls are sitting with us. I was polite and didn't want to embarrass those American's that invited me, but the next thing I know they had us checking into a hotel. I paid for a room and then let them go on upstairs while I hung back with the attractive Asian girl that had latched onto me. I gave her fifty dollars in scrip. Let me explain, we were not allowed to use dollars downtown we were given what was called script that the locals could change at the banks for their money.

It was late, almost the ten o'clock curfew, but I made my excuses and headed out for where I think the base was. I was hopelessly lost as my companions had taken me here and there. I found one of those strange things where you sit in front and the bicycle rider sits in back peddling along. I managed to tell him I wanted to go to the base. He said in his halting English that it was past curfew and he could get in trouble for just having me as a rider. I gave him twenty dollars in scrip and he took me within a few blocks of the gate and warned me that he could go no further and that I should just go to a hotel he would recommend and I could safely approach the gate in the morning after daylight. I thanked him and walked to the gate. I was wearing my uniform and my new captain's bars. The Vietnamese guards pointed at me and then pointed their mounted machine guns at me as I pretended to calmly just walk up to the gate and wait for it to be opened. I was correct that they would not gun down a white officer in uniform regardless of being past curfew.

5 Apprehension

That night in 1970 in Blytheville, Arkansas, I went out to the base and ate a dinner at the Officer's Club alone. I thought, "I won't do this again. Tomorrow before I come home I will stop by the commissary and stock my apartment with some food to eat there."

When I came home Friday night I had bought a dozen TV dinners, a loaf of bread, Miracle Whip, mustard, ketchup, some frozen French fries, a quart of Vodka, a fifth of Rum, a fifth of Jim Beam bourbon, some Coca Cola, and 7-UP for the Miss America Watch Party. "I wonder just how many single people are in this apartment complex. I wish it was just going to be Carolyn and I, but she invited all the singles in the complex. Why am I so obsessed with wanting to be with Carolyn. That makes no sense. She doesn't hold a candle in looks compared to the other two girls I have met. She doesn't have a great figure like Kelly. I like Jane's long blond hair. I have not even had a chance to talk with Carolyn much and won't have much chance tomorrow night with everyone else in her apartment. Whereas Jane and Kelly had more or less given me a green light, Carolyn had invited me to watch a TV show because she invited all the other singles and Jane and Kelly were with me when she did it. So why was I attracted to Carolyn when there were two good looking girls that were being very friendly?

6 Saturday Night

I went down to Carolyn's apartment at 6PM an hour early supposedly to deliver the Vodka, Run, Bourbon, and soft drinks, but really hoping to see Carolyn alone before the crowd came. There would be a crowd. There was a single lieutenant in the apartment between mine and Carolyn's that I had met Saturday morning, Jim Eversong. He had been invited and was going. He said that Jane and Kelly would definitely be there as would a second lieutenant John Filtch that did not live there, but might as well because he hung around the apartments when off duty so much he should have moved in. He came to all the parties, so apparently, Carolyn had invited John too. There were also about five others that I had not met that were also coming. There was one couple that had been living together for three years in a two-bedroom single level that were still not married.

Carolyn's apartment door was open so I knocked on the open door and said, "Knock, knock, your friendly bootlegger bringing booze for tonight."

Carolyn was back in her bedroom but yelled, "Come on in Hal, and just set it on the counter. I will be out shortly. I was out shopping and just got home. Just have a seat on my sofa."

That gave me a chance to see her apartment that was spotlessly clean. Her "sofa" was a metal folding camping cot with a thick piece of foam on top of a thin cot mattress. It was covered with a homemade fitted cover that came to the floor on all four sides and had some homemade bolsters for a back, of course with no arms since there was nothing to support an arm on a camping cot. The fabric was a mixture of mostly red with splotches of yellows going to oranges. Her dining table was a card table with two folding metal chairs. She had a wooden crate for a coffee table covered in the same fabric to match the "sofa". Her card table had a mixture of cheap miss-matched glassware. There was an overhead light plus a chrome free standing floor lamp with a two swivel lamps with one pointed up and one pointed at one end of the sofa.

My thoughts were that Carolyn must just be starting out. I had placed her age at close to mine, mid-twenties, so I wondered about her poor furniture. At least her furniture was clean versus I almost did not want to sit on my old ratty furniture I borrowed from the base. Her color TV was against the wall on a metal folding TV tray. There was a matching TV tray on either side of the "sofa". Each of those two had ashtrays. You have to remember back in the sixties and early seventies most young people smoked cigarettes. My parents did not smoke, but they kept ashtrays for those that did and they were born before World War One. There was no taboo against smoking back then. In fact, in college, I had started smoking because the classrooms had built in ashtrays at every seat. Even a couple of churches had ashtrays on the back of the pew ahead. The movie theaters had ashtrays on the back of every seat in the theater.

Carolyn came out of the bedroom wearing just a hint of makeup which I had not seen on her before. She smelled of soap and shampoo with a hint of some perfume that I later learned was "Wind Song", her favorite. It was warm and she was wearing almost knee length purple shorts and a short (not bare midriff) flowered purple top to match. She looked radiant. "Hi Hal. I was hoping you would make it.

Can I get you anything to drink, since you brought most of it?"

"No thanks. I came early to avoid the crowd, make my delivery and see if there was anything I could do to help."

"I think we are set to go, everyone should be showing up soon. So, how are you liking Blytheville?"

"I have met some friendly people, but it is not much to look at."

"That's Arkansas. Blytheville is one of the poorest cities in the poorest county in Arkansas. I stay busy because sixty percent of the people are getting some form of state help. There used to be lots of jobs for farming, but with farm equipment, and especially the cotton picking machines many have lost their farm jobs and there is not much else for them to do. They are not educated and have no experience even if there were jobs here. They don't have money to go somewhere else for jobs. A good example is that I have a client this week that I was told about. I went where they said he was and he was living in some old cardboard appliance boxes he had taped together as a one room house. His heat last winter was burning a fire in the dirt floor of his boxes. He worked for the same farm since he was fourteen and when he hit eighty-five the farmer had kept him on and housed and fed him for years with no job. The farmer got worried he would die on the farm and rather than explain his death just told him to go live in town. He never paid into social security and paid no taxes as the farmer did not have a job for him for the last twenty years and just housed and fed him. Now he was sick. I took him to a doctor in my car and the doctor gave him prescriptions for one hundred twenty-three dollars worth. The biggest welfare check I could get him was seventy-three dollars a month. He told me, "Miss Carolyn, I surely do appreciate you trying to help me, but with seventy-three dollars a month I have to continue living here and not buy those medicines. At least I can get me some new shoes, these wore through a year ago."

"I feel sorry for some of the older folks like that. What makes me mad is the young people taking advantage of the system."

"How's that Carolyn, by the way I like your name. My middle name is "Lynn" L Y N N, and yours is CaroLYN." Carolyn blushed. Just then Jane and Kelly came in with their offerings and that was the end of our conversation. Everyone quickly filled the room with some bringing their own folding or kitchen chairs and others camping out on the floor. I was introduced to everyone as "Hal" and I corrected Carolyn as I went by "AL" A - L. No 'H".

"Okay, 'AL' no 'H', you know Jim and Jane and Kelly. This is John Filtch from the base. He doesn't live here at night, but you can count on him being here if he is not at work or his on-base housing." I am terrible with names and I did not remember any new names that evening.

Carolyn stayed busy playing host, getting drinks, refilling snack trays, emptying ashtrays, almost before people could flip their ashes. A cigarette never rested for more than ten seconds before the ashtray disappeared to be replaced with a clean one. By the time the Miss America show was over and everyone had left, Carolyn had just about cleaned everything up. She had hardly talked with anyone except to offer refills and clean anything anyone left sit too long.

"Can I do anything to help?"

"No, I am about finished. If you will excuse me I go to an early church service in the morning. I think you met all the singles in the apartments and a couple of surprise guests. Not surprising, anytime anyone gives a party there are usually some uninvited guests that show up. A lot of young officers know that the apartments frequently have open parties on Saturday nights and there is not much else that goes on in this town."

"Can we sit and talk for awhile?"

"I would rather not. I don't mean to be rude, but I don't know you yet and someone might think there was something going on if I let you stay. I will see you around next week."

"How about tomorrow?"

"Tomorrow, as I said, I go to early church service, stay for the adult meeting and then I have to do my laundry to get ready to go to work Monday. Plus I have to return the serving dishes that got left. I'll be seeing you around."

I said goodnight. I thought there was a spark there, but I had just been given the bum's rush out the door. Carolyn seemed to enjoy the party, loved playing host, everyone liked her, but she had not really talked with anyone. She was a mystery to me. I think she liked me. Jane and Kelly seemed to recognize that Carolyn and I had a special spark and stayed clear of me all evening. They were somewhat remote and just one of the guests that all knew each other. Everyone had been friendly with me, but the subject was watching the color TV show of Miss America and the friendly, no money, betting of whom the finalists would be and who would win.

The next morning, Carolyn's faded old fastback Volkswagen was gone. When she said early church I guess she meant it. I had only two rum and cokes and then coke after coke so I was not hung over, but I had slept too late. What the heck, I might as well get ready to go to an eleven o'clock service. I had driven by several churches just driving around the small town of Blytheville. I had sung in the choir of a Methodist church in college so I decided to try them out. After the church service there was the minister and several deacons shaking hands with people as they left. The minister was friendly but two of the deacons held my hand a little too long and asked, "Is there some reason you can't attend the chapel on base. We don't really encourage single military members here. Now if you have a wife, bring her with you next time."

I would not be there again. I did not see Carolyn all the next week although I was watching for her. I did see Jane and Kelly who told me, "We see you really like Carolyn. We just wanted to warn you she does not date. If she is not having the party she comes to our parties and does just what she did last night, act as waitress and clean up crew. We all like her very much and would like to see her have a boyfriend for a change, but I don't think you will have much luck."

"You are serious aren't you? Was I that transparent?"

Kelly said, "Yes, you watched her all night. No one else mattered to you. I'll bet you don't even know who won the Miss America."

Jane enjoined, "If I were you I'd cool it with her. I don't know why, but you will scare her away and we want her to feel comfortable at our parties. If you like her that much play it slow and let her come to you."

Kelly said, "Carolyn has told us that she is seriously thinking of becoming a nun."

"Is she Catholic?"

"No, but she just doesn't date or have any guys over without a crowd at a party. She kids around with the other guys, but last night she didn't kid around with anyone. I think you upset her applecart and confused her. So just don't chase her too hard. Be outside and let her see you, but let her make the moves."

7 The First Miracle

(was the lightning storm the first?)

I did as suggested and put a chair out on the balcony to read my novels when I came home to my apartment from my work at the base. Jane and Kelly were right, Carolyn would drive in from work or shopping and go straight into her apartment and wave as she went in, then on Saturday of the next week she came down to my door and asked, "What are you reading."

"Oh I read mysteries, science fiction, adventure type novels. I don't have a TV yet, so what else can I do. When it gets dark I listen to my records and read."

"I take it you are more comfortable with your job at the base?"

"Yes, I have some great enlisted guys that have taught me my job. It is not all that different than what I have been doing for the last two and half years. The inventory is just a little different."

"Different how?"

"Most of the items are more expensive, but you count them and keep records the same why as before. It is actually much slower paced than in the past, which means I have more time to stay home and read."

"Do you ever fly planes?"

"Not a pilot. I went to pilot training, but ended up as a logistics officer. Long story. So, no, I don't fly any more except as a passenger. When I was in Southeast Asia I traveled around to a number of different bases over there, but in my first real job I could drive my car to places I needed to go for work and in this job everything is right here on this base."

"Say, I was going to cook lasagna tonight, and it will be way too much for me, would you like to come over about six?"

"I would love to. How about I get us some 'Lancers Rose' Wine to go with it?"

"Sounds good, see you at 6."

Wow! Finally maybe I can get a chance to know her better. I rushed out to the class six store on base and bought some wine then took it home, put it in the freezer to cool quickly from the summer heat of driving from the base in an open sports car with no air conditioning. It was September but in Arkansas it is still hot.

When I arrived at her apartment at exactly six she opened the door and ushered me to one of her folding chairs. She had several candles burning. She dished up some of the lasagna on both our plates and handed me a cork screw for the wine. I opened it and poured each of us a fruit jelly jar of wine (she had no wine glasses).

We talked about nothing and everything meaningless while we ate. "This is great lasagna. I would say it was like mother used to make, but she didn't. She was a great baker, but most of our food was pan fried steak, fried pork chops, fried chicken. We would have spaghetti but the hamburger was fried with some tomato sauce and spices over the spaghetti noodles."

"Did your mother work?"

"Not when I was younger, but when I was going into seventh grade, my father went back to college to get a masters degree to help with his teaching job and she went to work as a clerk to provide some extra income. I became the baby sitter for my younger brother."

"So your father is a school teacher?"

"Yes. What about your father?"

"He is mostly a retired farmer. My mother never worked outside the home."

"I feel like I have known you all my life but don't understand why I feel that way."

Carolyn blushed and said nothing.

A light bulb went off. "Have you ever been to Disneyland out in California?"

"Yes, but I was only 12. My father was always working back then so my mother took my brother and I out to California by herself."

"Really? I was there then too when I was 12. My father borrowed an old World War Two trailer made for a jeep and put it behind the car. We put our bags in the trailer, topped it with a mattress and then at night erected a tent on top of the trailer that my sister and I shared. We had a Nash car that made up into a bed for my parents to sleep in."

"You would not catch my mother in a tent. We stayed in hotels. Why did you ask about Disneyland? That was out of the blue."

"I think I saw you and your brother there."

"Oh come on. You would not remember that. And why would you think it was me?"

"I was going to get in line for the Mad Hatter ride and I think I saw you arguing with your brother who was refusing to go with you and said, "Mom said I was not supposed to let you out of my sight. And the Mad Hatter is too childish."

"I was right there within ten feet of that argument. I almost volunteered to ask if you could go with me until your brother said he was not supposed to let you out of his sight. It was a pretty boring ride I couldn't wait for it to end for fear you would be gone when it was over."

"Why would you remember that after thirteen years?"

"Because I thought you were beautiful and felt that I did not want to let you out of my sight again."

"Oh come on. You went on the ride by yourself and never saw me again. I never saw you."

"When I got off the ride I looked for you. I stayed at the ride watching for you and your brother to get off the ride until I decided you were long gone and never rode it. As I walked around the park that day I kept looking. Several times I thought I saw your platinum blond hair beside a taller dark haired boy, but you were always too far away for me to see where you went. Do you remember the crowds? I would get to that spot where I got a glimpse but you were always gone. I tried following for an hour and caught several glimpses way ahead and then another thirty minutes I didn't see you again. I was never sure that platinum blond I was trying to follow was you except at the Mad Hatter ride."

"What about your parents? They just let you go off by yourself?"

"They always trusted me to meet them at a designated place at the designated time. I always had a sense of where I was and how to find locations. Sorta like a homing pigeon."

"That's a good story, but I don't believe it."

8 Serious

"Jane or Kelly, not sure which one said you wanted to be a nun. Why?"

"I hate telling you this when I still hardly know you, but I have known since I was fifteen that I could never have children. I was not allowed to really date. I had to be home at 10PM even on special occasions. Every time I thought a boy might be getting serious I would tell them I could never have children and that would be the end of that. I grew up in small towns where there were lots of farmers who wanted lots of children so I was out. I actually talked to the Catholic Church, but they were not interested in me becoming a nun just because I could not have children."

"So?"

"What SO?"

"So get married and adopt. There are plenty of kids out there that need a mother that can cook."

"Going a little fast aren't you? I have served you one meal and you think I can cook. You don't want children of your own?"

"My job has nothing to do with psychology, but my degree was psychology and I happen to believe children are who they are because of environment not genetics. Oh sure, genetics can be a bad thing, but personality is environment. Intelligence may be primarily environment too. I have known many car mechanics that were whizzes when it came to cars but barely knew how to write their names. I also know people that can do very difficult math problems, but don't know to come in out of the rain. No, I do not mind adopting children. It would be easier for you to not have to go through the childbirth."

"Okay, Al. Note that I called you Al, not Hal. This is getting too serious. I have early church again tomorrow, so let's let things cool off a little, I will do my usual going to church and laundry and I'll see you next week. By the way do you go to church?"

"I sang in a choir all the way through college, but haven't really had the opportunity since. I have been to three churches here in town and they all made it clear that they did not want a single military officer attending their church."

"Why don't you come with me to the Episcopal Church tomorrow morning?"

"Seriously?"

"Yes, they will welcome anyone. I might warn you that the Episcopal Church ritual is very similar to the Catholic Church. We kneel for prayers and have a book of common prayer that we read out of. I'll help you through the service. Want to give it a try?"

"Absolutely. The only time I have been in an Episcopal Church was when a college friend invited me to go to a Christmas midnight service with him. I found it strange with a lot of people crossing themselves like Catholics. Not that I have anything against Catholics, but just could not be directed by the Pope."

"The Episcopal Church doesn't follow the Pope either or take the saints as seriously. Yes, I'm sure any church names saints, but we pray to God and Jesus, not to a saint. Think of an Episcopal Church as a very formal Methodist Church."

"What time do I need to be outside to meet you and what should I wear?"

"Early service starts at 7:30 and we want to be a little early so meet me out by the cars about 7:15. Dressy casual, not a suit and tie, but dress slacks and a nice dress shirt. Some wear ties."

"Okay, I'll be ready."

The next morning I was waiting in the parking lot wearing black dress slacks, a white short sleeve shirt and a paisley tie. I had on my black military dress shoes with a nice shine. I was amazed when she came out. She was dressed up in a light blue skirt with a white ruffled blouse, with makeup that made her look really pretty and had what I would call a doily on her head. I had never seen her with makeup. Over the blouse she was wearing a light blue short jacket type of thing that matched the skirt. As a guy, I know the jacket on a woman was not called a jacket but had some other name. It could never close over her chest and was cut away further at the waist. It was made that way. It looked great!"

"Wow! You look really nice. I feel under dressed. Are you sure I will fit in."

"Don't worry, the women like to dress up for church, not so much, the guys. You look just fine."

And here I thought I had fallen for the least attractive of the three single girls in the apartments. I was wrong, Carolyn put them to shame when dressed up like this. Her personality was shining through.

I found the service strange, like Catholic, but all in English. Carolyn kept me on the right page of the prayer book to read along. She also shared her Bible with me turning to today's readings. It was not so different from the Methodist Church in my home town but more formal than the one where I sang in the choir at college. I saw in the hymnal they had the songs I grew up with in the First Christian and Methodist churches, but the songs they sang in this Episcopal Church were different songs that I had never heard before. I could sight read most of the bass notes, but bobbled a lot of the words as I tried to look at both the notes and the words of these strange hymns. One thing I liked was a short sermon with meaning, but the allegories were humorous and easy to relate to.

After the church service she took me to the adult meeting in a large side room where they had cookies and coffee. They were a truly friendly group that were very welcoming. They obviously thought a lot of Carolyn and if she brought me, I must be okay to them. I kept my mouth shut as much as possible to sit back and observe and only answered direct questions as well as introducing myself as a supply officer. I did not tell them I was the Nuclear Ordnance Supply Officer.

On the way back to the apartment Carolyn asked, "So what did you think of the Episcopal Church?"

"I liked it and the people. They welcomed me unlike the other denominations in town that I had tried. I was surprised that they had ashtrays and smoking during the adult meeting."

"The Episcopal Church is not overly strict on what people do. They are even relaxing their rules on divorced people. They used to consider divorce a sin and did not want divorced people to attend, but now they do allow them. I'm not sure whether they allow a second marriage in the Episcopal Church though. I don't think so."

"Why don't we go out to eat Sunday dinner at the officer's club? I'm buying. I know they have a very nice Sunday dinner after church. But it is only 10:30. I think probably the probably serve dinner at noon because that is when the chapel service lets out."

"Okay, why don't we go to my apartment and have some more coffee, kill an hour, and then go out to the base. I drove to church. Let's take your car to the base because it has a base sticker to get on base without having to get a visitor's pass."

....

"Thanks, Al, that was a wonderful lunch. Do you come here often?"

"No, this was a first for Sunday lunch. I usually just eat TV dinners at home."

"That sounds boring."

"It is. I buy a dozen at a time, shuffle them with my eyes closed, but them in the freezer and then every evening I take whatever is on top. I like pizza, but it is hard to eat one alone. I understand the club has live music on Fridays. Why don't we plan on going to a pizza place on Friday night and then going to the club to see what it is like?"

"I have a co-worker who is married to the security officer here. Is it okay if I invite them to meet us at the club around 7PM on Friday?"

"The more the merrier, I don't know very many people here. It would be good to meet the security officer since I work with his people a lot."

"I thought you were a supply officer, why do you work with security a lot?"

"They guard my storage areas?"

9 Friends

I didn't see Carolyn all week. _ When Carolyn came home she went straight into her apartment. Jane came up and knocked on my door to complain about thumping base from my stereo and then hesitated and said, "The bass is not loud here. It is twice as loud in my apartment. Come down and see." (How does one learn English when bass can be a fish?)

I did and, yes, it was twice as loud. "I see what you mean. The floor must amplify it. I'll try raising the bass speaker off the floor to see if that helps."

I did, then went back to her apartment to see the results. It was still louder than in my apartment, but getting the speaker off the floor helped. "I'll play it lower. If it gets too loud, just bug me again." When I left her apartment, Carolyn was going to her car and gave me the evil eye. She didn't stop as I walked toward her. She proceeded to her car and drove away without looking at me.

When I got off work Friday, I waited for her to come home and asked, "Are we still on for pizza and the club?"

"Yes, what were you doing going in and out of Jane's apartment this week."

"My stereo was thumping her ceiling to where it was louder there than in my apartment so we were experimenting to see if we could make it more tolerable."

"Okay, just curious. What time are we going for pizza? My friend and her husband will meet us at the officer's club at 7."

"Would 5:30 be okay?" We ended up with eight officers and their wives joining us as the only unmarried couple. It was more of a show band with a go go dancer, but they played one song that Carolyn and I both loved dancing to, "Unchained Melody" that came out in 1965 by the Righteous Brothers. From that time on we danced to that song wherever we heard it. Might be in a parking lot, a club, a restaurant. I think the song cemented the growing bond between us.

For the next two months, we ate our pizza and met our friends at the club every Friday night. Carolyn went to visit her parents that Thanksgiving and we missed that Friday night. I skipped the pizza, but did go to the club. I left after thirty minutes of visiting with my new officer friends. Without Carolyn, there was no point in my being there so I went home and read a book. We resumed our Friday night ritual the week after Thanksgiving. Now we were asking for our song to be played every time, some times twice. We were now beyond saying goodbye to each other and into kissing and hugging a lot before saying good night. And I would go back to my apartment all hot and bothered. Now I was serious when I asked her to marry me, but she still put it off.

She surprised me, "Al, I know the base will be pretty much closed down from Christmas to New Years. Rather than sit here alone while I am gone, would you take off and drive me to visit my parents near Fort Smith, Arkansas?"

"Certainly." I had been planning to go home to see my parents, but I was not going to miss out on spending a few days with Carolyn. She had become my reason for being. I could not catch up with her at Disneyland all those years ago and now that I had found her again I was going to take every advantage I had to be with her.

"Don't get any ideas. I made the mistake of telling my parents we were dating and they insisted on meeting you.

They are very strict and I do what they tell me. This does not mean I am serious."

We drove my 1969 black Datsun 2000 two seat convertible sports car with the top up for the winter. It was a very comfortable, quiet, and extremely fast car. With a speed limit of seventy, I had to downshift to fourth to go up the hills as the car was very high geared. It would run nearly sixty in first gear, eighty-five in second, one hundred-ten in third, one hundred-forty in fourth and I have no idea in fifth gear The only time my Datsun was not very quiet was if I punched it and the carburetors sucked air making it sound like a loud exhaust. I never did that on the trip. I drove it like I would a sedan. We told each other our history during the three hundred mile five hour trip. We ate at a Stuckey's at one point taking an extra hour and forty minutes as Carolyn had to look at every item for sale on every shelf. Forty minutes of that was spent watching honeybees go in and out of a hive built into the wall of the Stuckies.

I did not learn much on the trip except that she had gone to Lindenwood University in Saint Charles, Missouri, a suburb of Saint Louis, then dropped out and worked as a clerk in a construction company in Fort Smith and then gone back to college to get her degree in social work at Arkansas Polly Technic College in Russellville, Arkansas. I assumed she dropped out of the college in Saint Louis to be closer to home and, because Lindenwood was an all girls school back then, maybe save some money to go back to college again. We drove past Polly Tech on the way or she probably would not have told me. She had wanted to be a school teacher, but did not have the grade point so settled for a degree in Social Work. After graduation, she got a job in Blytheville, Arkansas all the way across the state from her parents, but a job was a job and she could still drive home to visit.

We drove through the small town of Booneville with people looking at this small sports car when the vehicle of choice seemed to be ratty pickups. "We used to go to that drugstore there and get fountain soda's and shakes, and sundaes. The high school is up that road. We used to gather in that park with the basketball court, play the car stereos loud and drink beer. Don't tell my parents. They would be mortified if they found out that I was not just going to a movie in our little movie theater or getting a shake at the drugstore."

"Turn right here. See that large mountain, that is Mount Magazine, one of the highest points in Arkansas and yes, we went up there to smoke cigarettes and drink beer too. No, I didn't really have a boyfriend and always had to be home before 10 PM and couldn't go out at all on school nights unless there was a ball game or a special dance and I still had to be home before 10 PM. One time I kissed a boy outside the porch as he was telling me goodnight and my father was sitting in the screened in porch and yelled at me to get in the house right now and called me a slut for kissing a boy. I was sixteen and had never kissed a boy before, but he had taken me to the homecoming dance and felt obligated to at least thank him with a kiss on the front steps of the house. "

She directed me onto smaller and smaller roads until we were on a two track dirt road. By that I mean, two tire groves separated by grass in the middle. After about a mile we came to what I can only describe as a moonshiner's cabin by an old large wooden barn. Now, don't get me wrong, the cabin had new wood siding painted a light green. The barn was unpainted and old, but looked in good condition. We parked and she lead me to the door and opened it saying, "We're here."

Her father and mother came to the door and said, "We didn't hear you drive up. Where is your car?" Then he saw my little black sports car. "It is sure quiet for a car like that."

"Yes it is."

"It looks unsafe."

"It has a very heavy frame and a roll bar just in case it tips over, which is very unlikely. So it is safer than it looks for its size. It makes over thirty miles to the gallon, better than a Volkswagen."

Her mother pitched in, "You must be Al Clark. Carolyn has told us about you. You are an Air Force captain, right?"

"Yes, Mam, I am."

"Call me Ivy and this grouch is Roy. We're pleased to meet you. Have a seat on the sofa with Carolyn and tell us where your home is, where you went to school, and why you drive such a cute little car."

Even Roy warmed up to me as he quizzed me on my politics and what I had read. He was a reader too. I did not learn much about Roy and Ivy as all the questions were directed at me. As I told them my history I saw that this moonshiner cabin was very deceptive. The light gold carpet was very plush, the kind you sink into. The furniture was top grade and obviously expensive, no pressed wood or plywood here. The paintings on the wall were mainly oils and did not look cheap. The fireplace was field stone and immaculate with a large oak mantel. Later when we sat down for dinner the table and chairs were probably Drexel as was the furniture in the living room. I had dated a daughter of an expensive furniture store a few times and learned something about good American brands.

This was so incongruous with the almost non-existent furniture in Carolyn's apartment. I was perplexed but said nothing about the incongruity. Her parents turned out to be very warm and friendly and her father, in particular, got really talkative about the stock market, world politics, morality in the world. He even complemented me, "It is nice to meet a young man that I can talk with. Living out here in these small towns I don't have that many friends and the youngsters here just want to drink beer, fight, and carouse around." Ivy winked at me. Carolyn was trying not to blush.

I was given the second bedroom and Carolyn slept on the back porch. I wanted to trade with her, but her parents insisted that guests do not sleep on porches and the back porch was heated like the rest of the house.

When we were alone for a few minutes, Carolyn said, "You know that it was really because they could hear the second bedroom and monitor the door to make sure no one sneaks in at night. I told you they were strict."

The next day we opened Christmas packages. Carolyn had told me in passing once that her father occasionally drank scotch whiskey so I had purchased the most expensive fifth in the class six store and wrapped it before we came. I had learned her mother was a bird watcher which was why they lived out so far from town and I had bought her a couple of small paintings of a Blue Bunting and a Blue Jay that were in the base exchange. For Carolyn I had a gold chain with a cross in recognition of Carolyn's taking me to church with her. I had seen other Episcopalian women with similar necklaces. Roy gave me a book on Arkansas history and Ivy gave me a small darling photo of Carolyn in a nice gilded frame. She was dressed in an all white shin length dress with a fur stole around her neck and a white round hat and white gloves. Like a wedding dress, but she was probably in high school when the photo was taken. She did not look like the poor girl I had met. I wondered if the fur stole was real, probably rabbit.

It was cold outside, but Roy showed me around the farmyard near the house. He explained that the larger conventional house near the paved road had been theirs before, but there was too much traffic noise so he rented it out and refurbished the cabin here for the peaceful nature. "You can hear wolves at night off in the fields, but I have only seen glimpses of them in daylight. They stay away from people and look like skinny gray dogs. Ivy likes her birds. If you count them, there are twenty-three bird feeders in the grassy area across from the front of the house. If you go out at night, take a good flashlight, stay out of the grass, and watch for copperhead snakes. You do know what they look like don't you."

"Sort of like a faded rattlesnake, right? I went to grade school near the Okeene, Oklahoma annual rattlesnake hunt. So most of what I saw were rattlesnakes and I stay far away from them."

"Copperheads are not as poisonous, but they can still hurt and make you sick. This time of year it is too cold for them to be out of their dens much, but when we have a warm spell, they come out and lay on the road to warm up so we have to watch out for them. That's why we keep guinea hens. They will kill snakes if they find them. They will surround the snake to keep it from leaving and then peck it to death. They confuse the snake with so many targets surrounding it so the snake does not know which one to bite. Only drawback is that the guineas can be quite noisy."

Carolyn had stayed in with Ivy to give Roy time to evaluate me further. I knew that and wondered about it. Was Carolyn going to take the idea of marriage seriously? Was she letting her father test me out?

When we came in for lunch, Ivy said, "Al, you and Carolyn need to hit the road after lunch. I hate to run you off so quick, but they are predicting an usually large snowstorm for most of Arkansas all the way over to Tennessee. They don't plow the road from here to Booneville so you would be trapped here waiting for it to melt. There might be more snow up around Blytheville."

"Well, okay. I have the week off, but if you think we should head out we will." We did. By the time we got to eastern Arkansas we were down to about thirty miles an hour.

"I'm glad this car has a good heater, it looks cold out there."

"Yes. In fact I bought this car in Utah and it would frequently get to below zero there. Not only does it have a good heater, but does well on snowy roads."

"I guess I should tell you that I did not graduate from Booneville, Arkansas. After my father caught me kissing that boy on the front steps they suggested that I go to All Saints Episcopal Girls High School in Vicksburg, Mississippi. They didn't want me hanging around the country bumpkins, his name, not mine, living around here. That was fine by me. My parents can be a little overbearing. When we went to gym here I was the only girl in school not allowed to wear shorts even for gym. I was born in Madison, Wisconsin, but we moved to the little town of Walworth, Wisconsin near Lake Geneva. We only had about thirty kids in my class and the whole town was very straight laced. The teenagers did not sneak around drinking beer and smoking cigarettes. They did not have fights."

10 Another Coincidence?

"I played saxophone in the marching band there and when I went to Lindenwood Girls College in Saint Louis, Missouri. It did not go co-ed until 1969, but by then I was back in Arkansas. When I went back to college here at Arkansas Poly Tech I played my saxophone in the marching band again."

"Would you believe I played alto sax from eighth grade and then in college I joined the Reserve Officers Training Corps (ROTC) band. ROTC was mandatory for all the guys and being in the band meant that I could just stand in one spot playing my sax while everyone else had to march in formations. The band, naturally, already knew how to march in formation, so we only marched to and from the marching field playing our marching music while all the other students lined the daily parade route."

"You played alto sax too. Coincidence? Poly Tech was so different than All Saints and Lindenwood. It was co-ed for one. I didn't date there, but there was not even the potential at the girls' schools I went to. It was a big disappointment to my parents when I struck out on my own and went to work in Fort Smith, dropping out of college."

"That's two coincidences. We both like thunderstorms and we both played alto sax."

"Keep counting. Don't forget Disneyland. It was love at first sight for me and then we met again in our twenties in the same apartment building with only one apartment between us. Your degree is in social work and mine is in psychology although I haven't ever used anything I learned in college. We both drive small economical four cylinder cars instead of the typical big cars most people drive. We're both politically conservative, your father really is. Now we are going to the same church. Neither of us are big drinkers, but we do drink. We both smoke cigarettes."

"I can't count Disneyland. That is your story, that would be too much of a coincidence."

"I saw a beautiful young platinum haired girl arguing with her brother about the Mad Hatter ride and you were. I was drawn to you then and should have introduced myself, but I didn't. If I had, maybe you would have remembered me and waited around the ride for me to get off. Or maybe I wouldn't have gone on the ride. Or maybe your brother would have let you go with me while he waited for us. I choose to think that I was given another opportunity to meet you at a proper age and living near each other. It would have been impossible to see each other with you in Wisconsin and me in Oklahoma over 900 miles away when we were only twelve."

"Okay, but neither of us even remembers the exact date, only the month we were at Disneyland."

"I had assumed that you were from a poor family, until I saw the nice expensive furniture and the new Chrysler Imperial Lebaron."

"I am still determined to make it on my own. The only furniture I accepted from my parents was my bedroom set that you haven't seen. It was blond wood, that did not match my mother's idea of what furniture should be but when we moved to Arkansas when I was fifteen, she let me pick out my own as a consolation for the move from Wisconsin that really upset me. She was going to throw it out if I didn't take it."

"That's why we moved to Booneville. She wanted to come back to Arkansas to be near family, but thought going to Fort Smith high school with a thousand students would be too much of a shock, so Booneville it was, but my father had forgotten what a small Arkansas town could be like. We originally had one of the biggest houses in Booneville, but my mother wanted to move out to the farm. Maybe next time Roy will show you more than the barnyard." How much more, I had no idea until my second visit there.

By the time we got to our apartment building there was about three inches of snow in the parking lot which was nearly full with no tracks in the snow. Shortly after we got back, Carolyn invited me down to watch television with her. We sat side by side, like we had to sit close in the sports car. After awhile, she scooted over then laid down on the "sofa/cot" and put her head in my lap. "Hope you don't mind. It's been a long day."

I didn't mind. I didn't mind when she went to sleep with her head on my lap. I put my hand near her waist and was afraid to move for fear I would wake her. I was very happy that I was getting this private time, even if she was sleeping. It was after 9PM when she woke. "I'm sorry. I didn't mean to go to sleep, literally on you. Why don't I fix some sandwiches? It has been a long time since lunch at my parents. You must be starving."

"I wouldn't mind a sandwich. What do you have? And I didn't mind you dozing off. I rather enjoyed having you close and trusting me."

"Why don't you come back and see my bedroom furniture that I talked about?"

I jumped to conclusions and said, "Absolutely."

She lead me into her bedroom. The headboard was also a bookcase and the end tables extended the same bookcase another eighteen inches beyond the full bed headboard. She had a matching credenza on the opposite wall and a matching chest of drawers on the wall near the door. It was the blond wood all right. It fit her nicely. Nice quality furniture, but not flashy and rather old fashioned by today's standard. Obviously not cheap wood, maybe maple? Definitely not soft pine. I started to put my arms around her.

"Bad idea, Al. Off limits. You are tired after driving in that snow, let's eat our sandwiches and call it a night."

The next morning Carolyn knocked on my door, "You are going to Kelly's party for new years eve?"

"I haven't been invited."

"Now you have been. See you there."

11 Party

It was hard to believe so many people could pack into a one bedroom apartment. It just went to show the lack of entertainment in Blytheville, Arkansas. The guys were mostly air force officers and I don't know where the girls came from. I only knew the three I had met so far. The booze was flowing freely.

There was standing room only. The food disappeared quickly, but the booze kept flowing. Several of the young officers milled around me. Carolyn was doing her thing of cleaning up after everyone as fast as they messed things up. If someone set down their empty plastic glass, it was gone. If someone did not keep a hand on their ashtray, it was replaced by a clean one.

There were more guys than girls and I found myself in a gaggle of six other young officers. One of them punched me playfully in my shoulder and asked, "Getting any. We all know Carolyn and I understand she can be pretty loose."

I wanted to hit the guy. He obviously did not know Carolyn. I calmly said, "I've been around her a lot these last six months and I find her pretty wholesome and not loose at all."

"I'll bet. Maybe you can arrange some time for me to be alone with her. I'll bet I can get her loosened up some."

"We're exclusive. We're going to get married when I get her to say yes. So just keep your distance."

"Soooorrrryyyy. Don't get your dander up, I just know these local Arkansas girls like to party."

I guess Carolyn saw the almost confrontation and came and hung on my arm and pulled me toward the door and then out onto the balcony. "It's getting pretty stuffy in there. I haven't had a chance to talk with you even. How do you like the party?"

"I think we could use more room. Where did all these people come from?"

"The guys are from the base, but you know that. There are a lot of girls that live in Memphis and commute here to work and more that work in Memphis but come here looking to hook up with an air force officer. Our apartments are known for some good parties. It's too noisy in there for me, why don't we go watch the ball drop on television in my apartment. It is nearly midnight Eastern Time."

"Good idea. I like the party, but there is too much booze flowing. I hope everyone can get home safely."

She had made herself scarce since we returned from her parents and I was concerned about our relationship. Maybe seeing her parents had been bad, but this invitation to go to her apartment made my heart warm. The first thing I saw was that she had purchased a maple stained round, wooden dinette set with a Formica top and 4 matching chairs.

"You bought a table and chairs."

"Yes, I did. You like? My parents gave me a check and told me to buy it.

"It's nice."

We watched the ball drop in New York on television at 11PM Central Standard Time, midnight Eastern Standard Time.

"So, Al, do you want to go back to party?"

"We could stay here and watch New Years Eve in Saint Louis."

"I don't mind, I watched it every year with my parents."

When that was over, "I think the party is over, don't you think it is time to go back to your own apartment?"

"We could stay and watch the Los Angeles celebration."

"I don't think so. I have to get to bed and get some sleep."

"If you insist. Can I come down tomorrow to watch some bowl games?"

"Not before noon. We'll probably have company for the games. Good night now."

January 1st, 1971, I walked two doors down to her apartment and helped her set up for the football game viewing. She sent me to the store for some more supplies: more chips, a couple of bags of ice. She already had huge bowls of chips out on the new table with smaller dishes of various dips for the chips. Her kitchen countertop had an array of alcohol for the expected guests.

As people arrived some of them brought their own lawn chairs to sit in, others just sat on the floor. Like the New Years Eve party downstairs, this one was also crowded, but everyone was from the apartments except for some girl and boyfriends. The invasion from the air base or from Memphis didn't happen and there were several married couples that lived in the apartments that had not been at last nights party. There weren't quite as many people, but still a crowd, and I got to meet more of our neighbors. Carolyn knew them all and they all seem to, at least, know of me, and introduced themselves. At different times some asked me in private, "Are you going to marry her?"

My reply was always, "If she agrees."

The comments back were some variation of, "We are all hoping she will find someone and we have heard good things about you."

"Thanks, but it is not my decision. I have been asking and she keeps saying NO."

12 Change

Everything became routine. We would both go to work Monday through Friday. I would come over to her apartment regularly and watch television with her, some of the other singles would come by and visit with us for awhile. Sometimes we ate out and sometimes she cooked, and sometimes she said she needed some alone time. Every Friday, we would go to the officers' club to meet the same group of six to ten friends and have a couple of drinks. Sometimes we went out to eat with one of the other couples, but usually we went to our regular table at the locally owned Italian restaurant and get our half sausage and half pepperoni thin crust pizza. If we had not drunk much at the club we would get beers and sometimes a cola or iced tea getting home around 9PM kissing and saying goodbye until sometime late Saturday afternoon with church on Sunday morning. One Sunday afternoon one of our air force neighbors looked in the open curtains and then came in.

"What are you doing here? There is an airplane coming in with nuclear weapons in less than an hour and aren't you always supposed to be there to meet the plane and get it unloaded?"

"Don't worry, Jim, its only some radioactive iodine for the hospital. I only have to be there if it is related to nuclear weapons or plutonium for them."

"Are you sure?"

"Yes, I was notified three days ago and the hospital has their own people to pick up radiologic medicine."

"Okay, if you say so. I will leave you alone then, but don't say I didn't notify you." With that he left and shut the door behind him.

"Al, what was that about nuclear weapons. Are we going to war or something?"

"No, it is fairly routine to ship some out and some different ones arrive. Actually most of the plutonium comes by truck. I have to be there for any loading or unloading of any nuclear weapons related shipments. If it is conventional, that is non-nuclear, then the enlisted guys take care of it on their own."

"Why would they ship nuclear weapons here?"

"It IS a SAC base. That is why we have all those B-52's there."

"I thought they were just training B-52 pilots at the base."

"They don't fly with nuclear weapons unless there was a war, so all those airplanes you see are just training flights where they pretend they are carrying nuclear weapons."

"Is there any danger to the town?"

"No. They never fly with nuclear weapons on board and their take-off and landing runs are not over the town so if an airplane were to crash it would be out in the country."

"What about nuclear weapons on the ground? Could they just explode?"

"No. Even if there were a fire with nuclear weapons in the fire there would only be a low grade non-nuclear explosion of the TNT inside the bomb. I might throw some chunks of plutonium for a hundred yards but would not even go over the fence. It would be a mess for someone to clean up, but the odds of even that are very very slim."

For the next weeks, Carolyn cooled our relationship. "You are getting too serious and I have told you I am not getting married. I think you need to go find someone else. What about Jane or Kelly, they are still single and they were talking about hooking up with you until we started going together."

"I am not interested in Jane or Kelly. You are the one I was looking for since I was twelve years old. I found you and am not letting you go."

"That really isn't up to you is it? We can still be friends, but let's quit going out so much. I was perfectly happy before you invaded my space. Now we eat what you want and watch the TV shows you want. I want to go back to how it was before we met."

....

I still saw her from a distance but when she came home she went into her apartment, locked the door, and drew the curtains closed. In the mornings she opened the curtains, went to her car and went to work.

A couple of weeks later the air force got the bright idea of sending me off to an air force school for six weeks to learn the job I had already been doing for over three years. I didn't have a choice. I told Carolyn, "I am being sent to Denver, Colorado to a six week school. So I am leaving next week and won't be home until mid-April."

"Why are you going to school? Did you ask for it?"

"No, I didn't ask for it. Someone realized that I have not been to the school to learn the job I have been doing for over three years and guess they want to check off that box that should have been checked off years ago."

"Well, drive safely. Are we going to the club on Friday?"

I was a little surprised. It had been at least four weeks since we had been to the club. I was not without hope, but things had definitely cooled with her. I had mixed feelings about the school. I figured it was a waste of time in that I knew the job. I was not planning on making a career of the air force. A Nuclear Ordnance or Munitions Supply Officer was not a career path anyway, but maybe my being away from Carolyn for a few weeks would give me a fresh perspective. I had been feeling pretty much a failure. Here I had found that girl that I had been in love with since I saw her at Disneyland when I was twelve and it seemed like I had lost her again. "Absolutely. Pick you up at 5PM here, like before?"

"See you then."

That night and the following week were back the way they had been before she found out the SAC base had nuclear weapons and I was involved with them. Then I had to go to the school.

13 Separation

The week after that, I had to leave for the school in Denver. Wouldn't you know it? It snowed heavily in Blytheville, AR. I had waited until Friday to leave for Denver, giving me three days to drive there, get checked in to the Visiting Officer Quarters, and check in for school at 0700 Monday morning. I had planned to not leave until Saturday morning, but Carolyn had phoned me at work saying they were let go early due to the snow and "I think you should get on the road today giving you an extra day to drive to Denver. I am staying in my apartment alone regardless of what you want to do."

Well, the snow was a record setter. My little Datsun 2000 sports car was no match for 3 foot drifts across the road from my office in the bomb dump to the gate. I had been told the highway was plowed, but I would have to get out the gate. I had one of our deuce and half dump trucks from the bomb dump tow me out the gate and I took off. The highways were not bad. The snow had just about blocked Interstate 40 through Little Rock, Arkansas, but had not snowed much in the northern half of the state once I got further west than Blytheville. I went the northern scenic route through Eureka Springs, Arkansas. The roads were dry once I got thirty miles west of Blytheville. It was dark when I drove through Eureka Springs and I picked up a Plymouth Roadrunner Superbird with the big wing on the back. He was right on my bumper leaving town. I accelerated and took to the twisty turny mountain road. Going into the first corner the "Bird" was maybe five feet from my bumper. Coming out of the turn he was two car lengths behind. Going into the second turn I lost sight of him but when I got to the third turn I could see him coming out of turn number two. I didn't see him again until I got to the bottom of the little mountain and was a little worried about why. I stopped in the middle of the road, got out and looked back at the mountain. About half way down the twisty road I could vaguely hear tired squealing and could see his headlight crazily zigging around turns. I figured I was at least fifteen minutes ahead so I got back in my sports car and headed on west.

As I went from Colorado Springs toward Denver at 10PM I had the top down on my car and it felt good. I could not believe it was so warm. I had been driving fairly fast for nearly 12 hours. I checked into the VOQ and still had most of the weekend to roam around town and learn the base.

On Monday I got to the classroom early and wouldn't you know it. I knew the main and assistant teachers of the class. They were two senior NCOs, non-commissioned officers, or senior enlisted air force people that had been at 7th Air Force headquarters in Saigon, South Vietnam, when I was in Southeast Asia. They had been the ones that had taken me out on the town in Saigon. Their first comment to me was, "Captain Clark, what are you doing here?"

"Someone found out I had not been to the school and I got orders to come here. So here I am."

"What are we going to do with you?"

"Teach me all you can and try to keep me awake, I guess."

"Are you married?"

"No."

"Anyone serious?"

"I thought so, but I guess not."

"Well, I have someone you should meet."

"Is she smart? Does she have a good figure? Is she single and good looking?"

"Yes, to all the above. She moved here not long ago and has not hooked up with anyone. Maybe I'll call her and see if she will give out her phone for you to call. It is hard to reach anyone in the VOQ."

"Sounds great."………

So for the next three weeks, I called her and we went out to eat, movies, night clubs, just driving in my sports car in the mountains. The class was how I expected. The instructors were teaching out of the lesson plan. Whenever the lesson plan did not match the real-life work, I kept my head on the table, but raised my hand and got the usual response, "Captain Clark, go back to sleep and I'll tell them how it really works."

Then, Darlene, suggested that we spend the evening at her apartment. That was a mistake. We had some platonic fun together, but the minute I arrived there, I got the impression that she was going to want me to spend the night. I broke down and told her about how I had met Carolyn after years of hoping to find her and now she had turned cool toward me.

That was the end of that. Darlene excused me and sent me back to the VOQ and would not answer the phone after that. The second half of the class went similar to the first half, but I had to actually study a little bit. The class was now talking about managing munitions on the base supply computer. It had not happened yet, but they had tried. In fact, the first 4 pilot bases had failed and they were studying why they failed to successfully manage munitions like any other supply in the system. I spent 4 nights pouring over the books before the final exam. I was the honor graduate on both the first and second half of the class.

I planned to drive to my parents house in Enid, Oklahoma that evening, but did not get cleared out of the base until nearly 4PM and it was 600 miles to Enid. I phoned home and told my parents and they said it did not matter when I arrived, but to spend the night in a motel if I got sleepy driving.

For the first two hours, the road was under construction and the traffic was stop and go. I never got over 45 mph which meant I never got out of third gear and was usually running in second gear with frequent downshifts to 1st to keep from burning up the clutch lugging the engine. I finally got on the open road only to see a sign that said road work next 30 miles. There was an exit that said the name of a town in Oklahoma and I got off the interstate and headed south. At nearly 7PM, the farm roads were deserted so I kicked up my speed.

I was depressed about losing Carolyn and not feeling a thing for Darlene that really was smart and attractive, but after 3 weeks of dating regularly, we never kissed and then I made a fool of myself talking about Carolyn when Darlene invited me to her place for an evening of sex. I had no choice but to return to Blytheville Air Force Base and had three days travel time. I wanted to spend one day with my parents on the coming weekend so I said to heck with police radar, I'm going to see if I can make it home at a decent time. I kicked up my speed to 130-138 mph. My speedometer only went to 140 and I did not want to twist off the cable so I kept it just below the peg. Everytime I approached a town I started downshifting from 5th gear, rolled through town at the speed limit in 1st gear and by the time I got to the town limits I had collected a line of the hottest cars in town behind me. When I hit the town limits, I punched it and went up through the gears: 50 in 1st, 85 in second, 100 in third, usually when I hit 4th gear at 100 – 115, I had lost all the cars from the town, by the time I was hitting 5th gear at around 130 mph I had the road to myself until I hit the next small town where the parade was repeated.

I had aircraft landing lights on my front bumper. I could not use them below 50mph because even though I was using house wiring direct to the battery, the wire would melt unless I had 50mph air blowing over the connections. At any rate, when it got dark I think I could have seen a rabbit within 100 yards of the road at a mile in front of me. When I came over the "Glass Mountains" I could barely see some headlights turn off the main highway onto mine. His lights started blinking. I said to myself, surely not, but I cut the landing lights and his lights quit blinking. I turned them back on and he started blinking his lights again. It took nearly 10 minutes before we passed each other and I had slowed down to 70, just in case he was the police. The night time speed limit was 55 and I had been driving for hours at 130 or more. At any rate, I drove into my parents driveway just after 10PM which meant I had traveled 602 miles in 6 hours with the first two hours far below the speed limit.

I did not relate to my parents about Carolyn and I's falling out, but my mother knew something was bothering me the next day. I showed them it was not the class as I had my honor graduate certificate, but when she asked about my dating life, I told them I had finally met the girl I saw at Disneyland when I was 12, but things were not going well.

"Don't give up on her, your father dated me for over a year and I had known him all my life. You barely met this girl. When will we get to meet her?"

"Maybe never at this rate, but you are right. I will not give up on her. It was a shock to her that I work with nuclear weapons. She is not a dove politically. In fact very conservative, but just never considered someone working with nuclear weapons."

"Well, there you have it. Just be yourself, she'll get used to it."

14 Homecoming

The next day I drove on to Blytheville, arriving at night and hit the bed to sleep off the last couple of days. I got up and went to work at the base the next day, a Monday. I was tired, but I had been away from the office for 6 weeks and wanted to see about damage control. Naturally my first stop was at the munitions squadron headquarters to let the squadron commander, Lieutenant Colonel White, the maintenance supervisor, Major Russell and the admin clerk, Staff Sergeant Wills know that I was back from the school and going to work. The maintenance supervisor was responsible for the aircraft loading equipment and teams so basically everyone worked for him except for the Munitions Storage that worked for me. I had 30 people, he had 140 people. His job was to maintain all the munitions transport trailers to transport munitions to and from the aircraft and supervise all of the enlisted people who did that job and loaded the B-52s with munitions. The biggest routine job was to load the 20mm cannons for training missions and unloaded any unused ammunition and take it back to the storage area.

My job was to supervise the people in the Munitions Storage Area who made sure that we had sufficient ammunition for the 20mm gun training missions, that the nuclear weapons were always ready to go and other conventional munitions like small arms ammo was available for the base small arms training, security police squadron, and plastic explosives for the EOD (explosive ordnance disposal) unit, smoke grenades for local air shows, etc. I was in charge of all security for the storage and the security police that actually monitored the electronic alarms and provided armed security for the Munitions Storage Area reported to me while on duty even though they were supervised by the Security Police Squadron. To assure that all these requirements were met we had to inventory regularly to make sure that the flight line maintenance personnel had not fudged what they took to the flight line and properly inventoried and stored 20mm left over from training missions.

The admin clerk typed and filed all orders, including my trip to the school, annual leaves, and typing and filing any letters for the squadron, except what I produced in the Munitions Storage 6 miles away on the other side of the flight line and near the alert pad where the aircraft sat loaded with nuclear weapons and tanker aircraft loaded with fuel just in case we ever went to an all out war which everyone hoped would never happen.

When I finally made it to the Munitions Storage Area, my NCOIC (non-commissioned officer in charge), Master Sergeant Stanton had kept things running smoothly. There had been no alerts or exercises while I was gone so everything had been very routine. He handed me the stack of paperwork that had be signed by the Nuclear Ordnance Supply Officer (NOSO) which was me. All of it was routine and I had no questions about signing it. By 2PM I had finished and went out to visit the nuclear ordnance maintenance building. Master Sergeant Wilson was in charge of all the nuclear maintenance and things had been routine for him also. He asked me about the school and I told him I slept through most of it, but the mountains around Denver were sure pretty. "We had one snow while I was there, but it had melted away and the snow on the mountains was melting too."

I took off a few minutes early to stop by the grocery and pick up some TV dinners, cola, and miscellaneous supplies as I had been away for the school and left my refrigerator nearly empty. As I was carrying in my groceries, Carolyn got home and came over to help carry the groceries. "Aren't you going to come over and eat with me?"

"Sure."

As soon as I had put things away and turned around, Carolyn hugged me, "I missed you, AL. I didn't realize how much until you weren't there. You know the old saying, 'absence makes the heart grow stronger', well it's true."

....

That night after eating supper with Carolyn we sat down to watch some television until after the 10 PM news. Carolyn had snuggled up close and put my arm over her shoulders. I got up after the news and said, "Well, I guess I had better be going. It's a work night." I expected her to run me off.

"Why don't you just stay here tonight? I've missed you and want you to stay close."

I had no pajamas so I ended up sleeping in my undershorts. She backed up to me and put my arm over her and said, "This is enough for now, just settle down and sleep."

Easier said than done, but I did. I had a hard time actually sleeping next to the girl I had loved forever without doing anything further, but I was tired from my driving across the country and going to work again so soon and eventually did. All too soon, Carolyn woke me up and said, "You better be going before the neighbors realize you spent the night here and I have to get ready for work and I imagine you need to get ready for work too."

By the weekend, we had spent 4 platonic nights together in her bedroom with me getting up and sneaking back to my apartment while we both got ready for work. On

Friday, we went back to our routine of going to happy hour at the officers' club with our old set of happy hour friends then pizza afterward. When we got back to her apartment Carolyn wanted to talk.

"Al, before our relationship goes further, we need to talk."

"What about? I still want you to marry me just like I have repeated over the months. You are not worried about me being a Nuclear muntions officer are you?"

"No, that's your job. Someone has to do it. This is far more personal."

"Okay, what about?"

"Something you need to know about me?"

"You aren't married to someone else are you?"

"Silly, of course not. I need to tell you that I am unable to have children. If you want a family, I can't give it to you."

"Why not?"

"When I was growing up, all the other girls started having their periods and I didn't. I never had a small waist like some girls, but developed otherwise like them, but I never had a period. My parents took me up to Rochester and the Mayo Clinic there and they did a battery of tests and determined I have a genetic defect that did not allow my ovaries to develop, so I will never have a period, or be able to have children. I would like to have children, but it will not happen, ever. I even considered becoming a Catholic nun, but wouldn't take me because of the defect. I tried enlisting in the military, same result. So I went to college, got my degree and settled down to be an old maid."

"That is why I went off to an Episcopal girls' school, All Saints, in Vicksburg, Mississippi. After that I attended Lindenwood girl's college in Saint Louis, Missouri. No men to worry about. (it is now co-ed) But I didn't like being at an all girls' school. I got tired of the goings on and wanted more freedom so I transferred to Arkansas Poly Cow College which was also closer to my parents. I never got along that well with my parents. They were so strict and then wanted me to marry even though they knew I could not have children. They never like any boyfriend they ever met. Of course, I never got so involved with anyone but you."

"So...we'll adopt children."

"They wouldn't be yours genetically."

"So...how many men are divorced and act like dads to their wives children? It is not like men get pregnant and carry children for 9 months. Men are required to start the process, but I don't see how I would feel any different with adopted children."

"I want you to be sure. I did not want to lead you on any further if you wanted children of your own."

"I don't care about that. I just never want to be without you, ever. You are what counts. With me being in the military and a war going on in Vietnam, this is not a good time to risk having children and then going off to war again."

"You have already been there once. You wouldn't have to go again would you?"

"Not likely, but I can count on being transferred again. We should wait until I get out of the air force and get a civilian job before adopting children anyway. It's good you can't get pregnant. I sure would not want to have to go off , have something happen to me and leave you with children."

"Well. I'm still not going to say, yes. You need to give it some time to make sure you are serious about not having offspring of your own. What would your parents say?"

"They would approve of whatever I do. My sister and brother have already provided my parents with grand children, so if I don't, it won't matter in carrying on the genetics. Besides, if we adopt, they will be just as happy."

"I haven't even met your parents."

"I've met your parents and liked them."

"Not everyone does. My father is so business like and never liked any boy they ever met, until you came along. My mother is a neat freak and takes plates away to wash before guests even finish. She can't stand for anything to be out of place, but with you there, she didn't act that way. My parents are overjoyed that I met someone like you."

"I'm glad of that anyway. I think they would be good parents-in-law."

"You weren't put off by them living in a moonshiner's cabin?"

"No. It was just the style of the house. It had new siding, a new roof, and the interior was plush. It was hardly a moonshiner cabin once you got a second look."

"Next week is Easter, I think we should go over and see them this weekend. Will you drive me, just for the weekend. The weather is supposed to be warm and sunny, maybe Dad will take you around and show you more of the place."

"There's more? It was a nice cabin and the barn could have used some paint, but was sturdy and not in need of repair. The fencing was in good condition. What more is there to see? Of course, I will drive you. I wouldn't want you to drive it alone and leave me here worrying about you."

15 Easter Surprise

We drove to Booneville Friday. Both of us were released early because it was Good Friday so we arrived there at 4PM. Carolyn had me drive around Booneville for awhile before going to her parents' moonshiner cabin on the farm. She had me drive by the house they had lived in when they first moved from Walworth, Wisconsin. It was a stately large older well kept house with a large yard. One of the finest in town. I privately wondered why they had lived in such a grand house and then moved out to the moonshiner cabin on the farm. I didn't say anything. I presumed (wrongly) that selling that house gave them the money to fix up the cabin. I had seen traces of money, but had no idea how much. We did not get to her parents until nearly 6PM. Her mother had dinner ready for us when we arrived.

Her father came out of the house to greet us, "Hello, Al, it is really good to see you again. Carolyn told us how you went off to school in Denver for 6 weeks. In fact, she ran up her long distance phone bill calling us almost daily while you were gone. I'm glad to see you two are still together. Have you set a date yet?"

I was a little taken aback about the implication of marriage. "She has not told me yes yet. I keep asking, but she won't commit."

"Well you have our blessing. We don't want her to be alone forever."

Her mother came to the porch and announced, "Come on in, dinner is ready."

During dinner Ivy (Carolyn's mother) told me Roy would take me around to see the farm while she and Carolyn cooked Easter dinner. That night, I insisted on sleeping on the porch and Carolyn in the second bedroom. Her parents went to bed at 10 PM after hours of visiting and talking with Roy while Carolyn and her mother stayed in the kitchen talking. At 11 PM, Carolyn came out onto the porch and insisted on me quietly coming into the guest bedroom and joining her in the bed there. She woke me up at 4 AM and told me quietly that I should go back to the back porch because her parents got up early. They would not be upset by me being in her bed, but she didn't want to get caught.

The next morning, her mother cooked a farmer's breakfast with thick bacon, mounds of scrambled eggs, toast, jelly, and coffee. After breakfast, Roy led me out to his old pickup for a tour of the farm.

"The road to the house was partially gravel with grass growing in the middle of the track but beyond the barn was just a wagon track. We drove along the side of the mountain. Roy pointed to a ridge on the other side of the valley. "The farm extends to the Petit Jean River on the North and starts at the paved road you turned off of. I don't farm it anymore, but lease it out to the people in the larger farmhouse by the road. They plant hay and raise cattle on the land in the valley. That house near the road is rented out. We lived there while fixing up our cabin. Ivy wanted to be away from the road traffic and out at the cabin because she loves her birds. We have deer that come down by the house looking for food when it gets cold. We have wolves that you can hear at night hunting rabbits in this valley."

We had come about 3 miles on this wagon track when we came to a ramshackle cabin, a broken down small barn with leaning walls and a couple of chicken coups.

"There was an artist that lived out here last summer and painted the cabin and barn for some sort of rustic art exhibit. Understand he sold the painting for a bundle. I guess I rented out the cabin too cheap. At least he was friendly and didn't cause any problems. He came by about once a week when he went into town for groceries. He kept a post office box in town since they would not deliver all the way out here. See that fence out there about 200 yards. That is the end of my farm in this direction, but hang on, we will be going up the mountain here."

It was a steep road with rocks in the wagon track going up the mountain. When we got to the top, the wagon track was smooth, but was almost overgrown with grass. The wagon track wandered to a pond with clear blue water.

"You like to fish?"

"I have fished, but not too often. Usually I just keep casting and never catching anything. If we caught anything, my mother would clean and cook them."

"Ivy keeps this pond stocked with largemouth bass. There are some large ones there. Carolyn and Ivy used to spend hours here in nice weather fishing. They would only keep the ones large enough to eat and throw back the really big ones and the small ones. Carolyn would clean them and Ivy would cook bass two or three times a week. We need someone out here more to catch some of the turtles that are taking over the pond since Carolyn moved away to Blytheville."

After almost a mile and going past another pond they came to a rock house and barn. "This house and barn came with the 600 odd acres here on the mountain top. I am thinking of having a road bull dozed down to the road on the other side of the mountain and renting out this mountain top and farm for someone that wants a private farm. I like this house and barn made out of solid rock and mortar, but it is too remote from a road and Ivy would never want to leave our cabin. The house is in pretty good shape, but it would take some work to clean it up inside as it has been empty for over 10 years. While we're here, do you mind if I inspect it? I like to make sure no varmints have gotten in or hobos."

"I'd like to see it. It would be a great place to get away from everything. I love the view of the mountains and valleys from up here."

"Yes, it would, but not until I get another road up here. I really don't like traffic on the little road past our cabin. Of course, if you and Carolyn ever need a place....."

"I have worked on farms, but I am not a farmer."

"It would be a great place to raise some horses. Carolyn loves and knows horses. Are you a rider?"

"I have ridden horses, but would not consider myself a rider. I kept a neighbor's Palomino mare one summer, but I would have a lot to learn, and it would take some money to get set up and buy horses and equipment."

"You're right, Al, it would."

The house was darling inside. The floors were polished hardwood with a patina of dust, but otherwise beautiful. The rooms were small, the kitchen outdated by about 30 years, but probably serviceable if you could get propane delivered up here. It only had two bedrooms and one bath. The dining was in the country kitchen. The living room had a large window facing the yard with the barn off to the left side of the picture. "I'm surprised that painter didn't paint this place."

"I don't think he ever saw it. He was enamored with the old broken down cabin and barn. He slept out in a tent except during the worst weather. He spent January somewhere else. The cabin only has a wood pot bellied heater and a wood stove. The bathroom is an outhouse in worse condition than the house. We had better be getting back, Ivy will have Easter dinner ready about 2PM so we need to leave now to get back by one o'clock.

When we got back to the main cabin it was nearly 1 PM. We had been viewing the "farm" for over 5 hours. I had a new perspective. I had assumed Carolyn was from a poor Arkansas farmer. His "farm" had over six thousand acres. It was unimproved and most of it was timbered, but had to be worth a bundle. It made me wonder how he had come to own that much land.

At dinner I was politely asked by both Ivy and Roy about my background in growing up and in the air force. I told them that I went to several small schools where my father was superintendent. I played baseball, basketball, and football. I was a good student and sang in a really big and good mixed chorus, played band in part of my high school and in the ROTC band in college. After college I went right into the air force, was stationed in Oklahoma in pilot training, then Tooele Army Depot in Utah. Then I was sent to Southeast Asia and then Blytheville where I met Carolyn.

They seemed pleased that our paths had intersected. I did not tell them that I had been looking for her for 14 years before we officially met. We had to be back at work on Monday morning so we left in the late afternoon and got back to Blytheville around 9PM. Carolyn said she was tired and sent me back to my own apartment. Our relationship was great, but she sent me back to my apartment each night. She was not cooling off the relationship, but more concerned about gossip. We continued our routine of going for pizza and the happy hour at the Officers' Club with a trip to Memphis and the Rivermont Club about every two months.

16 Dodging the Bullet Miracle

Starting in Southeast Asia, in 1970, during the Vietnam war I started running fevers in the evenings, regularly above 102 and sometimes 104 or above. It would only last an hour or so then I would start sweating and feel clammy, then the fever would break and I would be fine the rest of the night and into the next day. I was afraid it might be malaria because the base had temporarily run out of Quinine that was available in jars at all eating places on base. You would just reach in and get a handful to take home with you. It was a few weeks without the Quinine when I started running the fevers. Taking the Quinine didn't help, but when I lost a lot of weight and the fevers were really bad, one of my NCOs had told me to go see the base hospital because I was sweating at work one day just sitting at my desk.

When I went in to see a doctor at the base hospital, my temperature was 106 and he wanted to check me into the hospital. The doctor said whatever I had was not catching and if I could continue working I should just keep coming in for blood work while they tried to figure it out. They gave me nothing for it. I did that for two weeks and quit going in. It had gotten better, but instead of temperatures of 106 it was usually down around 101-102 and it did not happen at work.

After returning from the school in 1971 and after Easter, I was called into the Blytheville Air Force Base hospital for a routine physical. It had been over a year since I had seen an air force doctor and since I worked around nuclear weapons it was an annual requirement, just like for pilots, so I went in.

The next day the hospital phoned me to come back in for some additional blood work. There was something wrong with the blood test from the previous day. Okay, maybe it was related to the evening fevers I was still having. I did not really want to marry Carolyn if I had something seriously wrong with me. It would not be fair to her and the relationship I had been nurturing for months that was getting more serious since my return from the school. Might it be catching or might it signify some serious disease? I never took a prostitute, like most military over there, but many of them took tetracycline for various diseases they picked up.

I got another phone call from the hospital that afternoon. When I went in, the doctor said he wanted me to come to the hospital every 4 hours, 24 hours a day, until they came up with something. "What is wrong with my blood tests?"

"We haven't isolated it yet, but there is something strange going on. I see you have been to several countries in Southeast Asia, Vietnam, Thailand, the Philippines and it might be something unusual. So I must insist that you keep getting the blood tests until we can ascertain what it is? It could be catching, but since the fevers are intermittent we don't really think so, but we need to know."

This interfered with my work and sleep. Dates with Carolyn had to be cut short so I could run to the hospital for a blood test. I did not spend the night with her so she would not really be aware of what was going on with the blood tests in the middle of the night and I did not want to pass on some mysterious disease. Whatever the cause of my night sweats, they had decreased in intensity.

Finally after 10 days or 60 blood samples I insisted on seeing the doctor again. I could not get in right away so I dropped by the hospital lab and talked with the head blood technician who was a technical sergeant. "The doctor hasn't told me anything, but I want to know why I am donating so much blood. Is it something serious?"

"Yes, Captain, it is very serious. It is life threatening, but I can not tell you what we found and we haven't figured out how to treat it. We have even sent some of your blood samples to Brooke Medical Center in San Antonio (one of the main primary military medical centers) and they can't figure it out either. I'll get you in to see the doctor. I think you should know what we have found. Okay?"

About 30 minutes later I was in the doctor's office. "Captain Clark, it is very important that you keep coming in for the blood testing. It is very serious. We have been using those samples to find out exactly what the problem is and now we are trying to find the right cure."

"And I want you to tell me what you have found or I will refuse to come for more blood tests."

"You must continue. I can order you to. ... Okay, I'll tell you what we are doing."

"When you first came in for your physical we didn't believe what we found in your blood test so we asked you to come back for more blood testing. On the second blood test we found exactly the same results. Since then we and the Brooke Medical Center, have been experimenting for a cure."

"We found 4 different strains of malaria in your blood. If you had just one, we could treat it. But if we were to use the standard treatment for type one and you also have type two, the blood coagulates in your body and you die from the treatment. If we treat type two first, the type one would not cause the problem, but you have types three and four. We haven't found a way to treat someone that has four types. I won't bore you with the scientific names for these types, but I assure you they are life threatening and unless we can find a way to treat at least one at a time you might not have long to live. We would have hospitalized you, but since you seem to have had these for a year and still getting along, we just want you to keep coming in every four hours so we can continue our research."

....

"Two weeks later the doctor called me back in. Captain Clark, are you still having those night sweats?"

"No, not for the last ten days or so."

"Well, I have good news and bad news."

"Well?"

"The good news is that the malaria has disappeared out of your blood stream ten days ago and has not returned. We have checked to make sure we are still running the same tests, but it appears to have disappeared. You can quit coming in for blood tests unless the night sweats return."

"So, what's the bad news."

"While it appears that your body fought off the malaria it could just be hiding. Sometimes when we chemically treat one of those strains it will retreat to a joint in your body until we quit the treatment and then starts multiplying again. It would appear that your natural body defenses have killed it off and may never reappear. It could come back anytime in the next 17 years and if the fevers start again go immediately to a doctor. Maybe they will have developed a cure. In the meantime, it appears you are totally free from malaria. I must caution you to not donate blood ever. The antibodies your body put in your blood that fought off the malaria are unknown to us, but could kill someone getting your blood, just I said our treatments could kill you. Since we don't understand what caused the malaria to cure itself, I would not even want to get blood plasma from you for fear of killing someone just getting plasma from you."

"At any rate, unless the fevers come back, you are free to go about living the rest of your life and you can thank God for your bodies defenses."

17 ORI

Then in August 1971, her parents bought her a new car and got rid of her old Volkswagen fastback, a Chevrolet Malibu with the small V-8. It was brown with a darker brown vinyl covered roof and a very nice looking car. Their son needed a new car so they bought him a Pontiac, and to be fair they purchased a Ford Country Squire station wagon for Carolyn's sister, her Malibu, and a new Chrysler Imperial LeBaron for themselves. (nice to have money). They did it now because they thought we were going to get married and knew I would not accept a new car from them. They didn't ask.

A week later, the air base had an Operational Readiness Inspection (ORI). That meant that I spent the first 48 hours on duty, dozing when I could at my desk or a desk in the nuclear ordnance maintenance building. The inspection did not go well. On Friday of that week all the munitions squadron officers were asked to go to our conference room to meet with the inspection team for our results. It had gone like a Keystone Cops fire drill, not good. Then the lead inspector said, "Captain Clark, you can leave."

"Why, I am interested in what you have to say and if it is about me I have a right to know."

"Captain Clark, I said you can leave!"

I got up and left wondering what was happening. Well at least, I thought, the base brief out was in the base theater on Saturday and I would go to the squadron early in the morning to see what I had missed with the inspection team that had made me leave the meeting. It was late when I got home and went straight to my apartment without seeing Carolyn.

When I came to work that Saturday I walked into the squadron and the squadron clerk was busy typing and instead of his usual friendly greeting he looked up and then ignored me. Okay, so I walked back to squadron commanders desk and not only was he not there, but his desk was cleaned off completely. I then went next door to the maintenance supervisor's office and found the same thing. Okay, so I walked on back to the maintenance bay and no one was there. I went back to the admin clerk and asked, "Where is everyone, the wing ORI briefout is in 30 minutes? Did they change the time.?"

The admin clerk then stopped typing and acknowledged my presence for the first time, "Well the squadron commander retired last night, the maintenance supervisor took an early out from the air force with no retirement. Master Sergeant...."

It seems like I was the only officer in the squadron not fired and the only enlisted people above technical sergeant were either transferred to bad assignments, retired, or separated from the air force with no retirement. Those families living on base were transferred to off base motels and those military members still in the air force were en route to their next, not so nice, assignments, Vietnam, Korea, Greenland, etc. This left their families homeless and having to find a place to live on their own until their spouses returned from their assignments.

I was the only squadron person at the wing briefing from the ORI team. The essence of the briefing was that the entire base had failed the inspection largely due to the total failure of my munitions squadron. The entire base would be closed for a week to determine if the base would be closed or returned to active duty.

When the briefing was over, Major General David Jones, commander of 2nd Air Force came to the microphone and said to the crowd, "Captain Clark, you are staying, everyone else can go home or back to your offices."

That did not bode well for me. I ended up with the wing commander (the top officer on the base) driving a staff car with Two Star David Jones in the passenger seat and me in the back seat. "Captain Clark, the only reason you are along is that certain nuclear weapons areas are not available unless accompanied by you. I do not want to hear from you unless you are asked a direct question."

"Yes, Sir"

We drove around the alert pad and then to the nuclear weapons storage area. The only words I spoke were to tell the security police that I was escorting the commander and the general as we passed through security.

Then General Jones asked me a direct question, "Captain Clark, can you give me a good reason that you and your NCOs were not fired so we could start off with a clean slate."

"Yes, Sir. The only problems the squadron had were not following written procedure and allowing the inspection team to overstep their authority and some poor plans for an ORI that would not relate to war time."

That got the general to turn around in his seat in the front and give me a malevolent stare at me in the back seat. "Are you telling me that my 2nd Air Force IG teams broke rules and caused the problems in this squadron."

"Yes, Sir. Except for the plan for the ORI, I am saying that. The problems we had with the plan I had written letters to the squadron commander about. The rest was allowing the IG team to intimidate the squadron into doing things they should have refused to do."

"Okay, Captain Clark. I'll make you a deal. I will give you one week to get ready and then I will send in the 15th Air

Force IG team to give you another ORI. If you pass, the base will remain open and we will fill the vacant positions to replace those people we fired. I will also fire my 2nd Air Force IG team members that inspected your squadron. If you fail, I will fire every member of your squadron including you. Do we have a deal?"

"Yes, Sir."

To the colonel, "Okay, colonel, take me back to my air plane and get ready for another ORI in one week."

After the colonel dropped the general at his airplane, he turned to me, "Captain Clark, I don't know what kind of shit you have gotten the base into, but if you fail, I will be after you for insubordination. You have tried to get into see me several times and literally forced me to sign papers for you, but now I know why I don't allow Captains in my office."

"But sir, certain nuclear weapons documents have to be signed by the wing commander. I was simply bringing the papers to you for that signature and it specifically says that I have to witness the signing so some staffer doesn't sign for you."

"Captain Clark, I think you better keep your mouth shut and just hope you pass this next inspection."

"Yes, Sir." And with that, he got out of his car and left me to walk to wherever I parked. It was closer to the squadron building than it was to my car near the theater so I went in to find the Staff Sergeant admin clerk still typing.

"Well I see you dared the general into giving us another chance."

"What are you still doing here and how did you know?"

"With all the retirements, early outs, and transfers there is a lot of paperwork for me to do. Everyone on base knows what you did because the wing commander went into his office cussing you out in front of his whole staff that had been waiting for him. Gossip travels fast. Did you really dare him?"

"Not really. He said he wanted to fire everyone and I just took exception to it. Is there anything I can do to help you?"

"No sir. I would rather no one disturb my piles of paper or I might misplace something. I am about finished with what I can do until Monday when base personnel opens."

"Would you initiate the squadron recall and ask all of the new section chiefs to meet me in the squadron break room at Oh eight hundred in the morning?"

"That is one reason I was hanging around. You don't even know who the section chiefs are as of today since all the section chiefs got fired except for the ones that worked for you. I figured you would want to get them together tomorrow."

"Good thinking. You are the one that has been working, but I am emotionally beat and going home for the evening. You don't need to be here in the morning, your section is just you and you have been working hard. I don't need to give you any new orders, you are already doing more than is called for."

"Oh, I will be here. I want to hear what you say."

18 She Said YES

When I got back to the apartments in town all the officers that lived in the apartments and Carolyn came running when I parked my sports car. The question was, "Well?" (Why was I kept after everyone was dismissed?)

I leaned back against my car and told them what had transpired. I also told them about the mass firings in my squadron, nearly 50% of the manning was gone.

"What's going to happen to the base when you fail. You can't possibly pass an ORI with 50% of your manning."

"When you go back into work Monday, tell your respective offices to please cooperate with us and back us up. I think they are looking for an excuse to close the base permanently, but I think we can pass if everyone goes along."

Carolyn just said, "Come over when you change clothes and tell me what this really means."

When I came over, she met me at the door with a beer, and told me to sit at her table where she had put out some chips, bean dip, and picante sauce. "So, what does this mean?"

"It means that we have this coming week to get ready then another week-long inspection. I am the only officer left in the munitions squadron so I take the full blame. That means that Friday in less than two weeks, I will either get the next week off or I will be sent to a bad assignment immediately, or I will be kicked out and unemployed in less than two weeks. Want to get married two weeks from yesterday?"

"Let me think on that, YES."

"Did you just say YES"

"YES"

"But what if we fail and I am sent off somewhere I can't take a family?"

"Then in a year, you will be back in the states and then we can be together."

"I might get kicked out and be unemployed."

"I have a job and that means you don't have to leave and I'm confident you will find a job in Memphis or somewhere where we can be together. Will we get a honeymoon if you pass the inspection?"

"Traditionally, the base gets a week off to recover from the ORI, so I guess I will get a week off and then, since I am the only officer, I will have to be here with no days off until they assign more officers. That could take months."

"Okay, I have two weeks to plan the wedding for that Friday evening after the ORI."

"It might be that Saturday at the earliest, and only after the ORI briefing.

"Well, can you take off a few hours this coming week so we can go get a marriage license?"

"Absolutely."

"I don't want a fancy wedding, how would you feel about just going to a justice of the peace?"

"Sounds fine to me. How about if we get Jim and Linda for our best man and bridesmaid and witnesses?"

"Absolutely. I'll make all the arrangements, you just concentrate on passing that inspection."

(no pressure ha ha)

19 Getting Ready for and the Next ORI

I met with the 47% of the squadron that had not been fired and set up some radical rules. When the ORI kicked off we would immediately send all nuclear weapons handlers home for at least eight hours of crew rest. The ORI team would be upset, but there was no nuclear weapons handling for the first ten hours of the ORI.

The ORI team had to brief the command, get settled in Visiting Officer's Quarters (VOQ), and get assigned staff cars to drive during the inspection.

Then the Alert Aircraft would taxi out to show that they were ready to take off and then taxi back to the alert pad. Then the ORI team would brief the remaining aircrews on what their training mission would be.

The nuclear weapons crews would not do anything for this first ten hours, minimum. I briefed everyone that while the ORI inspection team did not need escorting, we would not break any rules at all. When it came time to load an aircraft with nuclear weapons there are rules that state that no more than ten people can be in the no-lone-zone. That meant five nuclear weapons handlers and no more than five inspectors. No action would be repeated for the inspectors on that aircraft unless someone saw something done wrong and then that one action would be repeated. If more inspectors wanted to see any action they would have to go to the next aircraft load.

I knew this was going to upset the inspectors, but I told everyone to follow every rule to the letter and tell the inspectors to come see me if they objected. I pointed out that the inspectors were not in their chain of command, I was.

The inspectors complained to the wing commander, but since he had been there when Major General Jones assigned me as the munitions squadron commander, he had to back me up.

On Friday, of the inspection, I was told that we had passed the inspection with no discrepancies which was unheard of for a munitions squadron. The Second Air Force IG team had been assigned to other jobs in the air force and I was free to skip the Saturday brief-out so I could get married on Friday night and go on a honeymoon for the next week.

After taking off a week, they were going to close the flying part of the base, ship all aircraft and nuclear weapons to another base so they could resurface the main runway. After my week off I was going to not be able to take any vacation for at least three months.

BOOK TWO

20 Marriage

Finally. I asked her to marry me over a year ago and day is here. We went to an old justice of the peace and his wife. He claimed that he had sealed many marriages over the years and they had never ended in divorce. Jim and Linda, our best friends went with us for the ceremony which took very little time. Our photographer was Jim who used a little disposable camera for our wedding photos. He caught us looking at each other with the same look as photographs taken 45 years later with a few more wrinkles but the same loving look.

We only made it to Cape Girardeau, Missouri that night arriving at 10PM. We had not made reservations since I expected to have to go to work Saturday for the IG brief out on base. We did have a bottle of champagne we shared.

We got up late on Saturday August 22, 1971, and drove on to Saint Louis where we did have reservations for Saturday night. Since we got there early we went sight-seeing going up to the top of the Saint Louis Arch and seeing the museum under it. That night we had dinner on a paddlewheel boat on the Mississippi River. We forgot to take pictures.

We had not made honeymoon plans for a trip since I was afraid I would either be unemployed or have to go to work Monday morning, but since I had the week off, we drove on to her sisters house in Elgin, Illinois. Carolyn had taken me several times to visit Shirley so I knew her well and she welcomed us. Before we left the Chicago area I found us a motel and we had an evening dinner in a revolving restaurant with a live band. Then we returned home to

Blytheville, Arkansas and our jobs. Carolyn to her job as a state social services worker filling out welfare requests and doing investigations and me to my job as munitions squadron commander.

Shortly after we married a two bedroom apartment came available next to the swimming pool. All the two bedroom apartments were in one story buildings while the one bedroom apartments were in two story buildings built motel style with a single outdoor covered walkway from one end of the building to the other with end and middle stairways. The lower floor was a sidewalk under the second story walkway from end to end. Our original apartments were both on the second level. The two-bedroom gave us a place for all of our furniture. Much of mine was borrowed from the airbase which we returned. My Hollywood style bed went in the guest room and her bedroom set went in the master bedroom.

I spent many long hours shipping the nuclear weapons and most of the equipment to Loring Air Force Base in Maine while our runway was being resurfaced. I had to oversee the loading of every C141 cargo plane carrying weapons and the KC-135 cargo areas with the handling equipment. Many of the squadron personnel were sent to Loring along with the weapons. Gradually the squadron received new personnel to replace those that had been shipped out after that first ORI. There is a written rule that says the munitions supply officer cannot be acting squadron commander of a munitions squadron for more than 90 days, so on day 89 a lieutenant colonel arrived to take over from this new captain. While he was getting settled all of the nuclear weapons and the equipment was shipped back to Blytheville Air Force Base because the runway work was completed.

21 Meeting my Parents

That Christmas I was able to take a week off from work since we had a new squadron commander and my work was caught up. We drove to Enid, Oklahoma to meet my parents. As we walked in we faced the floodlights of my mother's 8mm movie camera. Back in those days it took very bright lights to expose the 8mm movie film in use by individuals. It could not have been pleasant for Carolyn meeting that brilliant light for the first time and not being able to really see anything other than the lights. My mother finally turned off the floodlights and my parents met my bride for the first time.   My parents were very non-judgmental people and it would not have mattered if Carolyn had two heads and purple, if I married her she was a member of the family. Then it was still photo time with the flashbulbs going off. My brother was there from college and shy. My parents house was nice, but only a two bedroom, one bath house with an eat-in kitchen. The one car garage had been converted to a TV room and my room when I was in college. The garage door had been replaced with a brick fireplace.

Bruce, my brother, was kicked out of his bedroom and took the TV/bedroom while we were ensconced in his bedroom that had been cleaned up for us with clean sheets. The heat for the house was a floor furnace which you never see anymore. Basically there is a metal grate in the floor in a central location, this one was at the junction of the living room, bath, and the two bedrooms...not quite big enough to be called a hall. If the bedroom doors were closed, you got no heat. The electric range heated the kitchen which had a doorway, but no door to the living room. Similarly, the

TV/bedroom had no door either. My mothers house was always neat, but cluttered with knickknacks on shelves, furniture, etc.

Good thing, Carolyn, was not uppity. She had been brought up wealthy with only the finest things, but she didn't care about those things. She judged on personalities and sophistication of the people themselves. We spent Christmas Eve there and Christmas morning then we struck out in Carolyn's Chevy Malibu for Fort Smith, Arkansas to see her parents later on Christmas day.

I knew her parents already, but this was the first time after our marriage. We had not invited anyone since we got married on short notice by the Justice of the Peace. Her parents knew we were going to get married and had already approved of me. After spending Christmas afternoon and the next day with her parents we drove back to Blytheville.

This was the start of 45 years of miracle laden, wedded bliss. The most perfect Cinderella marriage imaginable. We were never rich and never would be money wise, but we could not have been happier. I took care of Carolyn and we never wanted for anything, but Carolyn would have been happy anywhere under any circumstances as long as we were together, and the same said for me. Nothing else in the world mattered more to me than her. I had seen her when I was 12 and fell in love at a distance. I didn't actually meet her until I was 26. Her shoe size was 5.5 which also made her my Cinderella. She had decided she would be an old maid before we married because she couldn't have children and now we were until death do us part. But on with the story.

Shortly after Christmas, Colonel Billings ordered me to move into base housing. Rather than Captain's housing, we were assigned to field grade housing for majors and above. As a junior Captain we had a 3 bedroom house on base with all utilities paid except for the telephone which I had to have for work. The Colonel had not wanted to talk to a lowly Captain before the ORI, but now wanted me close by so that I could respond quickly to missions and answer any questions he might have.

Carolyn had not been able to keep pets at home because her mother was always cleaning and didn't want a pet in the house so she found some miniature poodles for sale and we named him Snoopy. He had papers, but we called him Snoopy. He was solid black. He was house trained almost immediately. He never barked until during a particular violent thunderstorm with the rain pouring a friend burst into the side door to the kitchen and surprised Snoopy. We didn't mind him not knocking with the rain coming down like it was or actually we wouldn't have minded if it was a nice sunny day. He was a friend and our house was always open to friends. In all our years of marriage we never locked our doors unless we were out of town or when we went to bed for the night.

22 Change of Plans

We had gone back to our routine except now we were living together as husband and wife. I had gone back to the routine of being a nuclear ordnance accountable supply officer. Accountable because I was the one that signed for "ownership" of all the nuclear weapons on the Strategic Air Command (SAC) base. My previous couple of jobs was as a MASO (munitions accountable supply officer) where I was accountable for all the conventional munitions on base. In fact my first real job as a lieutenant had been as the Air Force Detachment Commander on Tooele Army Depot. I had 900+ igloos of explosives and 40 warehouses of inert things like bomb fins. This was temporary storage for conventional munitions enroute to Southeast Asia and the Vietnam war. My next job had been the same on a base over there. Then to SAC where I met my love.

Carolyn was back to her job working for the state of Arkansas as a social services worker. Our friends were the same and we still went for Friday night pizza and the happy hour at the Officer Club on base. We still attended the parties over in the single bedroom apartments.

I applied to get out of the air force for my second time so that I would not have to worry about getting a remote assignment that Carolyn could not go to. There was still the possibility of going back to Vietnam or elsewhere without her. By way of explanation, an officer signs up for 4 years of active duty plus 2 years for every year of education paid for by the air force. I got none of my education paid for so I had signed up for 4 years so no one could accuse me of dodging the draft. All officers technically sign up for recall until they are age 60. Even though retirement comes after 20 years which would make me 42 if I stayed to retirement, I would still be eligible for recall to active duty until I was 60. To get out of the air force before retirement one must apply for a date of separation after their initial commitment. Mine was 4 years. The last time I had put in for a date of separation I received orders to go to Southeast Asia time stamped 4 hours prior to the time stamp on my request for separation. So I served an extra year and when I was assigned to SAC they would not let me apply for separation until after I had been back in the states for a year. I got married during that year, but as I was approaching another year I requested a new date of separation.

This time I received orders for a remote accompanied tour of duty with the German Luftwaffe on at Buchel German Air Base in the Eifel Mountains of Germany. The orders were time stamped 4 hours prior to the time stamp on my request for separation. Therefore, I was obligated to serve another 3 years of active duty. At least it was an accompanied tour where Carolyn could go with me. I only had a few weeks before I had to report. We decided to sell our cars here in the states and buy a German car that would be easier to maintain on the German economy since I was not even going to an American air base. We were only allowed 2000 pounds plus our suitcases which we would carry to the airplane.

Her one year old Malibu which was like new sold for book price. I had a less than one year old Mercury Capri which was German made, but American specifications. It did not have good handling so I sold it for what I still owed on it. I sold my black Datsun 2000 2 seat convertible with a roll bar racecar cheap. The buyer did not believe how fast it was until he was on the interstate near the base and a Mustang came up beside him showing him their first place trophy from the drag strip and gunned the engine, slowed down, gunned the engine and when the new owner of the Datsun decided to see how fast it was he downshifted to third gear (he should have used second gear) he caught up with the Mustang, shifted into forth beside the Mustang, left some rubber next to the Mustang that was near its top end then casually shifted into fifth gear just to show them he still had another gear. If pushed the Datsun would run to 140 in forth at the redline of 7000 rpm and leave rubber hitting fifth. I only did that once, having the front wheels leave the ground while the rear tires are spinning is not fun.'

Her bedroom furniture and table and chairs, along with my el cheapo bedroom furniture, all went into storage paid for by the air force until our return to the states in three years.

23 The Trip to Germany

Off we go on our first really big adventure. We have sold our cars, selected clothing to take with us. Naturally much of mine were uniform items that had to be in the suitcases for the airplane because our 2000 pounds of hold baggage might take weeks to arrive by boat at Bremerhaven, Germany, the main seaport for American items, then trucked to Buchel German Air Base (Luftwaffe). Carolyn packed a minimum of her clothes to allow me room for my uniforms in the suitcases. Just another example of her sacrifices for me over her lifetime. We had put our furniture and many lifetime memories in storage for the three years in Germany.

We had to rent a shipping crate for our miniature poodle, Snoopy. First we had to fly into Philadelphia to drop Snoopy off at the pet transport which the air force would not arrange or pay for. Fortunately, Germany has no isolation period as long as the dog has its shots. We rented a car at the airport, got our bags, and Snoopy from the baggage carousel in his crate. Then we had to navigate to the pet shipping company we had selected. In those days in 1972 there was no GPS or cell phones so it was maps and stopping at gas stations for directions. We got to see him for awhile and turn in the stateside air shipping crate and turn over a crying dog to the overseas shippers. Then we drove to McGuire Air Force Base for our military flight to Germany. We got there four hours early by design and were tired already from our long day.

Carolyn had never been on a long flight in a large airplane. It was a commercial airliner under contract to the military for the flight. They fed us well during the long flight. I had flown longer over the Pacific Ocean 4 times, and was able to sleep on those flights. Carolyn did not want to sleep so neither did I. We arrived at Wiesbaden Air Force Base, which was shared between military and civilian flights. After our arrival at 12 midnight, we picked up our bags. Then we took an air force blue school bus to the Visting Officers Quarters (VOQ) to spend the rest of the night until our ride to Buchel GAB arrived in the morning. We finally checked in at 3AM. Carolyn went to the bathroom and came out laughing hysterically. "What's so funny?"

"Come here and look at the toilet, Al, and you'll see."

What I saw caused me to laugh too. It was the first time that we saw a German toilet that we would live with for the next 3 years. If you go "number two" it lands in a little depression with almost no water and just sits there until you pull a chain that allows water from the flush tank mounted high on the wall. The water than washes off the little depression into a bigger hole in the front part of the toilet. Hilarious.

"I wonder if all the toilets are like that?"

"I hope not, AL, I don't know if I can get used to it just sitting there until you flush." We were exhausted and got into the bed and tossed and turned until morning.

Captain Dave Hill arrived at 10AM the following morning in his own car (POV – personally owned vehicle). He drove us over to a civilian baggage terminal in another area to pick up Snoopy that had flown in the cargo hold of a different airplane. We had warned him we had a dog. He spoke fluent German which made things easier and he had already found out where to pick up dogs that had been shipped. He was to be my military sponsor in the new overseas assignment and became an especially good friend.

He was a Mormon that had spent time in Germany on a youth missionary in Germany and then spent another 5 years there on military assignment and now was in his third year on another military assignment to Germany. He pointed out things to see on the road trip to the town of Ulmen, Germany which was near Buchel GAB and got us checked in to the Hotel Burgerstube.

It was a picturesque whitewashed typical German hotel in the small town of Ulmen about 10 miles from Buchel GAB. The inside was old, but kept like new with polished dark wood or stark white trim. It had a small dining room that served all 3 meals.

The concierge spoke a little English and they took care of us exceedingly well. As we had checked in on a Saturday we had the weekend to walk around the small town. The hotel had very good German meals that exceeded anything we have found in the way of German food here in the states. Our room was not large and had mainly white walls and, thank goodness, a private bathroom. One of the best rooms in the hotel. The bed had a thick white cotton comforter. We needed that because we had arrived in April and the heat in the hotel had been shut down for the summer, but our room was around 50 degrees. We had not packed warm clothing having come from Arkansas in April after it was warm there. We had to wear jackets at all times to stay warm and snuggle under that thick comforter in the room.

The dining room was warmer and fortunately the days were sunny and warmer outside than inside. We both felt very uncomfortable at first, but the hotel was very friendly. By the time I went to work on Monday, Carolyn was not scared to stay there by herself. She said she spent much of the time in the dining room that was warmer than our room. She actually got out on foot to visit a grocery store. Captain Hill picked me up to officially report in to the squadron. I could not go to work because my Top Secret clearance had not come through yet and it could be months even though I already had a Secret Restricted Data clearance for nuclear weapons from my SAC assignment in Arkansas.

Captain Dave Hill, took me around the German Luftwaffe base sight seeing and took me by the recreation area that was a double Quonset Hut with a two lane bowling alley in one side and a movie theater in the other side. The all ranks club was an old wooden building with creaky wood floors and dark. It had a small bar area, a little side room with foosball tables, a couple of slot machines and some poker tables. The ballroom, had a small raised area for a band maybe big enough for a crowded four piece band. We were the only ones there, but Dave had a key. It was a far cry from the Officer's Club at Blytheville AFB, Arkansas. This was an all-ranks club because there were only 8 officers and about 100 enlisted members in the detachment. Counting wives and children maybe 200 people total.

Carolyn asked when I got back to the hotel, "Where are we supposed to shop? I went to the town grocery store and all they had was hard crust bread like French bread, very little canned food, very little meat in their meat counter, no hamburger or hot dogs or lunch meat. Their vegetables are all fresh."

"We will have to make a trip to an American air base commissary."

"Where?"

"There is one at Hahn AFB on the other side of the Mosul River which is the closest and about 45 miles and then Bitburg AFB about 60 miles in the other direction. Hahn is our support base where the detachment picks up mail daily and where we do all of the official paperwork."

"Does the mail truck deliver groceries?"

"No, we will have to drive."

"We don't have a car yet. Dave is going to take the two of us to Bitburg AFB tomorrow where we can look at some cars. You didn't want me to get the Jaguar XK12, but they have an on base dealer for the BMW 2002 which I think is a pretty good car and Dave has found a used Porsche 911 at a German dealer that only has 15,000 kilometers on it."

"So what is 15,000 kilometers in miles?"

"You multiply by point 62 so that would be 9,300 miles, almost new."

"What is the difference in price?"

"The BMW 2002 is $4300 US and the Porsche 911 is $5000 US."

24 Fate – the First Time in Europe

So, after looking at the US spec BMW 2002 with air conditioning, leather interior for $4000 Carolyn saw the Porsche Red 1970 Porsche 911E with 911S magnesium wheels, Recaro leather seats with only 9300 miles for $5000 and that was it. It was a good choice. Let me explain, the 911S was the most powerful Porsche back then, but in Europe the 911E had more power with mechanical fuel injection and dual point capacitive ignition versus carburetors on the 911S. However, the E normally came without the other features of the S. Our E had the magnesium wheels, the Recaro seats and the full S gauge package. Dave had gotten us a special price from the dealer because of his fluent German. The previous owner had gotten a DUI which back then was a $3000 fine and loss of license for a year. That's why it was for sale cheap. The new price for one would have been $9400 which was out of my price range. For comparison an Oldsmobile 442 new was $4200 so $5000 for a used Porsche was good, but a new one was out of my reach.

We could afford it because the German government apartment we were getting was considered substandard therefore, even though we paid no rent or utilities other than phone, I got to keep my full off base housing allotment plus a special German off base cost of living increase. Our only expense was the car payment to my US bank back in the states, our groceries and clothing, and gasoline for the car which we used coupons for so we did not have to pay the exorbitant European gasoline tax of about $3 per gallon, so we paid 23 cents per gallon of premium.

Little did we know, but that Porsche was the right car for us. It gave unequivocal status throughout Europe. It gave you the right of way over everything else. As we approached borders, the guards were waving us through as I was downshifting for the borders. If cars were moving at all, traffic jams melted away in front of us. The best example was one time we had just left Switzerland headed into southern Germany and two trucks were driving side by side blocking the autobahn at 50kph (kilometers per hour or about 30 miles per hour. Cars were backed up for at least a mile behind them. As I approached the jam in the left lane, cars melted into the right lane to let us pass and then moved back into the left lane behind us. I didn't flash the lights European style, they just saw a Porsche 911 and moved out of the way. Eventually we were right behind the left truck still growling up the hill. I pulled over onto the shoulder, flashed my lights once and the truck slowed down, moved to the right lane to let us pass then moved back to left lane continuing to block lesser cars. I drove slow compared to most Porsche 911s. Carolyn made me stay under 160kph (about a 100mph) and usually around 140kph (87mph). We frequently had to dive into the right lane to get out of the way of all the other Porsche 911s traveling at 140mph. One time as we were entering the autobahn a big BMW Bavaria and a Mercedes flew past us. Carolyn wanted to see how fast they were going so I got about a half mile behind and sped up to 200kph (120mph) and when they saw me the car in the left lane slowed to let me pass. I did not really want to drive that fast, but was now obligated to pass them, so I did. I kept it up to around 240kph (150mph) until I could not see them any more and then got off at the next exit and drove under the underpass of the autobahn out of sight. I waited until I heard them roar past then some more before I re-entered the autobahn and drove my usual 140kph.

One funny thing we laughed about was the entry and exit signs of the autobahn. The entry sign said Einfahrt and the exit sign was Ausfahrt. When we got to Europe were no speed limits even on the two lane roads. Fortunately hitting the brakes on the 911 was like hitting a sand bank. You would be cruising along at 80mph and come over a hill to find two farmers stopped in opposite directions with their tractors blocking the road talking.

Sometimes, you would be climbing a twisty mountain road behind a semi-truck crawling slower than I could idle in 1st gear. I would try looking 2-3 corners ahead for oncoming traffic and then punch the 911. I would be next to the rear duels when I would have to hit 2nd gear at 7300rpm and then 3rd gear at 7300rpm before I got to the cab of the truck.

Some of the city streets were just wide enough for my Porsche 911. I had one of my enlisted people try to follow me one time. I did not know he was following, but he got stuck in a street with both of his door handles wedged between the walls. He had to get a farmer with a tractor to pull him back out to find a wider street.

25 Our First European Road Trip

Since I could not go to work without a Top Secret clearance I decided to use some vacation time to drive to Paris the second full week in Germany. We got our French gasoline coupons for US military for 23 cent per gallon of high test. European price with tax was nearly $3 a gallon. I had the maximum 60 days of vacation time I had built up with the intent of having the pay for those days when I got out of the air force. Since we went to Europe instead, I had most of the 60 days left and would have to take 30 days over the next year. I had used some leave to visit my and her parents before we left the states. The air force gave me several days of leave to travel to Europe which we did not use all of.

Remember, we did not speak the languages and GPS had not been invented so the best we could do was AAA tourist maps of Europe (I still have some). We could not sleep, so we took our bags and Snoopy and took off early in the morning for Paris, France. When we drove through Luxembourg the border guard stations were not manned even though the signs in English said we would have to stop for inspection. We drove on through. It was getting daylight as we entered France on a nice but deserted two lane highway. Shortly thereafter we saw a French police car on the shoulder and a policeman with a hand held stop sign came out to stop us. I had taken French in college, but dropped out after 4 weeks with an F. I was able to sort of understand what the policeman was saying because "passport" is passport. As Carolyn handed him her passport and I handed him my US military ID card, Snoopy practically jumped into the policeman's arms. We sort of talked about the fact that I had just arrived in Germany and we were heading to see Paris and "Yes, we had hotel reservations." I don't remember the rest of the conversation, but I was amazed that I knew and understood more French than I had when I dropped out of the French class years earlier. The policeman never looked at my ID or Carolyn's passport and he handed Snoopy back to us and told us to have a safe trip (in French).

26 Paris
Multiple Miracles and Adventures

Miracles happen again. Carolyn could not read maps. She did not want to drive into Paris traffic but have us stop at a commuter parking lot and take public transport to our hotel. We never saw the parking lot and were soon trapped in traffic. The street was marked as 4 lanes, but there was 3 lanes of traffic in each direction. When we would get to a stoplight we would have car door handles within an inch of our car door handles. We could not see any street signs so we had no idea where we were. As we stopped at traffic lights I would attempt to find out where we were on the map, but still could not find street signs on the cross streets. When I could see the signs they were either too far away, or in my rear view mirror.

I finally decided that before we went any further into Paris I needed to find out where we were because I "felt" we must be getting close to the hotel. I found a one way street to our right and turned. A block later I saw a P for a parking garage going back the way we came but a block off the main road. I pulled into the underground parking pay parking lot halfway down the 3 block (no cross streets) street. We locked the car and walked up to the street level to walk to the corner to find a street sign that I could identify on our tourist map. We had parked across the street from our hotel. Is that luck or a miracle?

We went back down, got our suitcases, and I disabled the car by taking its $75 rotor from the distributer. We checked in and ate at a street side bistro and then decided to get Snoopy and walk down the street to find some grass for him to do his business. About a mile from the hotel we arrived at the Louvre that was closed for the evening. In front of the Louvre was a large city park with wide paved walks and park benches. The park goes from the Louvre to the start of the start of the Champs-Elysees the famous street leading to the Arc de Triomphe the main high class shopping street.

Because of all the people on that main walkway we found a more private paved sidewalk along the outside fence. About halfway through the park we heard police whistles, shouting, and people running, so we stayed where we were and just kept walking. When we got to the other end of the park, the thirty foot high wrought iron gates were locked and in the far distance the Arch d Triumph was lit up. We had walked past some side gates so we went back the way we had come and found the side fifteen foot high wrought iron gates were also locked. Now we were feeling a little panicky since the park was locked with us inside and most of the streetlights in the park were turned off.

When we got back to the Louvre the fence was only about 4 feet high with park benches on both sides. The benches and steps of the Louvre were filled with French teens necking. We stepped over the fence going from bench to bench on the Louvre side. Someone asked, "Americans?" and I answered, "Yes". Then the cry went out that we were Americans who had hidden in the park after curfew to have some private time. Everyone of the teens applauded us. Carolyn was embarrassed. I did not deny that we had been necking in the park after curfew. A number of the compliments were in accented English. We got back to the hotel around 10PM. Was that a miracle or just another of our many adventures.

....

The next morning, we walked Snoopy back to the park again, then back to the hotel, then back to the Louvre to go in and see the famous art. We made it through most of the Louvre and were just sitting studying The Night Watch by Rembrandt when we noticed that we were the only people there. We decided to go out in the hallway and did not see anyone. I checked the time and saw it was about 5:10PM. Did the museum close at 5?

We decided we better head toward the front door. As we went the hallway lights behind us went off. As we got to the main lobby the last guard, keys in hand, was going out the door when I called to him that we were coming. He asked why we had not left when they gave the announcement and I said, we didn't understand it. I said, "Yes, we're Americans." I don't know what he said, but we came close to having "A night in the museum."

Was that another miracle that we did not get locked in or arrested or just another adventure?

27 Street Walking in Paris

The next morning, we took the dog and walked the mile to the Louvre, the half mile through the park, then walked the full distance of the Champs Elysees to the Arc de Triomphe. Along the way, a couple of older American women tourists made the comment about Snoopy. "Look how they starve their dogs. They should not be allowed to have them."

We didn't let them know we were Americans and every since Snoopy's plane ride from the states she had been forcing canned dog food down his mouth because he was refusing to eat. I started to tell them, but Carolyn grabbed my arm and moved us on before I could tell them.

After the walk to the Arc de Triomphe Carolyn was not up to climbing the stairs to the top and we couldn't take the dog, so I took the stairs, alone, two at a time while she waited below. When I got down, we then walked all the way to the Eifel Tower. Again, she told me to go on while she waited on a park bench with Snoopy. Because of the crowd I only made it to the first level and then worried about Carolyn having to wait down there by herself so I went back down. We had been walking many miles the last couple of days so we decided to take the subway to Notre Dame Cathedral. When we got down below we could not figure out what subway to take because everything was in French and my French that had been working so far failed. A French businessman saw we were lost and asked in good English if he could help. He told us what subway to take and what stop to get off and also what stop would be close to our hotel after Notre Dame.

Once in Notre Dame, we found a tour group going up a narrow stairway so we joined in behind them and once we started up the stairs you could not turn around because the spiral rock enclosed stairway was only wide enough for one at a time. Eventually we arrived up at the balcony with the gargoyles. The tour was in French so we went off to the side and took pictures next to the gargoyles. Unfortunately the film did not feed right and everything was double exposure and not good.

The tour group went out another door to leave and we waited a few minutes and then went to the door which was locked. We went to the other door where we had entered the balcony and it was also locked. It was starting to get dark, we could see heavy rain coming, it was already lightly sprinkling, and we were looking for the best spot to spend the night locked on the balcony until morning in the rain and getting cold. A few minutes later a janitor came up to empty the trash can and we escaped. Another miracle, or just another adventure. This was the third evening in a row we had almost gotten locked in a Paris landmark. The first night in the park, the only low fence had been at the Louvre and there were park benches on both sides making the exit possible. Then the Louvre and Norte Dame being the last ones out after closing time.

....

A trip to Paris would not be complete without a shot at the nightlife. We had booked a tour of the nightspots for that evening. Thank goodness, the bus picked us up right at the hotel. We first took a trip to the Folies Bergere for dinner and the show. We were seated right up against the stage. Midway through the show, some dancing girls came to us and took a Polaroid photo of us and called us "The Arab and one of his Wives". I was dark from Arkansas sun and most Europeans then were very pale in comparison. It was neat being the only ones in the huge crowd singled out. A miracle, or just another adventure.

From there we went the Moulin Rouge for another show

28 After Paris

The next morning we got an early start to avoid Paris traffic, by early I am talking we left the hotel at 5AM. We drove around the Arc de Triomphe while there was little traffic just to say we did and then on out of Paris toward the autoroute (vs the autobahn in Germany). I filled up with gas just before we got on the open highway headed south. I think Carolyn went to sleep before I got up to speed because I really motored driving between 160 and 200kph (100-120mph). She woke up when I pulled in for gas with the red light on the gas gauge blinking low. Our gas mileage had dropped to 16mpg at those speeds. Nothing passed us.

We spent the afternoon around Grenoble, France, spent the night in a motel and the next morning we drove on to Marseilles and then over to Monaco along the coast.

We drove through Nice on the way. We had always heard about the beaches there, but they were all gravel except for in front on some high dollar hotels where they had hauled in sand. On the border between France and Monaco we found we could change French Franks for one rate then walk across the border and change Monaco money for Franks and make an over 12% profit. There were a number of tourists walking aback and forth making that profit each time. I did it once just to verify that I could then we went on to our hotel in Monte Carlo, Monaco.

The hotel was on what the prior week was the start finish line for the Gran Prix. The next morning we got up early, went up to the palace, took photos of all the Yachts in the harbor then back to the hotel and the car for a drive around the route taken by the Gran Prix. Obviously, we could not drive that fast, but it was still fun.

That night we went into the famous Monte Carlo Casino. We dressed in our best clothes we had and just wandered around. We could not get into much of the casino without a pass where they had verified our credit, but even the main room we saw wagers of over $100,000 dollars on the roulette wheel and Baccarat tables. By having the Guards Red Porsche 911 the doormen and parking attendants treated us like we were somebody and not just a couple of relatively poor tourists. In fact, one of the doormen told us there was a tournament we could go to for a deposit of $100,000 in credit. I pretended that we had the money, but just wanted to see what kind of action was going on tonight. Another advantage to driving a Porsche 911 in Europe. We spent a couple of hours there, then walked over to one of the old grand hotels that had rooms at $3500 a night just to see the lobby. Then we went back to the casino, explained that we had just driven from Grenoble, France and were calling it an early evening.

The next morning we got up early and drove back toward Ulmen, Germany. Amazing how you can get around Europe quickly with no speed limits driving a Porsche 911. As we headed north we drove through the 11 kilometer tunnel through Mont Blanc into Switzerland. We spent the night in a Holliday Inn Hotel in Lucerne, Switzerland and that evening ate dinner on a paddlewheel on the lake there. It was much more elegant than the paddlewheel we had taken on the Mississippi in Saint Louis, Missouri on our honeymoon.

The next morning we headed home to Ulmen, Germany and our hotel there. It had been a tiring, but very fun week traveling in Europe while I waited for my Top

Secret Clearance to come through. The next morning going into Germany is where we found those two trucks slowing traffic on the autobahn except for letting my Porsche 911E go past.

We got home to Ulmen and the hotel before dark and had Sunday off. On Monday, I found that my Top Secret Clearance had been rushed through. Whereas normally it would take 2-3 months, mine had taken 2-3 weeks, or just over a week in Germany. I had replaced an officer whose father was commander of the Air War College that had gotten an early release from the assignment to go to an air force paid for law school. Whereas people normally had 6 months notice prior to that kind of assignment I had only weeks so they had pushed my security clearance through. Since I already had a higher than normal Secret clearance the upgrade was fast.

29 Daily Living in Germany

We also had a German government apartment assigned to us. I went back to the hotel and we packed our bags and moved into the apartment. It had all new Ikea type furniture including a king size bed (with two single mattresses). Someone had found us an over and under American style refrigerator freezer with a transformer to drop the power from 220 to 120 volts for it to operate. They had also gotten us a washer and dryer installed in a room in the basement under the apartment building. The building had multiple outside doorways that each had 2 downstairs apartments and 2 upstairs apartments. The kitchen range was German and very small with about a 1 cubic foot oven and three burners on top.

We had something unique from other Americans there. They had a water heater for the kitchen that would heat water only when they pushed the button and held about a gallon. Their bathroom had a larger hot water heater, but again, you had to push the button and wait hours for it to get hot before you could bathe. We had a 20 gallon electric hot water heater, with an automatic thermostat to hold a temperature, suspended over the bathroom tub which also supplied water to the kitchen and bathroom sinks so we always had hot water.

All of the apartments were heated by a centrally located coal stove in the wall that put out heat to the master bedroom and the living room with no heat in the 2nd bedroom, bath, or kitchen. We had to go down to the basement daily and scoop up coal in our coal buckets and carry them up to the coal heater. This coal stove in the wall between the living room and the main bedroom was intended to just heat those two rooms with no heat in the second bedroom, kitchen, hallway, or bath. I took the doors off the living room, kitchen, and second bedroom and we left the bathroom door open when not in use in order to heat the whole apartment. That meant using more coal which we did not pay for, but had to carry up from the basement coal room.

We quickly leaned how to keep it banked off and burning continuously. If you let the fire go out and the apartment get cold then you tended to burn it too fast to heat the apartment. When you burned the coal too fast, the iron impurity in the coal would create a chunk of slag, called a clinker, like a rock that was too big to get out the ash clean out door at the bottom and could only be done with the fire out. This required using a chisel and hammer to break up the chunk to get it out.

Most Americans did not keep the apartment warm at all times and ended up with clinkers almost daily. By keeping it burning slow all the time I only had to clean out the ash once every week or two and seldom had clinkers that did not come out of the ash clean out door. As soon as I got it cleaned out we would get it burning slow again to keep the heat on low, but without creating the big clinkers.

It was interesting in that the Germans burnt all of their trash in the heating stove. As you walked outside you could see black, yellow, blue, green smoke coming out of our neighbors chimneys but our chimney did not have much smoke.

The last year we were there the German government installed "central heating". Instead of each apartment in the building with 4 stairwells of 4 apartments with each of the 16 apartments having their own coal room, we would have one room in each building with a boiler burning heating oil that would provide hot water to steam heat wall radiators in each room, including the second bedroom.

The Germans complained at first because they would have no control over how much fuel was used. Using individual coal rooms they would fill the room for X marks and make it last the winter. Now the cost of operating the boiler would be added to their rent.

When I heard central heat, I thought of forced air instead of old fashioned radiators with the popping and cracking of heating and cooling and bubbles in the lines.

It was fun watching the German workers. They would start at 8 AM each morning and working hard and accurately, but at 10AM they took a beer break. Then as they installed pipes for the steam heat they would frequently mis-drill the holes and have to drill another a few inches away and then repair the hole in the wrong place. After lunch it got worse and then they would quit for the day at 2 PM. I saw the same thing from civilian workers on the German air base. The German staff, either military or civilian were always professional. It was just the civilian worker bees that were drunk by noon each day.

On the other hand, we had huge amounts of trash that the Germans did not have. We didn't burn anything but coal and an occasional newspaper to light a coal fire. We purchased a lot of packaged products like cans of food, boxes of cereal, etc. The Germans not only burned their trash, but did not buy packaged food. They shopped almost daily for what they were going to eat that day. They purchased fresh vegetables and bread so they had little trash.

This meant that their tiny trash cans that were about a foot in diameter and 3 feet tall were only have full on trash day. The Americans had a minimum of 3 of those outdoor trash cans and on trash night, used the empty part of their German neighbors cans. Our last year there the Germans installed a number of dumpsters instead of emptying all those individual cans. This solved our trash problem.

We found out immediately, that we were the only Americans on that side of the highway on the hill. All the other Americans in German base housing were in a low spot on the other side of the highway in old two story townhouses that had not had new furniture or paint or wallpaper in 20 years. It was called the American ghetto and we were "on the hill". Many American chose to use their housing allotment and cost of living allowance (COLA) to live in private housing off base. This was usually renting the upstairs or downstairs in a two-story house with the owners living in the other half. I was the only officer in government housing at that time.

....

Carolyn was a perfect air force wife. She never complained about being isolated from other Americans. She never complained about having to have me drive her to an American base to buy groceries because she didn't want to drive 45 miles on German mountain roads. We had no English speaking radio stations or television. At night, we would read books taking turns reading to each other. We read all of the James Harriot books about the British country veterinarian, like "All Creatures Great and Small". How she survived the loneliness those first few months I don't know. About a month after we moved in she took the dog for a walk and forgot to take her key. The apartment door was sprung to close quickly and automatically locked. She was shut out with the dog. Our German next door neighbors in the downstairs apartment came out to the stairwell and helped her take off the door handle so that the lock could be released and get back in. Our neighbor had not spoken with us because the wife was studying her English she had been required to take in public school in Germany. Carolyn and her got to be good friends.

A few months later I got a new NCOIC of the chow hall which I ran as an additional duty as the logistics officer. He was assigned to one of the two upstairs apartments in our stairwell since we were getting along with our German neighbors. Marge and Joe became fast friends. In fact 35 years later, Marge and Joe looked us up and dropped by our house in Florida. We exchanged Christmas cards every year since Germany. In the evenings, we would frequently play cards with either Marge and Joe Hills or our now English speaking German neighbors.

Interesting thing. Germans have to pay a monthly fee to their government to listen to the radio or watch television for over the air broadcasts. In fact, our expensive, all the options Porsche 911 had no radio so the previous owner, a German, would not have to pay a monthly fee for it. As American military we did not have to pay the fee, but we were too far from the military radio station to receive it and the German TV was in German naturally, but we did buy a German television set. It was interesting watching old American TV cop shows in German. Their broadcasting did not start until around noon and went off the air by 9PM, but we had a TV. We played a lot of 32rpm records those years without English speaking radio and television.

We watched the German Olympics on that German TV especially when they had the Olympic team from Israel taken hostage and the ensuing gun battle live. Most of our news was from the Air Force Times, a newspaper put out by the

Air Force to bring news from home. We also subscribed to several magazines.

As logistics officer, one of my many additional duties was to be in charge of the American school for dependent children at our detachment. That meant we had American grade school teachers that worked for me (technically). The German government bused our older children to Bitburg Air Force Base for junior high and high school each school day. At Hahn Air Force Base the high school kids were sent to an American boarding school at Wiesbaden, Germany Monday through Friday, so we had it better as our kids got home each night. If there was a football game or music concert after the school bus went home, the parents had to drive the 50 miles to pick them up. I negotiated and the German's agreed to delay the bus to let our students attend these after school events.

After being there several months, Carolyn realized that the American children had nothing to do in the evenings and weekends. I did the paperwork and Carolyn did the work of getting an official American Girl Scout Troop established in Ulmen, Germany, our home for the next 3 years. Each apartment in our building had basement rooms assigned. I cleaned up one of the rooms, painted the walls and ceiling, collected some used furniture and that is where the scout troop met. Carolyn did all the regular work of getting scout supplies and made all the plans for the scout meetings and 100% of the girls there attended the meetings. She got another American wife to help her with the meetings and finding supplies. I helped however I could.

The officer's wives (all eight) had monthly dinners and parties at each others apartments with the organization rotating each month. We had many months where you would go to one apartment for before dinner drinks and appetizers, move to another apartment (or two) for dinner, then another house for dessert. Military wives, especially overseas, have to be special women. The fact that we were not on an American installation, made it many times harder for them.

Many times we met at a German restaurant in Cochem, Germany. Ulmen was not large enough. It had one little walk up eatery where you could get Bratwurst and Pom Frites or French Fries served with mayonnaise, no mustard or ketchup. The other alternative was to eat at the Hotel we had stayed at when we first got there. I miss the meals they served there and I especially remember the Spiessbraten from this one out of the way restaurant just outside of Cochem. The first time an American military person would dine there the owner would bring out his photo album of famous people that had eaten there which included Hitler and various German and American generals over the years. Their Spiessbraten was pork filet stuffed with cooked onions and spices that was fabulous.

One time Carolyn and I had gone there alone and when we drove up to our apartments American wives met us before we got to the apartment to tell us there was an actual alert and that all military were to report to their duty stations. I grabbed a uniform and drove to the base in the Porsche hitting well over 100mph on the two lane. I slowed to maybe 80mph as I ran the stop sign and crossed the highway outside the gate. The German guards had heard my Porsche as I geared down coming toward them and were holding the gate open and waving me through. As I flew past the visitors pass building I saw a lot of American personal vehicles parked there. I was going too fast to stop and with the guards waving me through I kept gearing down and took the 90 degree turn just inside the gate at around 40mph before accelerating on the streets on base toward the alert pad where German airplanes were standing on alert. Again, the guards heard my Porsche and had both the inner and outer gates open and were waving me through. I thought I should not drive my personal vehicle into the alert pad so I slid to a stop on the grass outside the gate and ran through to the alert facility. When I ran into our alert room, there was no one except the one officer and one enlisted person normally on duty. They didn't know why no one else had shown up.

I called down to the visitor building where I had seen a lot of American cars and discovered that the German Luftwaffe had detained them at the visitor building and would not allow them in the gate. I talked to the German boss there on the hot line from the alert room to the visitor center and they let the Americans proceed onto the base and their duty stations. I guess another advantage of driving a Porsche 911. I had the only one at the Luftwaffe base and everyone knew it so the guards were willing to break rules for me.

Only a couple of officers were the right age to have children there. They were either young and waited to have children or older and their kids were in college. One couple had gotten pregnant while there and went to a German doctor believing that they were better than the Air Force doctors and a lot closer being stationed at a German Luftwaffe base for something for morning sickness, Thalidomide. A few months after returning to the states their child was born without hands or feet, Thalidomide. He became a Shriner after his child was helped by the Shriners. We lost touch with them.

We had another good friend that was on his second tour in Germany and decided he wanted to go visit Yugoslavia on vacation. We didn't need to tell anyone where we went so they drove there. They were waved through at the border entering and leaving Yugoslavia, but when he got back to the base he discovered that all his stuff had been shipped back to his home of record in the states and he and his wife had airplane tickets to do the same. He was an instant civilian after 9-10 years of service. Our security clearances forbid us to go to any communist country and even to go to West Berlin took about 6 months to get permission to even take the US military troop train to go to West Berlin. This made it obvious that they watched us closely when we thought we were anonymous when driving around on vacation. Either that or that they flagged him crossing the border even though it did not appear there were any Americans at the border and he was not stopped. The same thing happened to another officer there when he and his wife got permission to ride the train to West Berlin, but took a commercial tour bus into East Berlin. The tour bus was not allowed to stop on the east side. Both officers knew better, but thought there was no harm since they were loyal Americans and no one was watching, or so they thought.

30 Adventures in Camping

I had brought along a two-man tent in our 2000 pounds allowed because I had heard camping was good in Europe. We were not interested in anything in Eastern Europe since we had not seen Western Europe. After our first camping experience in Europe, most of our many trips were with that two-man tent, a small butane BBQ grill, and a butane lantern. Whereas we found the hotels to either be below what we wanted with only a few rooms in a small hotel with a shared bathroom down the hall, or in someone's spare bedroom. The other extreme was a nice American style hotel where the people were cold, did not speak to each other, and the workers were almost unfriendly. There were a few Holiday Inns that gave a 50% military discount and were similar to American hotels, but were seldom where we wanted to stay. Campgrounds were hugely different. Everyone was friendly even if they didn't speak English they would try.

Sometimes we someone would have a campfire with 3-5 nationalities sitting around trying to converse with each other. Someone would carry around a bottle of alcohol going from camp to camp offering a drink and then go to the next one. Camping was convenient and cheap. We stayed several nights at a campground in Rome on the grounds of the Savoy Palace. It cost 25 cents for the car, 25 cents for the camping, and 25 cents for each person so we could stay for $1 a day versus a Holiday Inn would be $50 a day even with the 50% military discount. Staying in someone's spare bedroom (Zimmerfree) would be $20 a night.

The first full day there in the Rome campground we took an "around the city" tour bus that came to the campground and then picked up some people at several hotels. As we rode around the guide would tell us in English what we were passing. I jotted down the city bus numbers I saw stopping at the tourist sites.

The next day we took the campground bus out to the last city bus stop near the campground and we took a city bus to the main terminal where we got on the appropriate bus number to take us to the Coliseum or Vatican City or wherever. We also did a lot of walking when things were within walking distance of each other. We did that for several days. At night, we would join in the comradery of our fellow campers. We met a lot of English speaking tourists our age from the Netherlands and Australia and Great Britain proper. We also made quick friends with other Europeans that spoke English.

One evening when I went to take a hot shower I took a lot of coins to pay for the shower. There was a long line and when I got to the front of the line the guy coming out of the shower explained that someone had a pocket knife they put in the coin slot so everyone could shower for free but I was to pass on to the next person the campsite number of the guy that owned the pocket knife to return it. Probably 30 people after me took a free shower with his pocket knife. The next morning after coffee I went to the campsite and sure enough, he got his pocket knife back.

One day we had a little shower while we were out exploring Rome and surrounding areas. When we got back a couple came over to explain that we had left our cookware out in the rain so they put it in our tent. They had also rolled up the windows on the Porsche that were not fully closed.

They were apologetic for having touched our stuff and we thanked them profusely for going out of their way for us.

Once a week we would spend a night in a nice hotel just to be able to sleep in a regular bed and take a long shower without having a line waiting outside the shower.

How many American girls in their late twenties that had been brought up wealthy would enjoy camping in a two-man tent all over Europe? Carolyn was one of a kind. By camping cheap we were able to travel more and buy more souvenirs while living within our means.

We made numerous trips to other places in German, France, Belgium and the Netherlands on weekends. Drive up Saturday morning early and home late Sunday night. On our Spain trip the plan was to drive all the way to Gibraltar by way of Madrid. When we got to the Spanish border they were just building a 4 lane and the two-lane was incredibly slow. When we got to the town of Figueres, Spain, in Catalonia ,along the Costa del Sol (coast of the sun) with nice sandy beaches on the Mediterranean we saw a campground sign and it was too late in the evening to make it to Barcelona that had been our plan. As we got off the highway, we saw the problem on the main road. There was a two-wheel wagon loaded high being pulled by a single donkey blocking traffic. There was too much traffic for anyone to pass and we had been following that donkey cart for miles without getting close enough to see the traffic problem.

Anyway, we found the campground right on the beach. We had gotten the tent set up when we discovered a big ant den close to the tent. Then the campers across the street started packing up their tent to leave. There had been a Land Rover sitting there with its air conditioning on. As soon as the other campers left, I moved everything to their now vacant campsite. The people in the Land Rover drove up, rolled down a window and said, "We timed you at 2 minutes and 38 seconds to move. Where did you get that tent?"

We slept late the next morning and went out to enjoy the beach and water. In 45 minutes our poor excuses for German suntan turned into a light burn and we had to call it quits. We decided to drive back into Figueras and see what was there. We drove to city center which was a totally vacant cobblestone square. We saw no other cars or people and wondered about driving into the square, but drove on up and parked near a Spanish Cathedral that looked interesting. Before we could walk up a priest came out to welcome us in Spanish and made it clear it was okay to leave our car there.

My Spanish is about like my French, not much. The priest explained that the wooden pipe organ over the main entry was the largest all wooden pipe organ in the world. He then led us back behind the alter to show us his collection of things. One thing that was above all others was a Bible in a glass box open to a page that I could read that the date of 1491 and Columbus's signature. The priest got the message across that it was Columbus's personal Bible that he left at the church before his voyage to America. Wow, was that another miracle. How many other Americans have stopped to see it or the wooden organ? Was our visit there a miracle? How many Americans have seen that Bible signed by Christopher Columbus? In fact, Google could not find the wooden pipe organ in 2017. I tried looking up more information about the cathedral in Figureres, but nothing there. The organ was so much larger than the one listed in Wikipedia it was not even comparable.

Later, we saw a sign for a bull fight in town so we went to it. It was bloody and we were the only American's there. Some people sitting near us got others to move so they could sit with us and explain the bull fight to us in English and translate the announcer. Another special experience few people get. Neither Carolyn nor I were squeamish, but, later, we both decided we didn't ever need to see another bull fight although we wondered whether a bull fight for tourists would be so gory. It's one thing to butcher animals for food, it is another to watch them tortured and people taking risks with their life and their horses lives for entertainment.

We went on to Barcelona the next day. The traffic was better. Two things that stand out about Barcelona. The first was our walking trip to see the Picasso Museum. We drove near where it was supposed to be and then parked in a Spanish Museum parking lot, got directions and started walking. There would be a sign on our right a few blocks down this street. After at least 2 miles we got to the Barcelona Zoo where the street ended. We walked up the next street over all the way back to where the car was parked and got directions from someone else and started walking down the original street. We got about half way to the zoo again and decided the Picasso Museum closed at 5 and we might as well give up and return to the car. About halfway to the car walking in that direction was a small sign about 4 inches tall with an arrow pointing down this alley to the Picasso Museum. That was the only sign and you could not see it unless we were walking back toward the car and looking up about 10 feet high on the side of the building at the entrance to the alley.

The alley was narrow so that we had to walk single file past a couple of small Spanish cars parked in the alley. If someone wanted to drive through every car in the alley would have to move. We came to a wider area where there was a farmer's market and got directions again. About two more blocks down the alley from the market we came to the Picasso Museum which was getting ready to close. We did a quick walk through and left. They had kept the museum open just for us and had already locked the door and we didn't want to delay their leaving any longer. I would have loved to have spent hours there.

The next day we were just driving around and saw these old Spanish style sailing ships, found a place to park, and walked over to them. We got a personal tour from a future crew member who explained that they were building the ships to recreate the voyage of Columbus and planned on being in the USA for the 500th anniversary of the discovery of America in 1992.

Years later in 1992 we had driven to Corpus Christi, Texas for a winter vacation and saw those same three ships sail into the Texas bay where they were going to be a permanent display. We mentally made the connection with those three ships we had seen in Barcelona, Spain and were amazed at the miracle that we were there in Corpus Christi where they were finishing their voyage nearly 20 years after we had seen them the first time. We drove down the next day to see them at the Texas dock. Over 100,000 visits to them were made over the next 10 days, but we got our own semi-private early tour of them by that same crewmember we had met in Barcelona as he remembered Carolyn and invited our two kids to see the ships and us to see them again, finished.

Another small miracle. I'm glad we did not have to stand in line when the official tours started the next day. In 1993, a year after we saw them a barge lumbered into them damaging two of them and they were moved on land. The disintegrating ships were destroyed in 2014.

We had spent 5 days in Spain and never gotten beyond Barcelona where we were to have spent the first night, and rather than face the slow traffic to go on over to Madrid we decided to go back and see more of France.

We took a different road than the one under construction so we were on a two lane mountain road when we got to the French border. Traffic was backed up at least a mile. There was a canyon and we could look across and see the Spanish border station. They were stopping every car and taking out all the luggage and going through it. Every so often they would take a car into a garage to do things like take the tires off looking for something. Our Porsche was packed with souvenirs where I had left a small hole in the back seat about a foot wide and 6 inches deep so I could see out the rearview mirror. Carolyn had her feet resting on other souvenirs in the front right seat. We commented that if we had to take everything out, we would probably never get it back in again.

The European Spec Porsche 911 did not like to idle and would carbon up terribly if I tried. The mountain road was too narrow to turn around with no shoulder next to the canyon and a rock wall on the right side. I would let the cars ahead move forward a ways and then start the car, drive it forward to catch up, rev the engine and then shut it off. As we got even with the border guards on the other side of the canyon one pointed at me and made a motion to go around traffic and come to the border. I stuck my hand out the window and pointed down at the roof of the car using sign language to ask if he meant me and he bowed at the waist in an exaggerated YES, and waved me around. I went by the hundred or so cars up the road, around the hairpin turn and back to the guard station where he waved me through without stopping. Another advantage of driving a Porsche 911 in Europe.

I didn't see anyone at the French side of the border. A few miles up the road we saw this huge walled city, looked at the map and found we were approaching Carcassonne so we made a side trip over there and walked around the city and followed a tour group in English explaining the history and particular things to see.

We had planned on staying at a hotel that night, but by the time we got into a larger town after walking around

Carcassonne it was getting late. I had marked a hotel on the map, but, as usual, we were semi-lost in the town. I saw a campground sign and we camped.

The campground looked like a subdivision with nice paved streets with curbs and frequent street lights like the old gas lights at the turn of the century but just a few tents here and there where people had driven over the curbs to set up their tents. My Porsche did not sit that low to the ground, but I was very careful going over the curb. I set up the tent in an open area under a fairly new small tree. We set up our little butane camp stove and heated a can of Dinty Moore stew and then I headed for the bathroom.

When I got under the lights of the bathroom I saw the whole building festooned with spider webs and crawling spiders. It was the same inside with spider webs and spiders all along the top of the walls. Carolyn was terribly afraid of spiders and was hoping she would not see them as I was dead tired from driving for 14 hours and had no other place to go other than try to find a hotel in a town where we were already lost in the dark.

Thank goodness Carolyn went to the bathroom taking the dirty dishes to wash with hot water in the sink area and didn't look up. She saw one spider near the sink and came out, "Al, there is a spider by the sink. Go in and finish washing the dishes and bring them back out. I'm not going to stay in there with a spiker."

Little did she realize there were thousands and thousands. Of them everywhere along the upper part of the building. I finished the dishes and we both crawled into the tent and slept soundly after our long day.

The next morning, she got up and went to the little campground store and bought some rolls. I stayed at the tent and heated some water for instant coffee and put away our camping gear in the Porsche.

Carolyn came back and we ate the rolls and drank the coffee. Carolyn happened to look up and see the webs and spiders in the tree we camped under. "Al, that tree is full of spiders. We have to get out of here. I'm going to the bathroom before we go and I want you waiting when I come out."

"She came out at a run. The place is crawling with spiders everywhere. Didn't you see them?"

"Look up at the eves."

"My God, Al, the place is crawling with them. I want you to go in and complain. They better not have gotten into our camping stuff. Maybe we should just leave it all here."

I went into the office and inquired about the spiders. The reply, "We are by the river and we don't have mosquitoes. The spiders are harmless and we want them."

I tried to tell Carolyn this as we drove north through France.

Another memorable thing on that trip was because I had gotten reservations at Mont Saint-Michael to eat at the famous restaurant and stay in the attached hotel. We drove our Porsche out there on the causeway, checked into our tiny plain room, toured Mont Saint-Michael, and then went to the restaurant for our dinner. Neither of us could read the menu and like many other European places, refused to speak English. This was supposed to be one of the primo restaurants in the world so Carolyn ordered the most expensive meal for two. I didn't want to order that because I could not read the French but I could read what a few of the other choices less expensive options were. I was not concerned about the price as with all of our camping we were not short of money, I was just afraid of what it might be.

I am not fond of seafood and will turn it down if given a choice, but Carolyn hated seafood. The first thing they brought out was a large fancy platter of oysters. Carolyn took one look and had me reject them. They then brought out a very large lobster and Carolyn cringed. She then got up and left the restaurant leaving me to try to explain in French that, no, we did not think the food was bad, but my wife had decided against eating there. I paid the bill and then when I found Carolyn outside the restaurant she had me get our luggage from the hotel room and we went back to the mainland and found a dumpy hotel to spend the night.

On another trip we camped next to another walled city in eastern France and we walked in the next day. You could not drive a car in as the streets were not made for cars. It was interesting, but I have never been able to find it on a map and never found out what it was called.

I could go on for many pages of our experiences in Europe. We could drive a lot of places and get home on weekend trips and I used up 120 days of saved and accrued vacation time while we were there. We had great experiences, loved every bit of it except that meal at Mont Saint-Michaels which was embarrassing, but made another memory. At this point I will just add a couple more things that happened in Europe and then get this story of our love and miracles back to the states.

31 Germany When Not Sightseeing

What did we do in Germany when not sightseeing or partying with our friends there? Buchel German Air Base had an impromptu skeet range. You parked on the top of the hill where they had a small shelter for rain. You went out with your shotgun and stood on top of an old German pillbox (where during the war they had machine guns to defend the base) and someone in the pillbox would use a clay pigeon thrower to fire off clay pigeons for the person on top to try to shoot. I had purchased the cheapest shotgun at the American Hahn Air Force Base gun club which was a 3 shot 12 gauge Winchester semi-automatic shotgun. The Americans and Germans would meet there once a month in nice weather to compete with each other. It was not Germans versus Americans, it was every man for himself and the comradery between the German and American military. We would empty our guns and then the next person would bring their gun and take their turn. We also took turns going down into the pillbox to shoot off the clay pigeons. Each person had the opportunity to try to shoot 25 clay pigeons that day, two or three rounds per shooting turn depending on whether their gun held 1, 2, or 3 rounds. The guys shooting the clay pigeons from inside the bunker/pillbox tried to make me miss by firing off not one, not two, but three clay pigeons which I had to try to hit before they fell to the ground. One of the few clay pigeons I missed completely was when they fired off 4 clay pigeons and my gun only held three shells. I usually came in first place with 25 of 25 hits. Carolyn, using the same 12 gauge shotgun usually hit 17 or more of 25 attempts and frequently came in second place. She was the only female that was there because I would not go without her and so to get me out to have fun with the guys, she would go too. She had been shooting clay pigeons with a shotgun since she was about 10 years old. Big gun, little woman, but more capable than most men. They laughed at her the first time, but after 2 or 3 times beating most of the 20-30 men each time, they accepted her as one of the guys although only 5 foot zero and light weight shooting a gun almost as long as she was tall.

Another adventure at home was when some other Americans made a deal with a German riding stable to teach the Americans how to ride German military style. Carolyn had grown up riding horses for show so naturally we went together. I am only a so-so rider, but just like Carolyn would do things that she didn't necessarily like to get me to do things, so I went to the riding classes with her because she wanted to. The Germans all had the full riding gear with special riding uniforms like you see them wear at the Olympics while the Americans typically just had blue jeans, the official riding hat, and official riding boots like the Germans had, but not the full uniform. I am not that big at 5 foot ten inches and 187 pounds, but my calves were too big for the tall riding boots. I had to slit the inside of both boots to fit over my calves and use rubber bands to make it look as if they fit.

It did not take long before the German Riding Master that owned the stable and all the horses put Carolyn on the monster horse. The only other person that could ride the horse was his daughter who used the riding crop unmercifully on the horse to make it behave. It would go in a circle to keep her from getting on and then try to buck her off until she subdued it with the crop. Every few minutes she would have another fight with the horse and have to beat the horse again. Other riders could not even get on the horse. I say monster horse, not just because it was unruly but because it was huge like the knights of old must have ridden with all their armor. It was built like a heavy thoroughbred, but was the height of a Clydesdale, just nowhere near as heavy and without the feathering around the hooves.

Carolyn asked if she could try to ride the horse. The riding master thought it was funny, but with the lack of her understanding German and him not understanding English he made the motion to go ahead and try. Little five foot zero Carolyn had to lunge off the ground to grab the English style saddle to pull herself up to where she could get a foot in the high stirrup. The horse tried to go in a circle to not allow her to get on, but she did. The horse then tried to buck her off, but Carolyn was stuck like glue. When Carolyn tried to use the riding crop like the daughter did, but not hard, the riding master said "Nine". Carolyn was not allowed to use the riding crop like the master's daughter, we just had it for show, but the horse quickly realized she was in control and behaved for her and went where she guided it without fighting her. The rest of us could gently use the riding crop to get the horse to move faster. Carolyn had no need of the crop.

My horse was the only other unruly horse, but normal sized if maybe a little smaller than the rest. My horse wanted to pick fights by biting the other horses or me if I got too comfortable. I am not a good rider like Carolyn, but I can manage to ride if necessary. I probably would have hit the ground if my horse had really bucked. I sometime got a little buck, but not serious.

After a couple of weeks of riding in a line around he indoor arena Carolyn and I were asked to join the all German advanced riding team. That was much more interesting in that not only did we ride around the outside of the arena but we also rode line abreast where every horse was beside another horse, twenty horses wide and not just at a walk or trot, but at full gallop.

One of the most difficult things was when the master would call out "Aus"   "Sitzen". We would be riding line abreast at a full gallop when he would call "Aus" and we would put one leg over the saddle so that both legs were on the left side, then a moment later he would yell out "Sitzen" and we were expected to bring the horse to a sliding stop, and land on both feet at the same time as all the other horses and riders beside the now stopped horses head still in our perfect line abreast of twenty horses. It was not hard for me from my little thoroughbred, but for Carolyn that would mean dropping six feet from the horses back to the ground and landing on two feet beside her monster horse. When everything was stopped, he would call "Ein", and we would put a foot in the stirrup and then he would call "Sitzen" and we were expected to be sitting on our horse. I could stand nearly flat footed and get a foot in the high stirrup. For Carolyn this meant leaping into the air to grab the saddle out of reach of her hands if she were only standing, pulling herself up to put a foot in the stirrup and then mounting the horse at the last command. That "Ein" command was not easy. Let me remind you that the stirrup is not a western stirrup, but closer to the English stirrup which is high off the ground.

He was proud of this huge monster unruly almost white horse. He wanted us to ride on his team competitively against other teams around Europe because little Carolyn was the only one who could ride that monster and she was so tiny in comparison to it. He could not show off this horse in competition without her, because only his daughter could control it and then with generous use of the riding crop which did not look good in competition and resulted in the horse trying to buck his daughter off until she beat it into submission and every few minutes having another fight. The horse behaved for Carolyn in that as tiny as she was she was very strong and the horse knew he could not even begin to dislodge her or fight her. So after the first time she rode him, the horse would settle down immediately. If anyone else tried, it was dangerous. Several German riders insisted on trying to trade horses, but either could not get on the horse or found themselves on the ground. Only three men tried in the months we rode with the team. They could not believe that little Carolyn could control the horse and they could either not get on or stay on if they got on. Some of the German team spoke good English and remarked on her horsemanship. She was only one of about four women on the team.

Unfortunately, when it came time for a competition, I was going to be stuck at work and could not compete. This was not fair to the German riding team we had practiced with, so we dropped out of the team and quit riding.

Carolyn did not complain, but when seeing a doctor to get a new prescription for TEDROL for her asthma the doctor told her she would probably have to have a hip replacement at some point. He said the air force could do it, but he would not recommend it at her age because it would wear out too soon. She should wait until she could not stand the pain and when they had better longer lasting hip joints developed. He prescribed Ansaid for it. It is an NSAID but worked better than anything else. I know because after an injury I tried some of her Ansaid and it was wonderful. I guess it was a small miracle that my job caused us to drop out of the riding team because her hip was taking punishment. Carolyn would never have dropped out until the pain was greater than anyone else could have stood. This way, it was my fault we could not continue riding so naturally Carolyn, as always, went along with me.

In 1974 the air force had an early out program at the end of the Vietnam War where they allowed any officer the opportunity to leave the air force regardless of time owed for education or whatever. I applied and a message went out a few weeks later that went to every base and detachment worldwide. It said, "All personnel applying under this program are hereby approved with their requested date of separation with the following exception, Captain Albert L Clark. Then there were 3 more paragraphs explaining that they could not let me go due my security clearance, unique training, and current assignment. I would have to finish my tour and a year in the states. Sound familiar. This was the third time I had not been allowed to establish a separation date.

The Germans came to us and said they wanted to close our all ranks club that got used very little. When the air force closed down the slot machines, our all ranks club got shabby. The USO had refused to come back again. I was given another additional duty to also be the club officer. There was an old club outside the gate at Buchel German Air Base and I got the Germans to let us use that club. It had a large horseshoe bar with a refrigerated room below for kegs of beer, a nice stage, room for about 75 tables of 4 in the main ballroom, a German style bowling alley in the basement. They agreed and went about fixing what needed fixing and then we moved in. I got some guys and a German truck and we collected old tables and chairs from other American clubs that were being refurbished and enough table cloths to disguise their shabbiness and mismatched designs.

I had multiple sources of supply. Since we also had a few US Army personnel I was able to buy things from the Army, the US Air Force of course, and the German Luftwaffe. I did a lot of horse trading and was able to buy things from one of these sources and trade for something else from another of these sources. Eventually I got enough table flatware and glasses to outfit the bar and the dining room. I hired cooks for extra wages that worked for me as military in the chow hall. Our dining room food was so good that soon we had a lot of German Luftwaffe Officers and their wives coming to our club to enjoy steaks and hamburgers they could not get on the economy. The Germans also liked our American red wines.

I got the USO to give us a trial run in the new club. When we had that first USO show the place was packed with our American detachment and all their kids plus German officers and we crowded in nearly 500 people. We made so much money that headquarters was talking about taking money from our little all ranks club with 120 members and giving it to big bases with hundreds of members. To counter that we started hiring expensive entertainment from the states. On Friday night there might be a concert for 25,000 in Frankfurt and on live German TV and the next night they were in our little club. We had to start limiting how many German's could attend even though they let us attend their clubs anytime we wanted and had to limit US military driving 50 miles to come to our little club.

As in everything I did, that was not a classified part of my job, Carolyn was my advisor, organizer, and sounding board for my ideas. In developing our new club she organized the wives and off duty military into self help projects to make the club our own club instead of just a cold empty building. The German Luftwaffe provided the supplies needed and the technical help with things like the electrical and heating systems.

During the week when we didn't have entertainment we had a steady flow of both our own service members and German Officers that just came to eat dinner. Where in Germany can you get Tex-Mex and good steaks for a reasonable price if you can find it? These are just not available in Germany. All my help were enlisted military looking for some extra cash paid out of club profits.

Our movie theater had been shut down and our two lane bowling alley had quit having leagues because the equipment kept breaking down. Guess what, another additional duty. I got new our old movie projectors overhauled, got some training for our enlisted folks hired by me to run the movies. We made arrangements with a bunch of nearby Army units to change our mail run so that each unit would have a different day for the mail run where they would pick up mail for everyone and deliver it to all the nearby US military Army detachments. While doing this, they would also pick up movies that had already been shown at one base and deliver them to the next base on the new mail route. This meant instead of getting a new movie every two weeks or one a week or maybe not for 3 weeks we instead now had a new movie almost every night and everyone on the mail route got the same great movie service. While this meant the daily mail run took a long day, each detachment did not have to do it daily and we had better service.

Again, while I was at work, Carolyn organized wives and off duty military to spruce up the place that had ceiling tiles and broken wooden stadium seats.

We had a good maintenance person who knew everything in our maintenance books. I slapped down a foot thick maintenance manual for the pin-setting bowling machines in the bowling alley and offered him 3 times minimum wage to try out fixing the bowling alleys out of our recreation services funds. To have the funds to pay him, we fired the contract maintainers from the manufacturer, that had to come from Frankfort, that were doing a terrible job and we now had reliable bowling and restarted the league bowling. A side benefit was we also had a great cash snack bar that served the now popular movie theater and bowling alley combination.

When I got ready to finish out my 3 years there and move back to the states, the German Luftwaffe honored me with their standard going away, a 5-course meal, live band and dance. German's spent either all of their career at one base or maybe left for 3 years and came back to finish their career. They served until they were 55 so they spent 30 years at that one base. A German going away party was a big deal. They also gave me a prized ($2) beer stein only given to retiring German military. I was the first American to receive this honor.

On the day we were supposed to leave, the German's said they wanted us to close the theater and bowling alley and if I could give them a design they would build a new facility close to where our barracks and headquarters building were. I have made contact with Buchel in the ensuing years and was sent some photos of the new facility I designed that day.

Carolyn advised me on everything from the new club, to the theater and bowling alley and everything I did that was not classified. She never questioned what my real job was.

When I actually left Buchel German Air Base in 1975, I was given a German going away party at their officer's club. One of my prized possessions is a $2 small beer stein with JABO 33 painted on it which is normally reserved for retiring German officers that spent most of their 35 year career at that base. I was the first non-German to get one. I have no way of knowing if others have gotten the beer stein. It has my name and my dates of service on Buchel GAB engraved on the pewter lid. Carolyn asked in front of everyone to stand by me as I was presented the beer stein. "An officer owes his success to his wife" as he German commander said.

32 Further European Adventures

We were gone a lot exploring the various Cathedrals and Castles of Europe. We made several four hour trips to Amsterdam and I think we saw every art museum there as well as wandering the streets. We visited the Hague, Brussels, Belgium and many other places on weekends.

The only other long trip we took there was our trip to London, England. Great Britain is the one place I would like to revisit someday. It was the only tour we took as a tour member in Europe. They had a special price for the U.S. military. We parked at our support base, Hahn Air Force Base, Germany and got on the bus to take us there.

I slept or read on the bus. It was cramped and boring compared to driving the Porsche and took hours to get to the coast where we boarded the ferry boat. Luckily, because we had so many Americans on the tour, the bus stopped at established bus stops with restaurants and restrooms instead of like a typical bus that would just stop and let the passengers out to relieve themselves along the highway. Americans are too modest. It is not far from continental Europe to the coast of England.

The sun was just coming up when we could make out the White Cliffs of Dover in the distance. We docked and transferred to buses again. This bus trip was more interesting in that the sun was out and the English housing was so different than what we had seen in the rest of Europe to date. Even the apartment houses were different with that packs of 6 to 10 chimneys close together instead of separated like in Germany. Some houses looked like they should have thatched roofs like in the story books and movies.

Our hotel was across the street from the Royal British Museum which was showing King Tuts treasures. We would like to have gone over there to see the exhibit, but the line, or queue as they call it there, wrapped around the whole museum twice. We did go over and inquire from some people on the outside line. They had been there all night and had been told they would be lucky to get in tomorrow. We were only going to be in England for days and the tour had places for us to go, so that was out.

The next morning when we looked out the window we could see the lines at the museum were still there. The tour took us on a bus trip around London, going to the "City of London" where there are hundreds of banks and ending at the Tower of London which is a fortress type of structure with the actual Tower inside the fortress. Underneath the Tower is where we saw the Crown Jewels guarded by the Beefeaters. It was really crowded down there. We wandered around the fort seeing the apartments of Anne Boleyn in fortress. It is near the Tower Bridge which many people think of as the London Bridge, but the Tower Bridge still stands in London.

The next day our bus took us to Windsor Castle. It was so foggy that we could not see the sides of the street. Finally, the bus parked in this town and we were told to cross the street, find the wall, and go to our righut along the wall until we got to the gate. We did. It was just a blank wall the color of fog. We could not see it from more than five feet away.

We got to the gate and I took a photo of Carolyn with a Royal Guard. We were guided through the castle and into the rooms they wanted us to see. We ended up purchasing some photos of Windsor Castle in sunshine since we only had hazy photos of the outside and dark photos of the dim interior. This was before digital photos so you needed a certain amount of light but were not allowed to use flash.

When we got back to London, we did some shopping and I bought a nice readymade three piece suit with two pair of pants. Then we walked for miles and visited some friendly London pubs and talked with some real Londoners.

London, compared to most of Europe, was almost like being in the United States. It looked British. The people spoke English with an accent. But we felt at home there. We could read the signs in English and ask anyone for directions naturally.

………………….

Of course we saw the tulip fields of Holland, drove along the dikes, and saw land being pumped dry. The picturesque windmills and Dutch villages were photo opportunities as we took multiple day and weekend trips to the Netherlands.

One interesting thing that was not funny at the time but was memorable in the Netherlands was when we were walking our miniature poodle and Carolyn let loose of his leash. Snoopy got too close to a dirt canal near a windmill and slid into the murky smelly water. I don't remember how I got him out, but he stunk up the car on the way home.

……………

Another point of interest was this miniature city where various cathedrals, famous streets, an airport with airplanes taxiing and tour boats on miniature rivers flowed past castles. That was worth quite a few photos.

33 German Highlights

We took a lot of trips around Germany. With no speed limits on the Autobahn and having a Porsche 911 put all of Germany within hours of our apartment. We went to Heidelberg, Germany and walked the castle walls. Heidelberg was one of the first places we went in Germany. It was also the site of our one car accident. We were looking for a road to take us to the castle and I saw a gas station to fill up the Porsche on the left side of the road. The river was on our right. I had to stop and wait for some oncoming cars before turning left. About six cars were stopped behind me as I blinked my turn.

Then I started crossing the two lane road into the gas station and heard tires squealing. As I looked to my left I saw a Mercedes sedan power drifting around the cars that had stopped behind me and coming at over 60 mph in a 30mph speed zone. I steered back to the right, but the Mercedes clipped my front fender. The police were called and the German Mercedes driver said it was all my fault. As an American, naturally I was at fault. The VW driver that had been behind me said that I had on my blinker and it was a double yellow no-passing zone so it was not all my fault.

We settled on each of us would fix our own cars and no one was at fault. The Mercedes attempted to drive away, but his bumper and fender were shoved into his right front wheel which would not turn. Several spectators pulled the metal away so the wheel could turn. He drove about a block and pulled over to the right with steam coming out of his hood as the radiator had been pushed into the engine fan. I drove my Porsche away with the most serious expensive damage being the turn signal plastic lens that wrapped to the side of the fender. It was not the plastic, but the chrome rim of the signal light. By the time I got it to a dealer for repair of the eight inch circle that was about one inch deep in the front corner of the left fender, I had bent the chrome rim straight.

After I got the repair estimate I called USAA insurance that insured U.S. military officer in Europe. They gritted their teeth and asked how much. $400. $200 of which was for the signal light. They were relieved. They said that 50% of the Porsches they insured in Europe were either totaled out or stolen in the first year. Anyway, this showed the strength of the Porsche versus Mercedes. His bumper should have protected the front end of his car instead of moving back a foot when just glancing off my Porsche,

A little background on driving a Porsche 911. If you are on a mountain road and see a corner marked at 25mph and try to go around it at 25mph like driving a sedan, you better hang on tight and be prepared for the heavy backend of the Porsche heading for the outside of the turn. If you are going into the turn at 35mph and just let off on the gas when the backend slides out, the car will leave the road tail end first. If you know how to drive a Porsche, you can enter that corner at over 100mph, hitting the brakes hard to get down to 70mph in the apex of the turn and leave the turn at over 100mph without any sliding or even a squeal of a tire. Hitting the brakes hard causes the car to squat down and spread the whole width of the tires onto the road. Acceleration causes the backend to squat and get amazing traction. I have passed cars on turns with all 4 wheels sliding by carefully using the brakes and gas pedal to drift around them. Adding gas moves you out and letting off carefully you drift back to your lane. Sounds dangerous, but the car was in perfect control at all times with being able to steer the car by adding or reducing acceleration.

Letting off the gas in a turn causes the rear wheels to tuck into center leaving only an inch or so of rubber on the outside edges of the tires on the ground causing the back end to uncontrollably slide as the amount of rubber on the road instantly goes from the several inch width of the rear tires to that one inch outside edge of the tire. The Porsche amazed me many times as long as I drove fast. Driving it like a sedan was dangerous.

……………………..

We spent several days in Bavaria, in southeastern West Germany. We walked up the long walk through the woods to Neuschwanstein Castle and then took the guided tour through the Disney Castle. It was built by King Ludwig II, the king of Bavaria starting in 1869 using mostly his own royal treasury and borrowed money.

Then we went to one of his palaces out in the middle of a lake, Herrenchiemsee, which is a partial model of Versailles Palace comprising over 90,000 square feet and has sculptured gardens surrounding it like the Palace of Versailles.

We saw Hitler's Eagles Nest and drove through Oberammergau, Germany where we bought a two foot tall four inch thick carved wooden grape picker that hangs on our wall. We stayed in a picturesque German hotel with a nice view of the mountains.

Along the roads of Germany, particularly in Bavaria are these little roadside shrines which are every few miles and frequently depict a saint. Great photo opportunities.

……………………..

You have to understand that Western Europe would fit on the eastern side of the Mississippi River. We could drive from West Germany to Spain in one day. With our Porsche 911 we could drive to Rome in a long day or Spain. It was 4 hours to Amsterdam, 5 hours to Munich, Vienna, Austria in a long day. Due to sight-seeing we spent two days to Vienna driving my $80 Volkswagen Beetle that would not exceed 80mph. We drove the Beetle because my Porsche had developed an engine miss on the way back from Amsterdam the previous weekend and the Vienna trip was pre-scheduled during the week.

Brings me to another story. When we got back to Germany after the Vienna trip I troubleshot the Porsche 911 and found a bad spark plug resister. I went to the Porsche dealer 80 miles away and told them I needed a new resister. They at first thought it was a language barrier, but I showed them in the parts book what I needed. They tried to say they don't list the resister as a part they can order and sent me back to their service department. The head of the service department had been the Porsche international racing team chief for years and spoke excellent, if accented, English. He did not believe it was a bad resister either. I insisted that the bad resister was on number 6 sparkplug. He said he would order a complete tune-up to include 6 platinum plugs, a 9 quart oil change, new oil and air filters, new brake pads on the 4 wheels, balance and rotation of the wheels, adjustment of the shift and clutch cables, and four wheel alignment. If it was the resister he would charge the equivalent of $15, otherwise it would be $300 plus parts. I had no choice and knew it was that resister because I had isolated the problem by moving it around on the engine to see when it misfired and left it on number 6 sparkplug.

A few hours later, he took it out to their half mile racetrack behind the dealership and I could hear the engine roar and tires squeal. He brought it back around, went up to the new car showroom, took a resister off the engine, brought it back, put it on number 6 sparkplug and went back out to the racetrack. The engine sounded better and tires squealed louder. He brought it back and said, "Resister on number 6 plug. Bring it back when it is due for an oil change and it will be $15 each time. So the rest of my time in Europe I took it in for the complete service for $15 each time which barely covered the cost of the oil. What a deal! He thought I could tell which plug from driving it and must be quite a driver. I never told him I had moved that resister all around trying to diagnose the problem.

34 Back to the States

My assignment was to another small unit, Saratoga Springs, New York. My German neighbors made the comment that it would be nice for us to drive over on weekends to visit our parents in Oklahoma and Arkansas from upstate New York. I still had a globe on the German government coffee table and I showed them how far we were going to be from home versus the size of Germany. "We never realized how big the United States is. No wonder we lost the war."

We had another American friend that was stationed in Oklahoma. His German neighbor flew to the United States and phoned them to ask to be picked up at the airport.

"Which airport?"

"Laguardia in New York."

"You need another airplane. It would take at least two days to drive to New York."

Carolyn really liked our new assignment. She loved horses and there we were across the street from the thoroughbred stables for the famous Saratoga Horse Racetrack, about 4 blocks from the harness track, about 6 blocks from the main racetrack. Saratoga Springs was nice in many ways. In the winter, it was a friendly town of about 25,000. Main Street was a two lane. When you turned on your left blinker at a light, the opposing cars would stop to let you turn left to not hold up traffic behind you. How friendly is that? The stores were picturesque on their own with exposed dark wood beams around the windows and doors with hand lettered signs, no flashing lights. The stores were small town friendly. We went to the Episcopal Church there which was almost formal Catholic Church in their service ritual with acolytes swinging smoking incense burners up the isle at the start of the service. It was one of the larger churches in town with beautiful stained glass windows and exposed dark beams up the walls and vaulted ceiling.

It was a radar site and my first real assignment without munitions. Instead, I had radar parts. Again, as logistics officer I was also in charge of recreation services which included a water ski boat, hunting rifles, a large weight room, golf club sets you could check out to play golf on the civilian golf courses in town. I also had the chow hall again which served families at least once a week for a reasonable, at cost, meal. A small commissary. Civil engineering which included water treatment plants for treating well water and sewage. We bragged that our sewer water left the base more pure than the city drinking water in most cities. I also had all building maintenance, road maintenance on base, and family base houses for the other officers.

We chose to live downtown in a nice apartment since there was not enough housing for even all the officers and the base houses were full. The married enlisted people all lived in surrounding towns in civilian housing. I was responsible for contracting for heating oil for the station and all of the off base housing. Our electric bill was several hundred thousand dollars a year and we were only paying one and a half cents a kilowatt hour versus nine cents a kilowatt hour for all private housing from the utility company. Our radar was thirsty.

I should mention that we had Carolyn's bedroom set and kitchen table and chairs, but we had to buy a sofa and living room chairs and tables. The sofa had removable cushions and drawers underneath for storage. We also bought prefab shelving that our daughter still uses today, 40 years later.

We also had a requirement to have 30 days of fuel for our generators in case commercial power was not available. Those tanks were large enough to generate for over 60 days. I used that as a way to buy fuel in the summer when prices were low so we would have a lower per gallon price all year around. By filling our heating oil tanks and our generator tanks at the cheap summer prices we could transfer excess generator fuel to our heating oil tanks to avoid having to buy fuel at the higher winter prices. The same fuel contract also allowed us to fill the off base housing fuel tanks with fuel at the cheaper summer price so when winter came every tank was full with cheaper summer fuel.

There were several other military members living in our civilian apartments downtown. Carolyn got with them while I was at work to visit and make crafty things. She spent lots of time just window shopping in Saratoga Springs. We had purchased good bicycles over in Europe and went bike riding out to the wonderful park in Saratoga Springs. I had saddlebags on my bicycle which I used to put our minature poodle to take to the park. We had many, just the two of us, picnics there. In the summer, that park has an open air concert area where the stage and some seats are under roof and excess people can lay out blankets on the grass in an amphitheater type area as the stage was surrounded by a manmade grassy hill so everyone could see and hear what was happening on stage. Not only did that theater have popular top ten music groups almost every weekend, but in July it was home for the Philadelphia Orchestra and August was the home of the New York Ballet.

They overlapped for a few days and we were able to watch the New York Ballet with music provided by the Philadelphia Orchestra. How great is that?

I had to drive past the docks at the lake twice every day as I went to and from work on the mountaintop. I bought a Sunfish sail boat. So on warm days in the summer I was able to change into a swimsuit at work and go sailing for a couple of hours on the way home from work. It was Carolyn's idea, which was just another example of her absolute selflessness. It wasn't the cost in money as I bought a nice used one. I thought we could enjoy it together, but she only went with me twice as she is afraid of open water. Again, she was thinking of me and took time away from the two of us being together. I never really thought about all the lonely hours when I was with people at work while she was sitting alone at home. What a great woman. I wish I could go back in time and not do the selfish things like sailing after work in Saratoga instead of being with her bicycling to the park.

Carolyn was in heaven when they had the annual yearling horse auctions in Saratoga Springs near the racetrack. We walked there that August. The auction barn is a horseshoe shaped brick building. One side is flat, the other sides round. There are huge picture windows with a 2 foot wide padded windowsill on the outside so spectators can sit and watch and hear the auction inside that piped electronically to the outside. Rolls-Royces and Lincolns and Caddys would line up disgorging the millionaire bidders at the front door. I think you had to have verified millionaire status to enter the auction "barn". The stage was on the flat side and just outside were exercise corrals where yearlings were walked around before entering onto the stage. The bidders sat in the rounded horseshoe in stadium style well padded seats where everyone could see. That summer the first colt from Secretariat was sold in Kentucky for $1 million, the first time a colt sold for that much.

A month later, in Saratoga Springs, two colts from Secretariat were sold for over $1.5 million while we watched, but it never made the news versus the nationwide news from the Kentucky auction.

One evening Carolyn and I were walking around the stables outside the auction barn and looking in at the horses. Each stall had a half door on the outside of the barns to hold the horses in but you could walk up to half-doors and look in at the horses Carolyn spotted one horse in a stall, "That is a beautiful horse. If we had the money and a place for the horse, that is the one I would pick."

A couple had come up behind us and the guy said, "I'm glad to hear that. I just bought him." It was Nelson Rockefeller and his wife. We talked with them like we were all the same class of people. He being from old money and me being the son of an Oklahoma school teacher that made more money than my father ever made, but not even close to being rich. When we left, Nelson asked, "Will you be here tomorrow night?" Was that coincidence, a minor miracle that we had a long conversation with a very rich person as if on equal ground?

I had to say no, it was a work night.

35 The Miracle Adoption

I have mentioned that Carolyn could not have children and we would adopt. Things had changed. When we went to Europe in 1972, adoption of a new born was easy, but in 1973 in Roe versus Wade, the US Supreme Court had legalized abortion so adopting a new born was very difficult.

At the end of that blissful summer in Saratoga Springs, Carolyn and I decided that we would explore adoption. When we contacted New York social service they nearly laughed at us and refused to let us apply. I got on the phone and called around and found New York Family and Children Services in Albany, New York, one of the tri-cities just south of Saratoga Springs. When I called, they said to forget it, adoption would take years and since I was military, I would probably move on before my name came up on the list. I explained that we had been overseas and when we left the states in 1972 it would have been easy. Could we make an appointment with a counselor just to get some counseling on the new now difficult process. They said, "Yes, but we would have to pay for the appointment and investigation. We won't be investigating, but we have no way to charge for just an information visit."

I readily agreed and the next week I took a day off work and Carolyn and I went there to meet with the counselor. We explained that Carolyn could not have children due to her now understood genetic defect where the second two cells did not divide correctly. When we left the states, Carolyn had been an Arkansas Social Services worker and they were looking for couples that would be willing to adopt. I had gotten orders less than a year after we got married and had spent the last 3 years in Europe only to come home to the states to find the rules had been changed.

The counselor said we could fill out the papers for an investigation of us, but don't expect anything in less than 3 years, and we would have to return to New York, but since I was military they would understand if I had to move away before the 3 years was up. She couldn't promise anything even after 3 years. We took the papers home, filled them out, and I took off work early the next day and drove them down before their 5 PM closing time. This was now early October of 1975. We had not used vacation time since returning to the states so at Christmas we used two weeks to go home to visit her parents in Arkansas and my parents in Oklahoma.

As we drove there, a blizzard came into northern United States. When we got to Buffalo, New York, the exits were closed with saw horses due to the blizzard so we could not get off the interstate. I had just put in a Citizens Band (CB) radio that fall and the truckers on the road said the border was closed into Ohio so we followed the truckers over the mountains to the south interstate across Ohio. By the time we got to Columbus, Ohio the roads had been plowed and were dry. The red car was almost white with salt and since it was an American Motors Pacer it was round and the truckers called us snowball on the CB radio.

We got home in January and had a hard time finding our apartment house because of snow drifts created by snow plows that were 6 to 10 feet high. I had to use my internal compass to get to the right area and we found a hole in the snow bank that went into the parking lot. Snow between the buildings was nearly up to our second-floor balcony with the sidewalks plowed out to get between buildings which was why the snow was so high. The snow plows for the sidewalks had thrown snow to the sides creating huge walls of snow almost to the second story balconies. People in the lower units had shoveled snow off their patios onto the building pile blown from the sidewalks.

We had only been back a few days when Carolyn got a phone call from Albany Family and Children's Services that they had a baby that we might want to come see about potential adoption. Major miracle. It was supposed to take a minimum of 3 years, if ever, and it had been less than 4 months since we applied. Of course, I took off work and we drove straight there. They had a 3 week old boy that had been born on December 21, 1975 and he was perfect. Technically they could not adopt him out until after they had had him for a minimum of 30 days, but would we be interested. Silly question.

There was a blizzard predicted again so miracle of miracles they offered to let us take him that night because of the predicted blizzard and that they knew the mother and knew she would be happy for us to have him. So here we are on the way home to Saratoga Springs. Our new son has nothing except an empty spare bedroom to go to. It is starting to snow hard. We stopped at Sears near the interstate to Saratoga Springs and go into the baby department carrying our son.

The clerks thought we were crazy to have a 3 week old son and be buying everything as if we never expected to have a child. They really got into it when they discovered that we really didn't know we would have a child adopted out of the blue. The clerks had fun guiding us to buy 3 and 6 month old things instead of newborn. We loaded up on baby formula, clothing, disposable and cloth diapers, baby blankets and sheets, walkers, car seat, and a crib with mattress which we had to strap to the luggage carrier rails on top of the AMC Pacer since it would not fit inside. We had to scrape a couple of inches of snow off since we had been in Sears for an hour buying everything a baby might need for a month or more.

That night I put together the crib in the living room and then pushed it down the hall to the spare bedroom across the hall from our bedroom since our bedroom was too small for our bed plus a crib. I could not make the turn into the bedroom so I had to take the crib apart again, move it piece by piece into the spare bedroom and assemble it again.

For the first time, Carolyn would not be a single wife living alone while I was at work and we were a family with children instead of just a married couple. I was happy to have a child, but Carolyn was ecstatic. She thought she would never have children and she had always wished she could be a mother to the point of starting and running that girl scout troop over in Europe.

I was happy to have a son to call my own, but I was very proud that I helped Carolyn become a mother. Both my parents and her parents made the trip to New York to see him. Carolyn made a good mother. We did a few things that were smart. We would wake him up and give him a bottle while watching the late night show with Johnny Carson and he immediately started sleeping through the night without having to get up in the middle of the night for a feeding. The first few nights he would wake and cry and Carolyn would instantly hear the first whimper and go in and pat him to reassure him he was not alone until he went back to sleep. While she spent many hours rocking him in the rocking chair her parents give us, she did not do it late at night and within just a few nights he would sleep until I got up for work in the morning.

When the weather started getting warm, I got a child seat for the back of my bicycle and moved the saddlebags to Carolyn's bike so the four of us could go have picnics in the park. Missy, Carolyn's niece, came to visit us for a week or so and played with Craig on the living room floor. Our poodle accepted him immediately. I took a large box and cut a door and some windows for a little playhouse in the living room and the dog and Craig would crawl in and out of the box.

The following winter, Craig was walking at about 8 months. We had bought him a dump truck that had a friction motor that sounded like a truck when he pushed it. He would partially stand and give it a push and the friction motor would sort of pull him along as he would push it along. Probably helped get him walking early. We bought him everything we could find that was age appropriate from a bouncy swing that we put in the hallway where he could bounce and push himself off the floor and bounce and laugh, stuffed toys, including Quack Quack, a stuffed duck that he sucked on when he didn't have a bottle or pacifier. Carolyn had to sew it up many times and we had to find replacement ducks. Now, 40 years later, Craig still has the remnants of the last Quack Quack.

The following winter there were rumors that they were going to close Saratoga Air Force Station, New York. I called some old friends and found that I was going to get an assignment as the only American on a Korean Air Base. A real feather of an assignment. Both of us would be treated like royalty. If I got up from my desk at work and grabbed a hat, there would be a staff car that would appear at the door before I got there to take me wherever I wanted to go. We would have a house with a wall around a large grass yard. If Carolyn looked like she might be wanting to go somewhere, by the time she got halfway to the gate a staff car would appear at the gate to take her wherever she wanted to go. They would take us sightseeing anywhere we wanted to go or to any restaurant we wanted to go to or to an American Air Force Base and when not on the American Air Base they would pay for our hotels, meals, or whatever.

It would be even more remote than Buchel German Air Base. When we had returned from Europe we had discovered that Carolyn's father had started having some heart issues. The Korean assignment was a two year accompanied remote assignment. I did not want to subject Carolyn to an even remoter assignment where there would be no other Americans and with her father's health in question, I did what I had to do to avoid the assignment which was to leave the air force by writing a letter to the promotion board for major to tell them I would not accept the promotion forcing them to let me out of the air force. On March 17, 1977, I was released and the air force would pay to have us moved to my home of record in Oklahoma, where I had joined the air force. I found myself unemployed during a serious recession and I had a little money to tide us over while I collected unemployment. The day I signed out of active duty I returned to Saratoga Air Force Station to say goodbye to everyone there and discovered while I had been gone that day, the orders to close the station had arrived and everyone would be getting orders very soon to go elsewhere.

36 Civilian

So, here we were in Norman, Oklahoma, an unemployed air force captain, his wife, Carolyn, and one year old son, Craig. Under normal circumstances an officer getting out of the air force knowing the date for a year or more I would have been able to find a civilian job to go to immediately upon separation.

My parents had a small two-bedroom house, but they had a separate one car garage with a work room in it. My father had converted it to a guest room with an electric heater and a window air conditioner. We moved in. Not too long later, I had an aunt in town that owned a nice older 3-bedroom house that was vacant which she would rent to us reasonably. So we moved out of my parents garage and into my aunts rental house across the street from another aunt and uncle.

It had several large trees with a couple of years worth of leaves on the ground and bugs everywhere. I bagged up 38 leaf bags of leaves for the garbage men to pick up. I found that it had been built over a sewage gutter that was infested with roaches and the house had spiders. When I sprayed a mimosa tree in front thousands of spiders dropped to the ground. I set off bug bombs in the sewer and sprayed for spiders in the house. Eventually we had it nearly bug free. At least weekly we played bridge with my parents and at least weekly we played bridge with my aunt and uncle across the street. We got a nice photo of Craig pushing a pedal car with our miniature poodle, Snoopy, supposedly driving. The aunt we were renting from did not want the dog in the house, but my other aunt and uncle that we played cards with never told her and since she lived in California never complained, although, I am sure she knew.

I had several cousins living in Oklahoma we visited with. We lived on unemployment checks and the money we had in the bank. I spent the days visiting employment offices and getting newspapers from around the country looking for jobs. I was unemployed for over six months when the unemployment checks would run out. I finally found an employer, but he was not offering the money I wanted to make so we set a date for me to come to work if I had not found the right job.

Just as my unemployment checks ran out after 6 months, that company phoned and asked me to come to work that night, a Friday night. I was to fly down to Dallas, which was only a 4 hour drive, get a rental car and show up at a warehouse near the Dallas Fort Worth Airport. So, at 7PM, there I was. There were over 200 semi-trucks waiting to get unloaded into what appeared to be a full warehouse. It was a fire drill. They had people there from the home office in San Francisco wringing their hands. As soon as I was introduced I took a walking tour, stopped the unloading since there was no empty floor space to unload anyway and got the forklifts moving to create isles in the warehouse to move things around. I put half the forklifts to work moving like things into basically piles of like things and making isles between. When we cleared out a little space I got the other half of the forklifts back to unloading trucks. By 2PM the next day we had all the trucks unloaded. By 8AM the next morning we were making air shipments out.

They expected it to be at least two weeks to make shipments out. On that Friday, one week after hiring on as an assistant to an assistant warehouse manager, I was promoted to full warehouse manager at double the salary from the first week. Vice Presidents of ARAMCO, the big oil company in Saudi Arabia had come in to see our amazing operation put together so quick and meet me. On the next Friday I was promoted to run a total of three warehouses in the Dallas area and a separate company of container shipments. My salary was doubled from the previous Friday and was now promised 50% more than I was making as a captain.

On Saturday night, we were meeting the air shipment schedule out, keeping up with incoming trucks and had organized the warehouse with location signs to tell us where things were so we could find them. We had isles wide enough to actually work through the warehouse to get to locations to find outbound shipments. That night I was offered a federal civil service job at Wright-Patterson Air Force Base, Ohio to be in charge of all Air Force military sales to Northern Africa as part of the Camp David Peace Accords. It would be a 50% cut in pay, but more important than this job. Before leaving that evening, a couple of the more experienced guys I had hired went around with me to inspect the ADT security alarms.

We used similar alarms in the air force so I knew how they were supposed to work. We found several doors where the sensors were misaligned and would not have worked if someone cut the locks and opened the doors. We made several calls to ADT until we were sure all the sensors were working and felt safe to go off and leave the warehouse empty.

I took the entire warehouse gang out to eat to celebrate our work and spend some of the new salary I had not yet been paid for.

On Sunday, the big boss from San Francisco called to say every warehouse, but mine had been robbed Saturday night making off with 50% of the SEARS store imports from one warehouse. Why hadn't I called? I explained that we had checked that all the alarms were working before we left for the evening, and late Saturday night I had been phoned by ADT to say that an alarm had gone off, but when they arrived, the door was secure and no one was around, so maybe the same bad guys had sabotaged the alarms on all the warehouses the company had around the country, but we had fixed ours before leaving the warehouse unmanned.

On Monday, the big boss offered to make me manager for the central part of the USA at a huge salary. I was to rent the entire floor of an office building anywhere in central USA and have complete hiring capability to hire whoever I wanted, and a company car of course.

I told him I was going to turn it down and go back to work for the air force as a GS-11 which was roughly equivalent to a captain and make less than my current pay let alone the new position. I gave them 10 days to find how to get along without me, but in the week I had worked there I had turned disaster into something that was working far beyond expectation and making double the profit the company had planned on.

In the meantime I had been working 18-19 hours a day, I was dead tired from all the time on my feet on concrete and barely had time to phone Carolyn on the phone back in Norman, Oklahoma. Naturally she would say everything was fine as she was very capable if lonely with just Craig, my parents, aunt Clara and uncle Lester.

I had just turned down being very highly paid to where Carolyn could have had a big house and all the things she deserved just so I could have a lower paying job that I thought was more worthwhile. Carolyn was happy with that decision. She wanted me to have what I wanted and she said as long as we were together that was all that was important. She would rather we be rich in experience and pride than wealthy. What a wonderful wife that I should have appreciated more. I did love her and appreciate her, but I did not realize how much until she died and I thought back to all of her sacrifices made for me. My parents were that way. My father had turned down good pay for being a good school teacher.

37 Settled in Dayton, Ohio

I accepted the federal civil service GS-11 position at Wright-Patterson Air Force Base International Logistics Center as US Air Force foreign military sales for northern Africa. This was to put me in charge of Egypt, Sudan, Zaire, Morocco, and technically Algeria, Libya, Mali, Mauritania, Niger, and all those small countries. However Egypt, Sudan, Zaire, and Morocco were the countries with real activity.

This was not a paid move by the government so that meant we had to pack our meager belongings that we could cram into our AMC Pacer and on the luggage rack. I had purchased a stripped tent trailer from Saratoga Air Force Station when they were directed to sell off their recreation services equipment so we packed the trailer with everything we could fit and find a mover to move the rest. Before we left Oklahoma I had made reservations at a centrally located Days Inn Motel which was a big mistake. I didn't know Dayton, Ohio and the motel turned out to be a red light motel with hookers everywhere and a not so clean motel. I was very disappointed in Days Inn. The first night there, Carolyn was attempting to bathe Craig in the bathroom sink and he slipped off, Carolyn caught him before he hit the floor but he hit his head on the edge of the Formica counter gashing the back of his head so at 10PM we went to find a hospital with no idea of where we were. So we found a hospital after getting directions then finding a hospital sign on the interstate and got back to the motel plus some stitches to his head about 2 AM.

I got up at 6 AM on Halloween, October 31st, 1977. Miracle or coincidence. It was the first day of a pay period so that was by chance I had to get up early to find the base and report in for work. Remember, no GPS in those days, only maps. Thank goodness, Carolyn was flexible and capable. Nothing phased her. I marvel now at all the things she did on her own without me.

I signed in for work, found where I was to sit, met my supervisor, and then was able to leave early. I found a dumpy furnished apartment just outside one of the gates to Wright-Patterson Air Force Base. I then drove back to the Days Inn getting there about 3PM and rescued Carolyn and Craig. I didn't want to make another gross mistake with the apartment so I took her to see the apartment. It was pretty bad, but most of the people there were associated with the air base so it was safe and the people were friendly. As it turned out, it was about the only furnished apartment with month to month rentals that I ever found there. All the units were furnished one bedroom/living room/kitchen/dining as one big room with stub walls separating the bedroom from the rest with the only doors being the front door and the bathroom. It was probably a failed motel at one time. There were no two story units and consisted of a street down the middle and about 30 yards of apartments on either side of the street.

Naturally, Carolyn said, "Fine." At least we were out of the "red light" Days Inn Motel in Dayton and now in Fairborn, Ohio, the small town next to Area A of the air base. The office for the apartments were just closing when we arrived at the office, paid two months rent, one month as a deposit and the next months rental, got the keys to the apartment. It turned out that these shabby one room apartments were largely rented to other people that had just moved to the base and had not found more permanent housing, so we were among friends.

We went back, got the tent trailer that was in the parking lot of the motel and parked it in one of the two parking spots assigned to that apartment. We unpacked the car, got Craig's crib out of the trailer and then went back and checked out of motel. Then we picked up some fast food and a few groceries at a store to take to our apartment. I set up the crib and we collapsed.

While I was at work the next day, Carolyn brought in stuff from the tent trailer, walked over to a convenience store a block from the apartments and got some additional groceries. The next day at work I was escorted around to meet the big bosses and sort of interviewed again. I was allowed to leave early again, so Carolyn, Craig, and I went looking for a house to buy. We found a realtor who showed us photos of houses for sale that were out of our price range or dumpy in questionable neighborhoods, or too far to consider driving to work at the base daily.

For the next several days, I put in a full day of work with a mentor to help me along learning the new job. Whereas before, I had my own supply system and everything I managed was right there to touch. I had managed the budget and daily funding. Now I had millions of dollars of foreign money to account for and no merchandise that I could touch because it was located at contractor plants and not yet manufactured or was stored at the air logistics centers, with much of it at Kelly Air Force Base in San Antonio, Texas or at Warner-Robins Air Force Base south of Atlanta, Georgia.

When I got home we drove around looking for houses and searching the newspapers for houses and then driving there the next evening after work. In driving around I found a used yellow Triumph Spitfire two seat convertible sports car that was cheap and bought it cash. That would be my work car and Carolyn would have the Pacer to drive during the day. We spent the weekend looking for houses. I drove the Spitfire to work the following Monday and Carolyn drove around looking for houses. Carolyn found a housing area not too far from the base that was a very nice and large housing edition that was populated by many people from the base. It was a Ryan Homes development. The streets were wide with lots of green areas between streets so the houses were not jammed in together. The yards were not large, and the houses were fairly close together, but many of them backed up to open grassy unimproved common areas.

The sales office was closed at 5PM so we could not go in. The realtor had never told us about this area. I absolutely approved of the addition, but we didn't know prices. The houses were mainly brick faced on the front with vinyl or aluminum siding on the rest of the house. Many had privacy fencing in the back yards or chain link fences. We really wanted a fence for our poodle so he would not have to be walked in the winter. So far the winter was not bad. No snow and not that cold. We could see multiple houses under construction and walked through some of them that didn't have doors yet to get an idea of size. The walls were just two by fours, but we could see the layouts. There were not many ranch style one story homes. On hills, a lot were split level with a garage and semi-basement under the main house above. Many were two story houses with the garage under the master bedrooms and a family room behind the garage.

We did not see for sale signs on the older or the newer homes. While I was at work, Carolyn went to the sales office and got brochures showing photos of completed houses with curtains and furniture for show. All of the homes were partly pre-fabricated homes with walls, roof trusses, siding, windows and doors delivered on semi-trucks and assembled on location for a house.

This sounded great to us. The cost of these houses was reasonable and the pre-fab construction would be quick.

The longest timeframe for a house was the concrete work. All of the two story houses were on a full basement vastly increasing the square footage. The lower level of the split level houses were basically a basement with an open wall for a garage door and a wall separating the basement area from the garage. That meant we could buy a new house for less than an existing custom home and be able to move in almost as quick as buying an existing house.

The realtor had explained that getting a housing loan and closing on an existing pre-owned house would take 3-6 months which seemed like a long time to live in that little dumpy apartment we were living in. Carolyn spent a couple of days looking for a better apartment for that 3-6 months, after we finally found a house we wanted to buy in a neighborhood we wanted to live in close to work. There were not many existing houses for sale approaching Christmas. Spring would see lots of houses for sale but it was now mid November and people were not looking to move around Christmas.

That Saturday we went to the Ryan Homes sales office. They had some basements already poured and with their financing we could apply for a no-down-payment VA loan right there and while waiting for financing they would complete home with the options we wanted and we could possibly move in by Christmas. We were limited to the houses where there was already a basement poured because of winter coming on. If we did not take one of the pre-poured basements we would have to wait until February to move in. All of the 40 houses currently under construction were pre-sold already and they had 10 other houses that had to be completed before ours.

So, to be able to get out of that tiny apartment by Christmas we were limited to basements already poured. After looking at the different plans, we ended up going with the second most expensive house for that subdivision, the

Vicksburg, which, if you counted the basement and the garage was about 3300 square feet. It had a two car garage under a large master bedroom that ran from the front to the back of the house with its own bathroom. One very small bedroom next to the master and across from the upstairs hall bath that would be a nursery if we managed to adopt a second child, one medium size bedroom that would be Craig's room, and a huge 20 foot by 12 foot bedroom above the living room for a guest room. The downstairs had an 18 foot by 11 foot family room with a brick functional fireplace with an outside ash cleanout, a half bath, a decent kitchen, a breakfast area just right for Carolyn's dining table and chairs when we got our stored furniture, a 20 by 12 living room if you didn't count the entryway and stairs to the second floor and a 10 by 11 formal dining area.

Our house payment with interest, insurance, and principle would be about $500 a month or nearly one of my two paychecks per month. My paycheck was about $700 every two weeks before taxes and health insurance. Basically we would have only $500 a month for utilities, groceries, clothing, etc. I still had nearly $10,000 in the bank and my civil service job should be secure with my veterans preference. In fact, the VA did not give me any cash but confirmed my status as a disabled veteran, so it would take a lot for me to lose my job. Both of our cars were paid for since I had the cash to pay for both when we bought them. The Triumph Spitfire was simple enough that I could fix it myself if it broke and the Pacer was only about 3 years old and shouldn't have anything seriously wrong for awhile.

Now, we just had to wait for the house to be built on the existing basement, find some furniture and appliances and just explore Dayton.

Disaster. As Christmas approached they still had not even delivered our house on semi-trucks and we couldn't get any answers, but it was obvious we were not going to move into our new house before Christmas as they said. Eventually we found out that the back wall of the pre-poured basement for our house had caved in after a big rain and hard freeze. Without having the weight and strength of the house itself, the concrete did not have the strength and had caved in. It was now too cold to re-pour the basement wall.

Naturally, Carolyn was stoic, never complaining while I was livid that the house I had promised her by Christmas had no scheduled completion date. I threatened to just cancel our contract and find something else, but Carolyn had picked out the brick, the color of siding, the carpets, and decided what curtains we would buy to match the carpets.

We decorated the apartment for Christmas as best we could with our furniture and decorations in storage. Our year of storage from my separation from the air force would be expired on March 17th and she was sure they would have the house finished by then. As always, Carolyn settled me down to wait it out. We went back to Oklahoma and Arkansas for Christmas with our parents. That used up all the vacation time I had earned in the two months I had worked.

38 Politics

By mid-January I was settled into my new job and working with almost no supervision. I was delivering C-130 cargo aircraft and F-5's to Egypt and doing the ground work on delivering C-130 cargo aircraft to Sudan. I had gotten to know our ambassador to Morocco and the Moroccan Embassy people over the telephone and electronic coded messages back and forth. The Moroccan business was primary deliveries of spare parts for their aircraft so was routine even though there were almost daily messages and phone calls back and forth.

The Egyptian activity was really ramping up because as part of the Camp David Peace Accords Saudi Arabia had agreed to pay for the Egyptian and Sudanese aircraft and spare parts. My idea to simplify the process of a fast ramp-up of activity was to establish an American detachment in those two countries who would be my counterparts rather than have to work through the embassies on the now multiple messages per day flowing back and forth. The ambassadors were having to translate supply terms to a not understanding foreign country staff and then figure out how to request the items from me back in the states.

This required recruiting a military officer and staff from our Air Force to move to those countries, set up an office, get housing, get furniture and vehicles, arranging for shipments to that country. Sudan was just in the talking stage so I did not have to set up anything for them yet, but it was coming.

They had finally delivered the first truck carrying the floor joists for our Vicksburg house so it was only a matter of a couple of weeks before we could have our house finally. When I had to go TDY (temporary duty) out of town, I felt I was leaving Carolyn in a good condition.

We had found the appliances, living room sofa, easy chairs, coffee and end tables at a store in Fairborn that did not look like much but was crammed with things. We didn't like much they had in stock, but when they found that we would be buying lots of things for a new house (with our remaining $10,000) they offered us a deal. We could look up anything in any of their catalogs, take the list price, take 50% of the price and add $20 to each item and they would order everything and deliver it to our new house. Shortly after we had picked out our dinning room furniture and a new bedroom set for our bedroom they showed us some Frigidaire appliances they had purchased from the factory when General Motors decided to quit making Frigidaire and sold off the brand to White-Westinghouse. These were the last appliances made by the Frigidaire factory in Dayton, Ohio. We bought a kitchen range, large over and under refrigerator (they did not have side by side refrigerator freezers yet) with ice, water, and three flavors of powdered fruit drinks through the door, and washer and dryer. They sold us these at 50% of the normal Frigidaire price and far cheaper than any other new appliances we could buy anywhere. They would hold everything for free until our house was finished. So it appeared everything was set.

My direct supervisor escorted me to Warner Robins Air Logistics Center at Warner Robins, Georgia to meet the C-130 manager and his staff that I would be working with to deliver C-130's to Egypt and Sudan. We flew down to Atlanta International Airport then to Macon, Georgia renting a car to drive the rest of the way to Warner-Robins. On the night of January 25th my supervisor and I had just eaten at the Warner-Robins Air Force Base Officer's Club and were having a drink. We were to leave to go to our airplane at 6AM the following morning to arrive in Dayton by 10AM and go home. As we were sitting there, a color TV in the corner was showing a bold blue line approaching Ohio and I got up and went to where I could hear the weather forecast. They were predicting a major blizzard for Ohio the next morning. My supervisor had gotten up and joined me to see what had arrested my attention and commented, "I don't think we will be going home tomorrow."

"We have to. My wife is stuck in a drafty one room apartment with no fireplace with my two year old son."

My supervisor would have been content to stay the weekend in Warner Robins, Georgia away from the snow, but agreed that we would try to get home. The next morning our flight had been cancelled and Wright-Patterson Air Force Base was closed for the rest of the week. We managed to get a later flight and at 3PM we were the first commercial airplane to land at Dayton the afternoon of January 26th, 1977. The previous night and morning Dayton had hurricane force winds with a foot of snow falling on top of 16 inches of pre-existing snow.

When we flew in the sky was still dark but the worst of the storm had passed. The parking lot had been partly plowed out. When I got to my Triumph Spitfire I could barely recognize it. I first cleared off the hood, roof and trunk to make sure it was my little car using my briefcase a scraper. I then pushed snow away from the driver's door so I could get it open. When I could get the door open it looked like an ice cave. There was snow filling the car up to the bottom of the windows with stalactites of snow from the convertible top. I scooped out the snow, again with my briefcase and frozen hands until I could get in, pull out the manual choke and turn the key. It fired right up. By then, my supervisor had found me and explained that his new Cadillac would not start. We cleaned out the passenger seat as best we could then knocked down the drift behind the car so I could back up into the plowed corridors of the parking lot. The roads from the airport had been partially plowed but it was slow going.

By the time we got to a gas station with coffee and a restroom, the engine had developed a miss. When I opened the hood there was no sign of the engine in that it was packed with snow. We knocked away some of the snow, got our coffee and headed for Fairborn, Ohio down the interstate highway that had been plowed. As we drove past Fairborn all the exits were closed with 10 foot drifts. When we got to the last exit, we decided we would ram the drift and see how close we could get to a Fairborn street that we could see had been plowed and walk the rest of the way if necessary.

My spitfire was really down on power and had been using gasoline at probably 8 miles to the gallon versus its normal 30+ miles per gallon. We weren't going to get far without getting gasoline anyway and it was miles to the next interstate exit. I got up as much speed as I could, about 50 miles per hour and we sort of drifted over the top of the 10 foot snow drift and down onto the street below at about 5 miles per hour. His wife met him at a bar in their 4 wheel drive and I went on to the apartment house after I filled up with gasoline. As I got to the apartments, there were snowdrifts almost covering the cars. The Pacer's 10 foot CB antenna and part of the roof rack were all that showed of the car. There was no place to park, but across the street it did not look like there was a car there so I got up my speed and drove up onto the drift until the car spun to a stop. I got my bags and made it to the apartment door. Carolyn had a friendly neighbor shovel out the doorway so she could get the front door open.

Naturally Carolyn was glad to see me and surprised I had made it into the airport at all. The last news she had heard was that the airport was closed. She said that the whole building shook all night, she put towels under the front door because snow was drifting under it halfway across the floor. Fortunately she never lost electricity, but the apartment had gotten down to 60 degrees because it could not keep up with the cold and drafts coming in. By the time I got there the wind had fallen off completely and the apartment had warmed to over 70 degrees. It was getting dark. The temperature that night was a minus 18 degrees. The next morning the sun was out and the temperature had climbed to a balmy 35 degrees. I went out to see if I could start my Triumph Spitfire. It started but would barely run with my foot pushing the peddle halfway to the floor. I opened the hood to see if more snow had drifted in during the night. It had not and seemed to be pretty dry. I took off the air filter and discovered one of the two carburetors was frozen closed explaining why it had no power. I took a large screwdriver and broke the piston in the carburetor free and then restarted the car which now sounded like normal even though still sitting on top of several feet of snow and a couple of yards from the plowed isle in the parking lot. It spun its way down to the plowed area and I took Carolyn and Craig down to get a nice warm meal in a restaurant and then to a store to buy a snow shovel. I spent hours shoveling out the Pacer. Some neighbors came out to help until it was free of snow and I could open the doors. I checked under the hood and it had been parked away from the wind and was clear of snow. It stared right up.

I then helped other neighbors shovel out their cars until it started getting dark. The next morning, we had shoveled out a parking spot for the Spitfire and took the Pacer for a drive around the area. We drove to where our new house was supposedly being built to find floor joists everywhere and no signs of work. One of my new neighbors, said he had been out smoking a cigarette when he heard a loud bang and saw floor joists flying through the air like my basement had exploded.

Monday I went to work. The temperatures were now cold but near normal and the sky was clear making the sun feel good. There were plenty of blizzard stories and a lot of people didn't make it in because they were still snowed in and waiting for snowplows.

I called Ryan Homes about my house and they knew nothing. Finally on Friday they said the basement wall had given way again and they had no schedule for fixing it saying it might be April before they finished the house. Naturally I threw a fit. Our furniture needed to be out of storage before March 17th or I would have to start paying for storage.

After another two weeks of nothing happening on our house, they went to work on it and had it completed quickly. We moved in the first week of March having spent four months in that tiny apartment. Carolyn never complained although she had to have been miserable. I was going to work and working with other people all day while she was primarily alone in that little apartment. I think she did a lot of shopping without buying much just to stay sane.

We got our appliances installed and furniture delivered from the store downtown and from the air force moving and storage contractor. I was working ridiculous hours primarily on Egypt and that left Carolyn to unpack everything herself and figure out where to put it. I left for work at 7AM and usually got home around 6PM. She would serve supper and then I would install shelves and help her with heavier objects then go to work the next day.

Unfortunately, I got recalled to work several times every weekend. The director of international logistics was the only one authorized to pick up and answer ops immediate messages, but he would read the message, then call me to write an answer since it would ask details only I could know the answer to. I would draft up the message, type it myself, since we didn't have secretaries working on the weekend, then he would sign the message and carry it over to the message center and send it off under his signature.

He got tired of that and even though I was only a GS-11 at the time he got special authorization from the 4-Star general commander of the Air Force Logistics Command to allow me to pick up the messages and send them out under my lowly signature. The rules read that you were to be at least a full colonel or GS-15 equivalent, but they made an exception because I was running the show in Northern Africa by myself and the colonels and generals on base really had only a passing idea of what was happening. The messages received were always under the signature of the American Ambassadors of those countries which is why they were authorized to use ops immediate priority on the messages. They had not invented secure telephones so the only quick way of getting answers was by secure teletype message services in the government. An ops immediate message required an answer within 24 hours which was why I was called into work whenever one arrived from any country in Northern Africa.

Carolyn finally had the house pretty well set up. We had the new bedroom furniture in our master bedroom and her old master bedroom set in the large guestroom. Our new furniture included a bunk bed for Craig's room. We had taken the sides off his crib for him to use while waiting for our house to be completed so our furniture could be delivered. We had one whole wall of his bedroom wall papered in a huge Star Wars diorama. I had taken him to the original Star Wars movie in a theater when he was only about 18 months old and he was transfixed and reached for anything Star Wars he saw in the stores so he already had a lot of Star Wars toys.

Craig was physically very advanced for his age, but really had not spoken much. One evening and I read Craig a children's story and was working with him on early reading books. Craig and I were looking out his bedroom window. I was started to get worried about his not speaking sentences until then when he came out with his first full very insightful sentence, "I wonder if there are other intelligent beings on a planet around one of those stars out there."

From that time on he talked like an adult. Instead of worrying about him not talking at over two years old he was now talking like a 1st or 2nd grader and reading books for a school kid.

I was overwhelmed at work. I was getting phone calls from President Carter, the Secretary of State, the Secretary of Defense, lots of undersecretaries and general officers as well as massive correspondence with the various Embassies. Every so often I would get called in to brief the 4-Star general commander of the Air Force Logistics Command and the director of international logistics would come along to just listen in. I was working on crisis mode primarily responding to the high rollers and unable to do the daily chores of my job. My inbox was usually over a foot tall and I had another 2 feet of unanswered mail that I put off for when I had time. Some of the other managers in international logistics would help me out reviewing the daily computer printouts of routine supply requests and issuing the shipping orders. I had no time for routine stuff.

Finally they created a new office for just Egypt and staffed it with 15 people to take some of the load off of me. The hard work on Egypt was already completed by that time and we had an in-country team of another dozen air force people. The only work left was tracking the day to day routine work of shipping parts and billing to the Egyptian funding account set up by Saudi Arabia. There was also a contractor team in Egypt now to help with aircraft maintenance. That was good since I did not have time for routine because Sudan was now taking a lot of time with more high-rollers as we set up processes and orders for aircraft and the initial lay-in of parts for those aircraft. Teams of contractors had to be set up for Sudan and an in-country counterpart for me in Sudan which required working through the Sudan embassy to find him an apartment, buy and ship US furniture to that apartment, acquire a vehicle for him to drive and set up telephones in his apartment and his office on the Sudan air base. That in-country manager was accepted whereas, the country of Sudan did not want what they considered "spies" from the embassy.

Carolyn in her stoic and efficient manner took care of all the shopping, cleaning, cooking, childcare, and paying of all of our bills. She was in a constant state of panic because after paying the monthly house payment there was not enough money left to pay all the bills.

In the Christmas season of 1978 all the high people of the Sudanese government came over to sign the deal for buying US Air Force aircraft and support. I spent several days briefing them on what I had done to date and what I had planned for their millions of dollars in Saudi money. They visited several other bases and ended up their last few days before Christmas back in Ohio. All the work was completed, all the document signed and they had the day free.

When they first arrived in the USA we all met at Warner Robins Air Logistics Center in Georgia. We had US Air Force drivers for the small fleet of staff cars we had arranged for them. They had all had training in the Soviet Union and heard about the USA having concentration camps for blacks in our country so they asked the US Air Force drivers to take them there. The drivers had no idea what they wanted so they then asked to be taken to the slums of Warner Robins but there weren't any so they took them to Macon, Georgia and tried to show them the worst.

The worst they could find was what they considered upper middle class housing in Sudan so the next night they asked to find the slums of Atlanta with the same result.

On the third night they asked if they could drive the cars themselves. They had international drivers license and were diplomatically protected so we turned over the keys to let them drive themselves. Over the next two weeks they drove around Georgia, California, Washington DC and finally Ohio without finding what they had been told in the Soviet Union training. By that time they were more trusting of us. I found out that after the first week some of them were picking up prostitutes and taking them to shady motels. By that time, we were getting civilian rental cars rather than risk them being seen in government tagged staff cars. They rented luxury cars instead of driving our bare bones staff cars.

The high-ranking Sudanese were living in general officer's quarters in the Visiting Officers Quarters and their assistants were in standard quarters. I went by to visit the big shots and then went down to find their assistants feeling claustrophobic in the standard quarters. The generals controlled the staff cars so they were trapped in their rooms. I invited the 3 major and lieutenant colonel assistants to come have dinner at my house to see how I lived. I called Carolyn to make sure it was okay and of course, as I knew she would, she was more than happy to oblige. They were overjoyed and called the high rollers and I ended up calling Carolyn twice more to up the number.

By the time we got to my house we had all 17 members of the Sudanese delegation which included, the Chief of Staff of their Air Force, their finance minister, the Chief of Staff of their Army (of 400,000 troops), their countries vice president, their military logistics chief. Interesting.

Carolyn cooked everything she had from the refrigerator and freezer and much of the canned goods. We did not yet have a dinning room table or chairs so they ate wherever they could find to sit at a card table and 4 chairs, at the breakfast table chairs (the breakfast table had all of the food she cooked and empty plates and glasses and silverware), the family room sofa and chairs and of course the living room.

We ended the evening with Carolyn playing Christmas Carols on the piano and all 19 of us singing the Carols. They were all Muslims, but they saw the piano and asked Carolyn if she could play some Christmas Carols since we had our tree set up in the living room. Even though prior to their visit they thought the USA was a bad place, they had learned differently and had learned the carols when they had gone to college in England when they were young. Craig was asleep before they had all arrived, but if you look at our photos, you will see much of the Sudanese military sitting around our Christmas tree.

After a year of intense work, I finally got all the key ingredients installed in Sudan and since there was an Egypt division working everything in Egypt my work was finally getting routine. We were allowed to hire some new college graduates and I was given first choice. After trying out several that seemed like children I chose a female college graduate from the bottom of the list. I had tried the three that were the most highly qualified in college courses taken and grade point average and now was being told to choose because since I had first choice, all the supervisors were waiting for me so they could choose. Sight unseen I chose the young female graduate with the poorest grade point average and the worst list of college courses. I was extremely overwhelmed the day she reported to me and I gave her a job that I figured would take her a week based upon the other three trainees I had. Since I had no time to babysit her, I spent about 15 minutes explaining what I wanted her to do and thought that would keep her busy for a week. At noon, she came to me and said, "What should I do now. I finished that job."

I reviewed what she had done and marveled. By choosing the one that had the fewest correct college courses and the lowest grade point average of the 20 new college graduates, I had a winner. I spent 30 minutes showing her how I created message and letter replies to routine correspondence and how to find the answers and suggested that she try drafting some responses. Before I went home, I spent an hour reviewing her afternoon's work and signing out the correspondence. You would think she had been working there for years or was somehow intuitive and reading my mind. Her correspondence even looked like I had done it myself.

I had been promised a promotion to GS-12 before I finished my first year there and a staff to supervise instead of just one new college grad, but promotions in international logistics were frozen as well as additional hiring. After I had been there for 15 months I came up on the promotion roster to get a GS-12 over in the Acquisition Logistics Division working logistics for research and development programs nearing delivery. While not as high profile politically it sounded interesting and would give me a substantial raise to help pay the bills at home. Our $10,000 saving was long gone and Carolyn was getting new credit cars to consolidate older maxed out credit cards and delay payments. We were nearing bankruptcy so I left my high profile job of dealing with the President, the Secretariats, the general officer commanders and took that new GS-12 position.

Again, it was starting over in the learning process, but the promotion was needed and there was no indication of when the promotion would come through in international logistics. After I left international logistics they replaced me with 12 workers and a supervisor by reorganizing all the international logistics offices.

39 R&D

I started my new job and Carolyn found some relief from our growing debts. I started out studying what had been written for managing the logistics portion of Research and Development (R&D) projects. Before long I was writing the logistics procedures required in managing R&D efforts. It does no good to deliver a new airplane without spare parts, trained maintenance people, and repair manuals. The R&D managers would just as soon leave the support for new systems to the original builders of the new airplane, but that is terribly expensive when you have to pay well over $150,000 per maintainer instead of $35,000 for a government employee who, after training and with good manuals, will do a more conscientious job. If all spares come from the original manufacturer the spare parts are very expensive. Many of the parts are commonly available and the prices are competed among many potential suppliers.

In a few months, I was teaching some of the classes in the Air Force Institute of Technology training new R&D managers in the procedures I had written. It did not take long and I was being sent out to the various R&D programs to study them and how they could be better managed.

A common problem in all big projects is schedule management. How many R&D programs run over schedule and consequently way over budget sometimes to the point that a program is scrapped at a loss of billions of dollars because it just got too expensive. I was allowed to visit commercial projects to see how they managed programs. Somehow I got the attention of the Assistant Secretary of the Air Force for Logistics and he gave me a blank check.

I started working with a couple of in-house government software programmers and we developed scheduling software for the old technique called Program Evaluation Review Technique with Critical Path Analysis developed by the US Navy in the 1950s. It worked good but was very manpower intensive and hard to maintain. Essentially you develop a flow chart, guestimate how long each job will take and decide what jobs must be complete. Number one problem managers make is not recognizing the critical path (timeline). They work on the wrong priorities only to find that the thing driving the schedule was something else. Number two problem is that they spend their funding on something other than the critical path and run out of money. Number three is allowing criteria to change from the original contract without realizing the impact on the critical path which causes a delay in the development and delivery dates which sometimes means updating the requirement while in R&D. This means adding in new technology greater than planned for. The delays this causes means there will always be new technology developed to again delay the system delivery. Number four is delivering an incomplete system that cannot be supported because there are no operating or repair manuals and trained personnel to start using the new system. Number five is delivering a non-working system that has not been fully tested.

When I visited these R&D programs I used their brains to develop a good flow chart and critical path while reviewing their plans to make sure they were as complete as possible. For some bigger R&D efforts that meant visiting them again a few years later to review their plan to see if they were sticking with it or helping them adjust their plans to take into account what they have changed or learned.

Many of these trips to program offices around the country required Carolyn to run the house and raise the children while I was gone. A "bimbo" or "arm candy" would not have been able to do this. While I was having lots of people contact, Carolyn was stuck at home with kids and running the house, paying the bills, overseeing repairs, etc. I am not saying she wasn't beautiful, but it was her mind and attitude and so much more that made me love her and appreciate her.

In addition to her being a cub scout leader for our son or girl scout leader for our daughter, she was always quick to volunteer. One year she took on chairman of the school carnival to raise money for school supplies. It took her months and I helped as much as I could but she did all the planning and most of the work with some help from other mothers. It was a great success and was a school record. She also spent time with the church groups making crafts for sale to raise church money.

Everyone thought the world of her and knew how capable she was. More than once she took a group over as the president until she could find someone else to do it. She was frequently the treasurer due to her accuracy and honesty. Everyone knew that if you could talk her into being the planner and organizer the event would set new records. When someone else took over she was disappointed in it and sorry she didn't be in charge for at least one more year.

Carolyn was a very crafty person from doing macramé, needlepoint, ceramic pottery which we still use, or sewing, she not only tailored clothing for girls going to a dance, but 15 years later the church is still using costumes she made for our daughter in Christmas pageants 20 years ago.

She was a good housekeeper keeping everyone in clean clothes and sheets, dusting, vacuuming, mopping floors, but never felt she did enough because her mother and sister went overboard. Carolyn didn't mind the kids or visitors making a mess. She wanted everyone to feel comfortable to be themselves in our house. Carolyn always worried about other people rather than herself.

Carolyn had good taste in paintings on the walls, not expensive, but good quality. She had Tuxedo China, crystal glassware, Oneida sterling silver, but generally used her everyday stoneware, stainless steel (that nearly matched the sterling silver). She had a sense of color and style that belonged together. She preferred plain white walls and used furniture and pillows for color. Most of our wood items were Cherry with Early American baseboards, doors, etc.

I always wanted Carolyn to have everything she desired, but she was happy with anything. She was hard to shop for because she worried about others and not herself. The only jewelry she ever wore was a Timex watch and her ring.

The only ring I gave her was a wedding ring. She had a diamond ring her mother gave her set in platinum with 3 matched high quality ½ karat diamonds. Because we got married on short notice I never bought her an engagement ring, but I could not match the elegance of the 3 diamond ring she wore with her wedding band. At one point she had her wedding band made into a ring guard for the diamond ring. On our 40th anniversary I tried to make it up to her by finding 4 rubies that matched in size and cut to the diamonds and then paid $800 to melt down the ring guard that had been the wedding band and had a ring manufactured with the original 3 diamonds and the 4 rubies in mixed platinum and gold. She was very proud of that ring and I was proud that I made her happy and sort of made up for never buying her an engagement ring. I took out a jewelry rider insurance policy but it is now in a safe deposit box at the bank. Someday my daughter will probably sell it for the estate if she doesn't keep it for herself.

When it came to Christmas, Carolyn always said she had everything she wanted except maybe a replacement toaster. If I found an old church key bottle opener in a tool box, cleaned it up, wrapped it up, and gave it to her she would give you that happy smile as if she had always wanted one and you were so thoughtful to have given it to her. I want to cry when I think about how selfless she was.

40 The Miracle of Our Daughter

Our first house was two stories plus a basement. There was a laundry chute to the basement where the washer and dryer were. Part of the basement was filled with metal shelving that I bought from a going out of business store and had our Christmas, Halloween, etc. decorations. Carolyn liked to decorate for all the holidays so we had about 30 large boxes of decorations, 15 for Christmas and the other 15 for all the other holidays.

The largest part of the basement Carolyn used for holding scout meetings, cub scouts for our son and then later girl scouts for our daughter. After getting settled in Dayton and after my promotion where we were not hurting so bad for money, we decided to try to adopt again. We tried several agencies. The state would not even talk to us about a new born. We wasted many evenings going to adoption training and having day visits in our home by Lutheran Children Services. They insisted that we join and donate a lot of money to the Lutheran Church to continue working toward adoption. Carolyn did not like their people, what they were forcing us to pretend to learn and had lost interest in their church. It was mutual and they turned us down.

During a home visit their investigator was sitting in the living room and our son would peak in and run, then come back, peek in and run again. The home investigator thought that he was abused or something and just told us to drop out of the program. They even implied that we were unfit parents. When we asked our four-year old son about his actions during this visit he replied, "He had a beard like Abraham Lincoln, but was too young to be him and Lincoln died years ago. I was scared of him. I thought it was a ghost of Lincoln."

We could not be mad at our son, he did look like a bearded young Lincoln, and of course the investigator would not believe our young son would be so insightful to have this reaction. Our son was near genius intelligence and we had worked with him to teach things most four year olds would never have understood, like the history of the United States, geography, etc. We encouraged Craig to be outside and playing with other young kids, but Ohio winters were too cold for the other kids so we spent the bad weather teaching our genius son things he was interested in.

Carolyn was extremely upset. "How can they say we would not be good parents?" I knew it was because the Lutheran Church just wanted lots of money from us and even though joining the church was written in their guide as not necessary our not joining was a major factor. Carolyn took it personally, but I just learned to hate the Lutheran Church. What they were trying to teach us about adoption was stupid. I could parrot it back to them, but did not believe any of it.

It took me a lot of time, but I eventually found Children and Family Services of Dayton, Ohio which was related to Family Children and Family Services of Albany, New York where we adopted Craig at 3 weeks old. Almost a year had gone by before I found them and Carolyn had been upset for that long. We applied with them and they repeated that it might take years, but a few months later we had Christine, our daughter, at only 6-8 weeks old (I don't remember exactly). We already had the small bedroom next to the master bedroom made up as a nursery. Unlike when we had nothing when we got Craig. The walls were either painted or wall papered for a child. We had Craig's crib and other children furniture. We had bought a new, very high quality child size table and chairs we could use as a baby learned to sit and play or learn at a table.

This made Carolyn happy again and to hate the Lutheran Church more for putting us through months of meetings to disapprove us. It made me happy to have a little baby girl and for Carolyn to be happy again. I don't know how to find a Children and Family Services anywhere, but I highly recommend them to anyone. The only expense is a small $500 application and investigation fee and court costs for the adoption. They investigate you to make sure that you will be good parents without trying to indoctrinate you in some strange belief. Apparently they get private funds somewhere to help the girls who are giving their children up for adoption and paying for the medical care during pregnancy and childbirth. I never thought about where they got their funding and didn't care until after we had our two children.

Again, another miracle. Our son was born on December 21st, near Christmas with brown hair and blue eyes. One concern about adopting again was that the second child might look nothing like our first child and have a birthday in the summer, not close to Christmas for a birthday party. Miracle, our daughter has brown hair (darker than our son, but brown) and blue eyes. Not only that, but her birthday is December 24th, Christmas Eve, even worse than her brother's.

Bad thing about both birthdays being so close to Christmas, it is hard to have kids come to a birthday party over school Christmas break. Particularly for our daughter. We would have a birthday party planned and then her friends would not attend even though they had RSVPed. Many times, when she was supposed to have 6-8 girls at her party we would just make it a family outing to a restaurant with no guests. They also did not get presents that most kids get from other kids at their birthday parties. At least our kids could commiserate with each other over their lack of a successful birthday party. I know it made Carolyn and our kids sad and I felt bad for them. Carolyn took it worse than our kids did.

As the kids got older we quit trying to have other people for their birthdays. We would just wrap all their presents, put them under the tree, have something special and a cake at home for their birthday and then let them pick which Christmas presents they would open early for their birthdays. Of course we made sure that they were not allowed to pick the packages of underwear or new shoes for their birthday. Our son, would not change his pick one year, but when he opened a package of underwear that time, he took our advice for what not to open next time.

41 Our Passive Solar House

I was worried about Carolyn having to go up and down the stairs from the second floor to the basement to do laundry. I was afraid she would be carrying something and fall down the stairs and get hurt. We had spent years looking at house plans and had many books of house plans. Our two story house with a basement was expedient when we moved to Dayton, but now that we were settled and had no plans to ever move again with the air force, so we started looking at house plans again.

We both loved our neighborhood that was largely military and consequently very friendly, but several of our close friends had moved on with the air force and we had to befriend the new people. We liked the location because our house backed up to a large green area with a little creek running through it. I mowed the grass all the way to the creek on my side of the creek and the width of our house lot. It was over a block to the houses on other side of the gentle valley. Several neighbors liked it and the third year of me mowing the grass to the creek, they mowed theirs also.

Carolyn was not all that hip on moving, but I was concerned about the three flights of stairs for her. Her hip had been hurting more every year since we got married. The horse riding and jumping off the monster horse probably didn't help nor the many miles we walked sightseeing in

Europe or sleeping in a two man tent with just a thin air mattress.

I could see the stairs were bothering her and, with me being afraid for her on those stairs from when we moved in, I pushed for finding or building a ranch style house with just one story.

We both liked an open floor plan and I wanted lots of glass to not feel enclosed and to provide some solar heating. Carolyn took all the plans we had looked at over the years and used a piece of graph paper to come up with a floor plan we both liked. It was essentially a large u-shaped house with a glass enclosed porch filling in the U so the overall outline was a rectangle. The garage was sort of stuck on the front of the rectangle and wide enough for 3 cars so we could have a side storage room in the garage. It was long enough to park the full size Chevy van and still have a work bench in front of the van. Versus the typical 20X20 it was 25X30. I took the plans to some builders to price. We had paid $57,000 for the two story house of 3300 square feet counting the basement and garage and the lowest price from a builder was $140,000 for 3200 square feet counting the garage. Our house had gone up to about $85,000 in value, but $140,000 plus a building lot was just out of reach and that was with a bare concrete floor and no light fixtures. After seeing a couple of houses that cheap builder would build it for I could see the shoddy work and would not want to live in a house he built.

Interest rates had gone up to 10% for a building loan that would convert to a mortgage of the same rate. My current house had an 8.5% Veterans Administration loan which was assumable which would help sell my house since interest rates had gone up to 10%. I really wanted to build that house for Carolyn and get out of what was essentially a three story house. We went looking for building lots.

I found a new housing area outside of Fairborn, Ohio that had streets for 80 one acre building lots but only 6 houses. The owner lived there in a very nice two story about the size of our house and he offered a one acre lot near the end of the only cul d sac for $18,000 and said he would help me find contractors to build my house for something I could afford if I was willing to do some of the work.

The plumber was living in one house he built and had another there that was vacant and looking for work to keep from going broke so he would do the plumbing cheap. The carpenter built McDonald's restaurants in Ohio during the week but was highly recommended and his helper was a foreman for a big tract home builder in the area. They could only work on weekends. The concrete guy for the concrete floor, driveway, sidewalks, etc normally built apartment houses, but had crews that were not working due to the interest rates and housing slump. There was a master electrician that was retired on social security, but did good work. All of these contractors offered me a great price if I would pay in cash for each stage of construction. I am sure they did not want to report the income on their taxes or the electrician on social security. There would be no written contracts except for material which I would have to buy and have delivered to the job site at the appropriate times. My warranty would be the threat of reporting the income I was paying in cash to the contractors. I would pay cash in stages at each point when the county building inspectors passed an inspection and I got a new "draw" from the bank on the building loan. Of course, at each "draw" I went further into debt without a house to move into if we could not finish.

I got several bids for heating and cooling systems. Most of the houses being built had geothermal systems where they had to have two water wells. The housing area was not on city water but had a great aquafer under it. They would pump water out of the ground at 57 degrees into a 4,000 gallon tank in their house taking up space, use a heat pump to extract heat or cool, and then pump the water back into the aquafer in a second well. The prices I got from multiple contractors was $20,000 for the geothermal plus the cost of two wells drilled and plumbing down to $3500 for an air to air heat pump system with electrical resistance back up heat. That air to air heat pump supplier did most of his work supplying the big tract home builders, but again, because of the housing slump caused by the high interest rates, they would take on my private job. He explained that he was recommending the 2.5 ton unit because I had so much glass. I said, fine I will take the 3 ton unit for $3800. This included all the duct work and an electrostatic air filter. I figured I would rather have too big a unit rather than one that was too small to heat and cool the large house.

The contractors made up a list of material they would need and I went to multiple lumber yards for estimates. Lowes was the cheapest, they would deliver for free, and if I didn't like the quality they would come pick it up and give me full credit.

I had drawn up blueprint size drawings of Carolyn's 8X11 graph paper drawing, but I needed actual blue prints to get approval from the county inspectors. An architect would be expensive but as I was getting bids for roofing shingles and trusses I found a draftsman working for one of them who took my drawings and made up blueprints to satisfy the county. I only paid him $200 but he got the commission for the shingles, tar paper, and trusses.

Carolyn had to keep our old house ready to show. The first realtor we picked did not seem to be trying to sell the house so we found another and within two weeks we had a buyer. I already had the construction loan pre-approved at 10% convertible to a mortgage and they would give me cash after meeting different inspection milestones to pay my contractors. Based upon my estimates that I had gotten with me doing a lot of the work, I had a loan approved for $93,000, a whole lot less than the cheapest general contractor at $140,000. We may have to live with bare concrete floors, but we could build our house.

We moved out of our three-story house, put a lot of stuff in storage and moved into a town house with a 90 day lease figuring we might have to renew it several times. One house in this housing area had been under construction by a general contractor for 9 months and was still not finished and it was a much cheaper split level house. We had boxes everywhere in the townhouse that made it hard to walk through. Our daughter had not started to school, but our son had so we enrolled him in the school he would attend after the house was finished,

We broke ground in late August. I had the electrical, plumber, and heating contractor all scheduled for the second weekend. I also had the county inspector scheduled. It looked like a fire drill. From laying the footings the previous weekend, the concrete contractor had hauled in 75 dump truck loads of gravel into the footings for a base for everything else. So as soon as the plumbing and heat vents were in the floor, the concrete guy was pouring fresh concrete floors over the top while the inspectors were trying to inspect while running from the fresh concrete. It was a Keystone Cop chase from one end of the house to the other with each contractor and the inspectors trying to stay ahead of the fresh concrete floor being poured. We did it. The concrete contractor gave me a special deal that if I would let him pour the driveway right then and pay right then he would use highway grade steel reinforced concrete on the driveway that would stand up to a bulldozer driving on it when dry and threw in a 12 X 26 patio in the back and a sidewalk from the front driveway to the patio and from the driveway to the front door all at the same time at the same price as just pouring a standard two car driveway at the end of house construction. That was really a smart thing to do and I don't know why all contractors don't do it. Usually people build the house, then pour the driveway last. By having it done first, the contractors were able to park their vehicles on concrete instead of mud and deliveries could be made into the garage during all the construction phases. Having the sidewalks and back patio made it good for everyone to get in and out of the house, moving things in and out.

Everyone loved the fact that we had all that concrete already in and I am sure that as they built more houses in the future they would have the driveway while building the house. That had not been in anyone's plan, but the concrete contractor wanted to finish his job all at once and collect all his money up front rather than have to come back to finish. He would only have to come back at the completion to do the final grading of the lot with a bulldozer but no more concrete workers or trucks having to come out there.

The next weekend was the three day Labor Day weekend. I carried every piece of wood at least once, the carpenters had hired a young helper so the four of us built all the walls inside and out, got the roof trusses on and covered with roofing pressed wood by the end of the third day. The county could not believe that we had the roof on only 3 weeks from ground breaking. It started raining that week.

The next weekend my carpenters took their weekend off from their regular jobs and were there when it got light. They expected that the pressed wood on the trusses would be destroyed from the rain and were amazed that it was basically untouched. A regular plywood roof would have had to have much of it replaced. By the end of the weekend we had the roof covered in the heaviest duty tar roofing material I could buy and shingled with the longest guaranteed asphalt shingles I could buy and the six flat skylights installed over what would be the sunroom/porch. We got all the T-111 siding nailed up to enclose the house and keep out the rain. Another very long but amazing weekend of work. And then the rains came.

It rained regularly for the next 8 weeks, but the concrete was all poured and the house enclosed. While the electrician was putting in the fuse box and wiring the walls, I put in and wired all of the plug-ins and light switches except for three-way switches which the electrician did. I had him put a computer next to the fuse box which controlled special things to keep our peak billing low. As it got cold and our peak electrical usage would increase, it would cut off the power to the hot water heater near the bedrooms and then the other hot water heater near the kitchen, laundry, and 4th bedroom and bath at the other end of the house. Yes, since the house was so long I had a hot water heater at both ends of the house so we would not have to wait for hot water. It required only a cold water line from one end to the other saving enough money to pay for the second hot water heater at the bedroom and two bath end of the house. The plumber made a mistake and installed two water lines not believing that I had two hot water heaters planned. So, I had a spare pipe under the concrete in case something happened to the line in daily use getting plugged with lime deposits or rusting.

I had priced the insulation for the house, but I hired an insulating contractor working for one of the tract home builders that supplied and installed massive amounts of insulation cheaper than I could buy the minimum requirement and do all the work myself. I had R-50 or better of fiberglass in the ceiling versus I had priced R-30 cellulose (used paper) and did not have to lift a finger while saving about 30% over doing it myself.

I had figured months of putting up drywall that I had never done before, but that same tract home builder came to my rescue and brought better quality drywall, installed it, textured the ceiling about 40% cheaper than me buying the material and doing it myself. I don't think he was that particular when building tract homes, but I had to kick him out when I thought it was perfect and he wanted to redo some of it because he considered it less than perfect.

In the end, we had come in so much cheaper than planned, that I put in $6,000 in light fixtures, special ordered carpet they had to make for me in Georgia because while they had samples, they did not really manufacture and sell that high grade carpet. What wasn't carpeted was covered with extreme high grade linoleum that cost more per square foot than the carpet. The "linoleum" was extremely durable and had the color design all the way through rather than just on top like regular linoleum. We had that put throughout all the hallways, bathrooms and kitchen areas.

My biggest job besides being free labor in carrying lumber was staining what seemed to be miles of baseboard, door trim, etc. I stained much of it behind our townhouse and moved it to the house in the van until it got too cold, then I did the rest of it in the new house before the drywall and flooring. That and installing the intercom system, the TV cable to most of the rooms and the plug-ins and light switches was all the physical work I had to do.

We still had enough money left over that when spring came we put in a 20X40 foot in-ground swimming pool.

Because of my scheduling and having great contractors working for cash by the job schedule versus hourly, we got the house built in 12 weeks which meant we got to move into our house before our 90 day townhouse lease had to be renewed.

What did Carolyn do? She kept up the kids, the townhouse and was out at the new house daily while I was at work cleaning up after the contractors, helping with some of the wood staining and varnishing, answering questions for contractors and inspectors when I could not be there. She also had the kids outside picking up scrap lumber, nails, etc.

Of course, we all worked on spreading grass seed, planting bushes, etc. when the house was finished. Carolyn accepted our furniture from the movers and had the movers place things however she wanted.

When it started getting warm, we had our concrete contractor back to put in the swimming pool and six foot concrete deck around the pool with our leftover money from the construction. So when the cheapest shoddiest general contractor we found quoted $140,000 for a bare house with bare concrete floors and no lighting fixtures, we bought an acre of land in a new housing addition of nice houses, built our house with expensive flooring, $6000 in lighting fixtures, a wide strong driveway not included in his bid, and an inground pool with 6 feet of concrete around it and landscaping for a total cost of $111,000. The cost we paid for what the contractor bid was probably 60% of his bid or less.

We built the house at a good time and locked in that 10% building loan convertible to a 10% mortgage because within a year the interest rates went to 16%.

To give you an idea, our family room was 28 foot square with a kitchen covering most of one wall and separated from the rest of the family room by a 15X4 foot countertop with bar stools that was ideal for having large pot luck dinners. That room connected to the large living and dining room areas that were 18X26 in total. The living room dining room area had a glass wall to the 12X26 foot sunroom and the family room had a double glass patio door to the sunroom. At the other end of the sunroom was the master bedroom also having a double glass door. The back of the sunroom were a series of either fixed or movable glass doors and had the 6 skylights in the cathedral roof.

This worked great for heating and cooling. In the winter the sun would shine through all the way to the front wall of the living / dining rooms. Our first winter there, we had a high of 26 degrees <u>below</u> zero. Carolyn had the sunroom closed off until she saw the wall thermometer said 95 degrees so she opened the glass French doors to the living and dining room and the sliding glass doors at either end and the sun room heated the whole house with the heating system shutting off until about 5PM as the sun started going down. By having time of day billing and the computer control on some of the heavy electric users in the house our heating bill was less than half of our neighbors in smaller houses with their expensive geothermal heating systems.

In the summer, the only cathedral ceiling was in the sunroom and the top two skylights could be opened to let out the heat and had ceiling fans to further draw heat out of the standard 8 foot ceilings in the rest of the house.

When it started getting warm I put up wood stockade fencing around roughly a quarter of an acre from the back of the house to the property line and half the width of our lot. The ground was so hard I had to use a pickaxe to start a hole so the rented gasoline post hole digger could drill a hole for each post. Mix ready mix concrete in a wheel barrow and pour around each post one by one until all the posts were in. Then there was hauling each of the 6x8 foot fence panels and using lag screws to fit them to the posts. As I was finishing this fence Carolyn offered to help me position the fence panels for attaching to the posts. This was a big help until she threw her back out. I lifted her by her elbows from behind and popped it back into position, but she decided not to help any more with that project. I was concerned she would have back problems after that, but within 48 hours she had no more pain and never had a bad back. It was the only time I ever saw her admit to pain or unable to do something.

That summer, I offered to use our house and yard for an office party. The party kept growing until we had hundreds of people coming for a huge pot luck summer party. We had to get a large party tent from the base to have borrowed tables and chairs for the dinner. All the food was on our 15X4 countertop and the 19 foot counter on the back wall. Except for when the general officers were giving speeches under the tent we typically had 70-100 people in the house, twenty or so in the pool and another 30 playing soccer in the open half acre of our yard. The party was a big success and back at work I was presented a hand drawn depiction of the party with me floating in the swimming pool with a cigarette and a drink. It was signed by 50-60 people including some of the general officers that attended.

42 Air War College

After finishing building our house and getting moved in and settled, I had decided that I need what they called professional military education (PME). I had never planned on making a career of the US Air Force, but I had spent over 10 years on active duty and now was approaching the 20 year mark to be eligible to retire from the reserves at age 60. I was nowhere near that age, but I only lacked 5 years to earn the points necessary to retire with my twenty total years of military service to qualify for retirement.

While on active duty I had applied twice for Squadron Officer's School (SOS), but could not attend due to either being reassigned or so short manned I could not be away from work. Now that I had so much time invested and had been promoted to a Major (0-4) without any PME I needed to make lieutenant colonel before retirement. In addition, it would help me get promotions as a civil servant to have that extra military schooling.

I was too old for SOS which was a prerequisite for Air Command and Staff college which was a prerequisite for Air War College (AWC). Therefore I could not take any PME to qualify me for lieutenant colonel. AWC would give me the equivalent of 48 semester hours of graduate school and substitute for a masters degree in my civilian career. A position came up where they were going to allow in a few civilians with only the grade of GS-13 instead of the normal GS-15 or full Colonel requirement. As a civilian I did not have to have SOS or Air Command and Staff College (ACSC). It was a seminar program where I would not have to go away from home for over a year, but would count the same. I would have to study on my own time and attend every other Saturday at the air base for a seminar with full Colonel selectees. I was the only civilian in the class. I was outranked by everyone there, but I had the backing of General officers.

The second semester brought a problem. They decided to enforce the rule that civilians had to be GS-15's to continue in the class, but if a Major had taken the first semester and was on the lieutenant colonel selection list they would be able to complete the second semester. The rule was that to take the first semester as military you had to be a lieutenant colonel (0-5) and coming up for potential promotion to full colonel (0-6)

Even though I had taken the first semester as a GS-13 civilian I was not going to be able to take the second semester. When they increased the grade requirements for the first semester they never increased the requirement for second semester so as a Major (0-4) the loophole allowed me to take the second semester even though I was not a selectee for lieutenant colonel (0-5).

I did well in the class. The books were really multipage 8 ½ X 11 booklets or chapters that made a pile about 4 feet high. One chapter that got my attention was named "The Chaos Factor". Most of the other chapters I had real world experience in so they were easy. This one was easy because it captured my imagination. Each semester required a term paper. For the second and final semester we were given a free choice on topic. My topic was war with the Middle East. I spent many weeks researching the material for it. I knew that everyone was saying that Russia was the enemy, but I felt it was more likely that we would go to war in the Middle East.

My term paper was rejected in early 1987, "We would never send military equipment and troops to the Middle East." That was going to leave me with a failing grade and a year of study wasted. I still had some time so I whipped up the story of going to war with Russia with no personal research and got a passing grade to graduate.

This qualified me for lieutenant colonel in the reserves to allow me to complete my 20 years for retirement and also qualify me for federal civil service promotion to GS-14.

Again, Carolyn had to run the household and allowed me the study time to read my 4 foot high stack of booklets, study for tests, and do two term papers. I neglected her and other things because I still had a full time civil service job that normally took 50 hours a week or more plus a lot of travel out of town. It was 48 graduate semester hours in 14 months while I was still working 50 hours a week at my job.

43 Moving to Oklahoma

In 1988 Carolyn and her sister Shirley took turns going to take care of her parents as they were in and out of hospitals in Fort Smith, Arkansas. Carolyn would either take the kids if they weren't in school or leave them with me. One time, my parents drove from Oklahoma to take care of the kids while Carolyn went to Arkansas to care for her parents. Then Shirley would come relieve her and Carolyn would come home.

Finally, we had her parents sell their house and move in with us in Ohio. They refused, but did agree to move into a senior living apartment that was brand new and not too far from our house.

Her father had dementia bad which was why someone had to go stay with them whenever one of them was in the hospital in Fort Smith. Her father had type 2 diabetes and the doctors never gave him medications for it. He got to where he could barely see and had to give up reading which was a major thing for him. Then he got so deaf that you could not talk with him if there was any background noise. He could only hear part of the television if you turned the volume up to where it was painful for anyone else. When family got together he would just find a quiet corner and sit. When I saw him that way I would go over and talk with him for hours, if possible, when I was not required to be with other family. I think it was being nearly blind and nearly deaf that caused his dementia versus Alzheimer's. I had studied isolation for space travel in college and knew that it did not take long for an astronaut to become debilitated due to the isolation.

I think the move to Ohio and him not being able to converse with others his age due to his being near blind and near deaf caused it to accelerate. After a few months we moved them in with us in our house when he got away and was found walking down the highway.

An opportunity arose where I could have a partial career change by taking a regular R&D manager job instead of a traveling consultant to R&D management. It looked good on my resume to prove I could do it, and my travel should be less. I would be the first civilian Deputy Program Manager for Logistics in the government. It was usually for at least a lieutenant colonel looking to be a full colonel or a full colonel looking to be a general. There were several potential jobs and one was in Oklahoma only 3 hours from Fort Smith, Arkansas. I would be able to live near my parents for the first time in 23 years. We thought it would be good for Carolyn's parents to be able to visit their old stomping grounds in Arkansas. It was supposed to lead to two automatic promotions to the highest grade in the federal civil service other than the senior executive service (SES) which were largely political appointees.

Because it was short notice, I had to leave first and leave Carolyn there to sell the house, take care of the house, mowing the acre lot, handle the packing when the house sold, and then driving the kids and her parents to Oklahoma. The housing market was not great with the double-digit mortgage rates so we sold it cheap, but with enough money for a minimum down payment on the new house and pay off our credit cards. Carolyn had designed that house herself and I had contracted out most of the work acting as the general contractor as I mentioned before. Our teenage son refused to mow the lawn with our riding lawnmower and Carolyn, being only five foot zero did not really fit the lawnmower, but she got it done.

We bought a house in Oklahoma that had 5 bedrooms and 4 baths. One end of the house had 2 bedrooms with walk-in closets, a full bath and a separate heating and cooling system. The plan was to have her parents use one bedroom as a living room and the other as their bedroom, and next to the kitchen. Her mother would not do it because her father had gotten worse and did not recognize that our daughter was his grand daughter and he was not himself. We found them a really nice two-bedroom apartment.

Nearly two months had gone by since I had left for Oklahoma and Carolyn's sister came down to drive her parents' car and them to the apartment. Carolyn left a few days later after the movers had come and packed up our belongings. Apparently her father gave Shirley a lot of trouble on the trip acting like a child being kidnapped. I could not have taken this job in the time available except for Carolyn being so capable. Carolyn never believed that I was so proud of her for making this move by herself. I was very proud of her and knew she could do it. Her older sister always said she was too dependent upon me, but I knew better.

I thought the move would be good for all of us. Where we moved was an outstanding and exclusive neighborhood. Our son had started running with the wrong kids in Ohio and our neighbors were the right kids. Most of our neighbors were medical doctors. Our next door neighbor drove a Ferrari, his wife a Mercedes station wagon, and the daughter had a new Porsche. One of the houses a block away was built by Conway Twitty, another house was lived in by Nadia Comaneci and Bart Conner, the Olympic gymnasts, another was part owner of several grocery stores.

I would be blocks from my parents, and we could take Carolyn's parents to visit people in Fort Smith on weekends. I was supposed to get a substantial pay raise and the move was completely paid for by the government.

Things did not work out. The Berlin Wall fell, my major programs in secure communications were deemed unnecessary with the Russian adversary gone and therefore none of the promised promotions. Carolyn's father's dementia got out of hand. Carolyn's sister was afraid of him, but tiny Carolyn put him in his place. When he would start to have a temper fit, she would push him back into his chair and tell him to just sit there and he would. After only a couple of months, her father had to be put in an Alhziemer's unit to protect her mother from him. She still refused to move in with us where Carolyn could control him, but only her and I knew she could.

Roy, her father, caused havoc in the nursing home. He had no idea who his wife was and thought she was his sister, little Carolyn was the big gorilla that made him behave, but he always knew my name and our kids, but he didn't really know me. He would greet me with, "Hello Al, glad you could come visit me. Is Craig still swimming competitively (he could have been Olympic if he had been serious and did go to the U.S. Junior Olympics for six years.) and how is that beautiful daughter of yours, Christine? Is she still playing the viola?" And then he would blow it by asking, "Do you still have that 36 Buick we used to go riding around in?" I mean I would love to have a 36 Buick, but I was his son in law and he thought I was an old friend his age.

He fell and gashed his head while I was out of town on a trip. Carolyn had to take him to the hospital. The hospital sent him home and he died 2 days later of Sepsis from an infection where he had stitches.

A couple of months later, I got a chance to take Carolyn with me on a government trip to Oahu, Hawaii. The trip was officially 5 days including travel time, but I was asked to stay over for another meeting the following week. Things beyond anyone's control ended up with Carolyn and I spending 10 days in Hawaii at mostly government expense with me actually being at work about 5 hours.

While we were there, Shirley came down from Illinois to help watch the kids and her mother who was now alone in the apartment. When we got home we found that Shirley had taken her mother to the hospital for general pains. Carolyn lost her mother less than a week after our return from Hawaii,

I had left for Oklahoma in later May, Carolyn and family came to Oklahoma in late July and she lost both of her parents before the end of the year. This was not a good move for Carolyn.

Our son was immediately invited to the rich kids' parties where they had indoor pools, but he gravitated to the wrong kids. In Ohio he was on the air base youth swim team that was highly competitive with a coach that had been an Olympic swimming coach. In Oklahoma, it was the high school swim team which was one of the better ones in the state. Craig might have been able to go to the Olympics but he did not take it seriously. He went to just enough practices to not get thrown off the team. He always had high state qualifying times but at the state he would not even try really hard except for the relays when others were depending on him. I saw him with near Olympic times when it came for his turn in a relay. He would dive into the pool a quarter of lap behind from the last swimmer and be half a pool ahead of the team in first place when he finished his turn. Many times the anchor swimmer was able to keep enough of that lead to win. On individuals, he would barely make the consolation heat in the finals and then be so far ahead that his time would have placed him in the top 4 in the state if he had been in the final instead of consolation heat. In fact, with some competition in the final heat he might have set some records if he really tried. Where others could hardly get out of the pool he would finish without being tired. While the other swimmers had to rest up before swimming again, Craig would be walking around joking with his team mates and swimmers he knew from the other teams.

Christine was only starting second grade when we moved and it was a good move for her. Carolyn, naturally, took over a scout troop so Christine would make friends quickly, always doing for everyone else. I should have done more for Carolyn all her life if I had known what to do. She was so capable and independent I usually felt in her way when I tried to help. I never did learn to fold a fitted sheet even with hours of instruction over the 45 years we were together.

At any rate Christine took up the viola in the school orchestra which she played until graduation in 2000. She was on the honor roll taking honors classes. We thought Craig was the smart one and from IQ testing he was much smarter than Christine, but where his grades were mainly B's and C's hers were near straight A's taking advanced classes. Her senior year she got 20 hours of college credit driving to the local community college. The only high school classes she took her senior year was English and Orchestra. She had to not go to summer school for English to give her another year in the Orchestra and allow her to hold off graduation until she was 18 in the 2000 year class. Otherwise she would have graduated at 17 and missed that last year of Orchestra.

She tried out and made the state youth orchestra, but she had too many things going and decided she didn't have time to go to the city several times a week for practices. She was the Worthy Advisor in the local Rainbow for Girls and the Queen of Jobs daughters which are both masonic organizations for young girls. She was a state officer in Rainbow for Girls which necessitated a monthly weekend away from home visiting other assemblies in other towns around the state. When she was 14 she was the Oklahoma Representative to Texas and gave a speech in front of the Texas state assembly in the Houston Astrodome Convention Center. She could read a two page speech twice and repeat it word for word a year later if necessary, Her speech at the Astrodome was word perfect without notes and properly formally acknowledged all the Texas state adult advisors, high level members of the Texas masons, and the Texas girl officers for their state. It was about 15 minutes and captured everyone's rapt attention with no talking from anyone except when they were called on to acknowledge Christine's acknowledgement of them.

Christine continued holding an Oklahoma state office from age 14 to 20 when she had to leave Rainbow for Girls due to being 20. For her senior year in high school, her best friend in Rainbows was the Grand Worthy Advisor (president) for the state. When not elected to an office by the other girls, the adult advisors made her an official advisor to the adults. She could probably have been the state worthy advisor except her friend was a year older and had the political support of her high-ranking parents in the state organization and they could not let two girls from the same town hold that highest office two years in a row. Christine was almost embarrassed by the masons when she graduated from high school winning multiple scholarships totaling over $20,000. Some of the scholarships were from businesses that had no relationship with free masonry but that wanted to promote women and came to the masonic girls organizations to find young accomplished high school graduates with good habits and high morals who would represent ideal womanhood.

Christine also gave up scouting those last couple of years and Carolyn turned over the troop leadership to her assistant troop leader. Where our son kept us busy with his competitive swimming meets around the state and going to nationals every year, Christine took our time with her activities. When Christine went to college that left Carolyn alone with the dog while I was working. Christine graduated with a Bachelors in 3 years and went on to grad school in New Mexico.

My jobs consisted of earning the money, making sure our frequently older cars were totally reliable. For 16 years her main car with a full size custom Chevy Van which she drove daily and we took on trips. I went through a variety of older second hand cars. That Chevy Van was the last vehicle we bought new and had well over 200,000 reliable miles on it. The only time we had to stop on the road was when some kids put some dirt in the gas tank that plugged the little filter on the inlet to the carburetor and the only tool I had in the van was a pair of vice grips. I fixed it at a gas station by removing the filter and just letting the dirt go on through unfiltered for a few years.

I took care of the outside of the house, cleaning the swimming pool, fixing the little plumbing jobs, contacting service people to get the heat and air serviced. In 45 years I only had to have an appliance fixed about 5 times, like the ice maker in the fridge, a new sink disposal (2), a clothes dryer burner (2 times). I cooked on the grill at least once a week on average: more in the summer than in winter.

She did most of the cooking, grocery shopping, and dish washing in the dish washer. Before the dishwasher it was a two person job, she washed, I dried. However, we had a dishwasher in our first house after being married 6 years. Because of my frequent business trips for the air force, she did most of the raising of the kids.

Carolyn's hip that the doctor said she was going to have to have replaced in 1974 was now bothering her more in 1990 after we moved to Oklahoma. Then it started actually locking up on her where she would get stuck half way to standing and have to spend up to 5 minutes getting her hip straight to stand. I had two co-workers who had hip replacements. One woman walked really funny with her hip joint causing her to walk crab-like and the guy using a cane and limping badly. He retired and came back six months later as a contractor walking like most people would run. He had no limp and I asked him what he had had done. He had gone to Oklahoma Bone and Joint Hospital and they had replaced the badly replaced joint with one of theirs and it was like dark to daylight. Instead of limping with a cane he would practically run you down he was walking so fast. I called his doctor and using him as a reference, got Carolyn in to see him the next week. He said Carolyn needed both hips by XRAY and scheduled her for the hip locking up two weeks later. Carolyn's friends were glad she was not getting the joint replaced by the local doctor in Norman, but had not said anything.

Carolyn was scared, but the next day after surgery they had her walking with a walker. A week after the surgery we went to the local hospital's brand new rehab center with a cane and asked about getting her rehab there instead of going to Oklahoma City. They said, "Sure. How many months ago did you have the hip replacement?"

Answer, "Last week, just about this time of day."

"Where's your walker?"

"They didn't give me one."

Carolyn took their rehab for two weeks and worked at home with the instructions from the hospital for home rehab and then quit the official rehab. When the stiches and clamps were removed by the original surgeon and he cleared her for swimming rehab, I used the pool heater to warm the whole 20,000 gallon pool behind the house and she started swimming laps using the breast stroke kick with a paddle board to keep her afloat which caused her to move that new hip just right.

Four months after surgery, we were visiting her sister in Illinois and she got on a horse for the first time. I had to help her on and off the horse, but it did not hurt her and she was glad to see she could straddle a horse again. When she saw the surgeon he said, she shouldn't be riding. He was not worrying about the hip he had replaced, but the other hip that she going to have to have replaced soon.

About 4 years later, we heard that surgeon was going to retire and if she wanted to have him do the second hip she needed to have it done right away or get his son, who was also an orthopedic surgeon at the same hospital. So she got the second hip done. She did not do the home rehab as well with the second hip and it was never quite as good, but you would never guess she had two metal hip joints and did everything anyone else could do and never had a limp.

I was close to retirement when I came home from a trip a day early and found that when I was out of town she loaded a 357 magnum pistol and put it under my pillow and had a 20 gauge double barrel shotgun leaning against her nightstand whenever I did not come home. She always told me she was a scaredy cat, but I never believed her in that she seemed fearless. And to think, I did a lot of traveling. Never leaving her for more than a few days and calling her daily from wherever I was, but I had no idea she was loading and sleeping with guns,

I always bought houses in what I considered very safe neighborhoods. We never had anything stolen or any evidence of anything being taken. We left our cars unlocked most of the time and no one ever disturbed them. Only one time when we were in Germany there was a rumor about a peeping tom and one night I heard giggling outside our bedroom window. I got my 357 magnum pistol, turned on the light as I pointed that big gun toward the window and said, in English, stay away from my apartment. No one ever had any more rumors of a peeping tom in the German housing area.

Whoa, brandishing a gun in Germany? A little story on that. In the next door two story apartment building a young German officer found someone trying to steal the hubcaps off of his car in the parking lot and he emptied his handgun trying to shoot them from his second story balcony. The German police that we only saw 3 or 4 times in our 3 years in Germany came the next morning in their Volkswagen Bug and asked him about firing off his handgun in the housing area in the middle of the night. He explained, the police searched the woods across the street and told him that he needed some more shooting practice, they found bullet holes in the trees, but no evidence he hit the bad guys. Would our police be so understanding here in the USA. No wonder the crime rate is so low in Germany, or it was before all the immigrants came in. Look it up, "Germany has one of the highest rates of gun ownership in the world, but one of the lowest rates of gun related deaths." If most homeowners have guns, the bad guys better stay out of homes.

I pulled my last reserve duty in 1989 completing the required 20 years of service for retirement and in the spring of 1990 I was officially separated from the reserves having received the points and time necessary for retirement, but a reservist cannot draw that military retirement pay until they reach their 60th birthday which would be April 2004. I had spent 10 ½ years on active duty as a reservist before returning to federal civil service. To make that time calculate toward my civilian retirement I had to pay the government for the money I did not pay into the retirement system while I was in the active military. I took out a second mortgage on the house to pay in the $25,000 so I could count that time for civil service retirement thus increasing the years in the calculation from 26 ½ to 37 years which raised the percent of my working pay for my retirement check from under 50% to 68% of the average pay for the last three years. I could have drawn full federal civil service retirement at age 55, but I was still working. I had 60 days annual leave built up and could only carry over 30 days leave so I arranged to retire from federal civil service in early January 2004 before the end of the pay period. That meant I could collect 60 days full pay the day I retired by selling back the accumulated leave and my thousands of hours of sick leave would add time to my calculations for a retirement check. That extra money was enough to easily carry me over until I could collect that first air force reserve retirement check when I turned sixty four months later. Therefore my 68% civil service retirement check plus my 44% military lieutenant colonel check would give me roughly what I was making when I worked full time. To continue working my salary would be $1.78 an hour more than not working and still having the expenses of going to and from work and being away from Carolyn.

44 Examples of Miracle Vacations

We took many family vacations. This is an example of one of our vacations while we were in Oklahoma. Our tent trailer had to be scrapped, and we could not afford a new one but still wanted to take vacations so we went to a family size tent.

We wanted to see Canyon De Chelly in Arizona so we packed up the old 200,000 mile Chevrolet G20 custom van and our family tent, sleeping bags, food, air mattresses and took off. We drove through to the Canyon in one long day arriving just before dark and camped in the nearly deserted National Campground there. We got up the next morning and drove around the rim of the canyon stopping many times for photos and looks through the binoculars. Then we decided since we were so close we would drive on over to the Grand Canyon. We went north and could see Bryce Canyon and Zion Canyon rock formations as we drove along the south side of Utah. Then we drove through that famous road through Monument Valley.

We arrived at the east end of the Grand Canyon just before sunset. We drove into the first lookout and found we were the only ones there. We wondered where the mass of crowds you see on the news were, because we had the parking lot to ourselves. We walked out to the viewing point, took photos and moved west to the next parking lot and viewing point. At the third lot, we didn't bother with a parking space since we were alone so I just parked by the entrance to the trailhead to the viewing point. We did this until we got all the way to the campground after dark. We drove up to the ranger station at the entrance to the campground and asked about a camp space. The ranger told us they had been reserved for nearly a year and recommended driving on out of the park and trying to find a motel. I knew that they had said to make reservations a year in advance, but we had always been blessed with good luck, miracles, God's grace or something.

I said, "Okay, we will just drive in and make a u turn and leave."

As we drove in, a couple of young college students waved us down. "We heard. We have an empty camp space. There were a bunch of us coming out here to meet at the Grand Canyon and we did not realize how big the camp spaces were and reserved three of them. When we got here we discovered that they were so huge that we could park all seven cars and set up our five tents in one and so we have two spare camp spaces. We paid $10 per site. How many days do you want it for?"

"Two nights should do it, here's two twenties to give you a little profit."

"We only paid $10 that's not necessary."

"No problem, you saved us the time of driving into town, trying to find a motel, and the cost of the motel."

The next morning we woke at the first hint of daylight so we decided to head back the way we came and watch the sunrise over the Grand Canyon. Just like the night before, we had the parking lots to ourselves. When we got to the little store at the east end they were still not open. We waited, got some donuts and coffee and headed back toward Grand Canyon Village. When we got to the first parking lot west of the little store, the parking lot was not only full, but people were parallel parked on the main road and walking toward the parking lot and the lookout point.

Every parking lot and viewing point was like that all the way back to the campground.

We had missed the crowd and had everything to ourselves. If we had left the campground any later it would have taken hours with the traffic and the parking. As it was we got all our photos at the prime sunrise times and missed the traffic and walking from our van to the lookouts.

When we got back to Grand Canyon Village, my daughter and I decided to start walking on the trail to the bottom of the canyon. Carolyn was just going to stay around the lodge and the van because she did not want to walk for miles on a slope. Christine and I walked for about an hour with a lot of people slowing us down. We had not brought any water or snacks and could see it would take hours to get down to the bottom and decided we did not want to spend the day that way so we spent an hour going back up. Then we met with Carolyn and decided we would drive down into the town. As we were leaving the park, there were miles of cars waiting to get their pass to enter the park, but we had the road to ourselves.

We watched an IMAX move with a simulated eagle's flight through the canyon that was taken from a hang glider, went to a museum, ate lunch and headed back to the Grand Canyon. We drove right on through flashing our pass to the rangers at the entrance. There were miles of cars lined up to leave the park finishing up their visit there. Again, we missed the traffic by going the other way at the right time.

We visited some Indian ruins along the south rim of the Grand Canyon and then as it was approaching sunset we took a shuttle trip to the west end of the park to see that end of the park at sunset. We had sandwiches with us and after taking our photos discovered we had missed the shuttle. As we started walking back toward the lodge a shuttle came by picking up stragglers like us and drove us back. Hey, God was always with us so we didn't need to worry about getting stranded miles from the campground at night.

The next morning we decided that we had seen what there was at the Grand Canyon unless we wanted to go to the bottom and did not want to spend the day that way.

We decided to continue on west and go over the Hoover Dam and on to Las Vegas. We drove into Las Vegas near dark, camped on a hot gravel camp ground, got up and walked the strip and drove to some other areas of casinos like downtown Las Vegas. The next morning, we decided we had seen enough of Las Vegas and headed west again. We drove through Death Valley and found ourselves near Sequoia National Park in California and decided to go see the Sequoia trees.

Naturally, the ranger said there was no camping available when a couple came in to say they were leaving early. We took their spot near the upper restrooms and showers. A prime camping spot. Who needs reservations with God pulling a small miracle on a regular basis. We cooked out and took showers and turned in for the night. About 3AM I felt something pushing against my head through the tent and some snuffling like a big dog. I was afraid a large dog was going to relieve himself on the tent right near my head so I swatted it through the tent and it ran away. We got up around 5AM.

Everyone was talking about the bear that came down through the whole campground knocking down tents and causing confusion. It was not attacking anyone but running from something. Everyone was trying to straighten bent tent poles or re-stake their tents and find their sleeping bags that had been dragged down the hill. I did not say that maybe I caused it. I thought it was someone's dog running loose in the campground. Apparently I had swatted the nose of the bear who took off from my tent causing havoc all the way downhill to the other end of the campground. We drove around and looked at the magnificent trees and decided we needed to head home since I had only taken off for one week which meant counting the weekend days we only had 4 days to get back home. We took off again headed east now. As we drove into Las Vegas there is a long hill. Thermometers on businesses showed over 120 degrees and while the van was not overheating the air conditioner was cutting off from time to time as we pulled the hill in the heat.

We decided to stay in a hotel and wandered around the Las Vegas strip visiting the famous casinos. When we got back to the hotel I got each of us a roll of nickels to use in the slot machines. It was not long when Carolyn and Christine were digging into my winnings to feed other machines. At one point playing nickel poker I was up to $126. We finally gave up and went to bed and took off east again in the morning. On the way to Oklahoma we stopped by the Dinosaur National Monument, the Painted Desert, the Petrified Forest, and back home. So 5 days of vacation time, with weekends 9 days, we saw a lot of the western USA and several national parks. A typical vacation. A miracle in getting camp spaces at Grand Canyon, Sequoia National Park, the Petrified Forest and no car trouble in a Chevy van with 200,000 miles.

Another long week was driving to Elgin, Illinois for a wedding, driving from there to see the South Dakota Bad Lands, Mount Rushmore and because of rain after seeing it we drove on to Devil's Tower and then went on to Yellowstone National Park, and back through Colorado.

All our trips were adventures and charmed. We did not need to plan our trips a year in advance like many people do, we could just blunder around, spur of the moment, and trust our luck or God to make things work out the best way possible.

45 Moving to Florida

A little over a year after I retired and started working as a poor realtor my sister-in-law's husband died. Carolyn had just flown down to see her a few weeks earlier. Then my father died. I already had a cruise scheduled so Carolyn and I left on the cruise after the funeral. While on the cruise I got a job offer to move to Tampa, Florida for roughly my retirement check. This meant I would have $90,000 in retirement plus $90,000 salary and Carolyn's sister had just lost her husband 150 miles away, so we said yes by email from the ship. When we got home we bought a new 5th wheel trailer to live in Tampa, put our furniture in storage, and the house up for sale. Two weeks from returning from the cruise we were living in the 5th wheel trailer on payments and I was working in Tampa as an R&D manager for electronic systems for the special forces (Seals, Green Berets, etc.). Similar to my job managing secure voice then the AWACS radar plane R&D but on a lower dollar value scale. This job required some travel too. It had been a year since I retired so they thought it would take a year to get my Top Secret clearance back, but apparently, the government had been watching me in retirement and it only took 2 weeks (a miracle?) which was unheard of.

Carolyn started working with realtors to find a house around Tampa and all we got was disappointment. Either it was a run down house in a bad neighborhood for $300.000 or a nice house next to a quick stop gas station with bars on the windows and doors surrounded by slums for $400,000.

We finally went further and further out and found Sun City Center which is an over 55 community of just under 20,000 population with all ranges of prices for houses from $8,000 for a tiny condo to $700,000. We would look at houses on the weekend, but by Monday they were sold and not on the market. After about the 4th weekend we found a house that was subpar compared to our previous houses, but in good shape in a good neighborhood for a price only slightly higher than what we sold our house for in Oklahoma and said, "We'll take it."

The only thing wrong with the house was that it only had two bedrooms and two small bathrooms, with a small kitchen and other small broken up rooms that had been closed in or added on since the house was built. The other thing was that it was called the Pepto-Bismal house because that was the color of the kitchen cabinets that had mirrors on every door, the front door, the awnings, and the garage door. After we bought the house we figured we would have to buy all new cabinets but found out from a friendly neighbor that they thought they were good oak under the pink paint and mirrors.

We had a chain link fence put in the backyard immediately for our two dogs. Carolyn had me order green vinyl covered chain link to help camouflage it for our neighbors that did not have fences. In fact the house behind ours was in one of the 75 different homeowners' associations in Sun City Center and most prohibited fences. That limited the houses we could look at when shopping for a house. We needed to be able to put up a fence.

I bought a nice wood front door to replace the hot pink metal door and then stained and varnished it. Carolyn and I took turns stripping paint off the cabinets and peeling off large mirrors on every cabinet door. Carolyn ended up handling the movers that brought our furniture from storage in Oklahoma and much of the paint stripping. I did all the staining and varnishing. I replaced the master bathroom cabinet top and sink and added some wood medicine cabinets to replace a large fixed mirror.

While we were doing this we had moved our 5th wheel trailer to Cockroach Bay, which sounds bad but was actually a nice trailer park. Most of the lots were for snow birds and some of the 5th wheels and park model trailers had probably not moved in 20 years. A snow bird in Florida is someone that has a home somewhere in northern United States or Canada and comes south to Florida in the winter. There are probably a million snow birds but it is hard to track because Florida has no income tax so many snow birds own a home in Florida and claim Florida as their state of residence even though they may spend more than 6 months each year up north. Canadians lose benefits if they don't maintain their residency in Canada by spending at least six months in Canada and there are over 80,000 in the Canadian Snow Birds Association but that is only a small percentage of Canadian Snow Birds.

I commuted to work from the trailer park and Carolyn commuted to our house in Sun City Center until we had the cabinets finished and the furniture moved from storage in Oklahoma. Again, Carolyn had to take care of most of the move and deciding where the furniture would be placed. When I came home from work after we moved in, I hung the pictures wherever Carolyn told me. As always, Carolyn turned the house to a home.

The previous owners had a small vinyl sided room added onto the house with what had been triple sliding glass doors to the outside now dividing what they used as a dining room with a chandelier above their dining table. Carolyn decided the living room was large enough for both the new sofa and loveseat we bought in Florida and our dining room table, 6 chairs, china hutch, and server. We had donated our old living room furniture except for the coffee and end tables before the move.

The separate room was not used as a dining room but became the computer and file cabinet room and temporary guest room with a hideaway bed. Christine's old day bed and trundle became the TV room sofa along with an old reclining, glider chair we had from Oklahoma and the "game table" and 4 cushioned leather chairs we had inherited from her parents. The game table and chairs were the only quality living room furniture being name brand good quality wood. The "game table" was lower than a dining table and 6 sided. That is also where we put our bookshelves and television. We ate most of our meals on the game table where we could watch television.

The television room looked to be what used to be a porch that had been closed in sometime in the past with windows on two sides. There was an add on porch behind that covering what had once been the patio. The porch was large and I ended up spending many hours out there, reading and smoking my cigarettes not allowed in the house.

46 Heart Attack

We took another cruise in September 2006 to the Eastern Caribbean. Carolyn knew that I wanted to snorkel, but I would not do it without her. I tried to convince her otherwise that I wasn't interested but she insisted that we sign up for a sailboat, snorkel, beach side trip. Carolyn did not like to be on water except on a cruise ship which she loved, but here she was on a large catamaran with 20 other passengers and 5 crew. Sailing out to a snorkeling area was fun, but when it came time to snorkel, I suggested we just stay on the boat. I was worried for some reason. I have always had premonitions of both good and bad things and this seemed it might be bad, but the wind and water was calm and you could see the bottom of the sea from the boat.

Carolyn did not like to even wade in lakes except Lake Geneva in Wisconsin where she grew up that had very clear water and all her friends were in the water. She was a fairly good swimmer, but preferred the swimming pool. She seldom went in our pool in Ohio and the only time she used the pool in Oklahoma was after her hip replacements for rehab that worked great.

At any rate, for my benefit she went into the water without me and I followed as quickly as I could. This snorkeling trip was her gift to me, she had no interest in snorkeling, but wanted me to have the experience. I was trying to catch up to her as she had a head start when a thunderstorm came over the mountain on the island and the wind came up with lightning actually hitting the water which harmed no one because everyone was too far away, but

Carolyn panicked and with the wind blowing and waves I lost sight of her.

Apparently, the lightning had scared her and she was swimming toward the beach but the wind had created a current that pushed her far to the right of the closest beach. When I finally saw her she was in trouble and doubling over in the water. I fought through the waves to her about 50 yards away and I am not a good swimmer, especially with a life vest on, that we both had. When I got to her she said she couldn't breath and her chest hurt. I started trying to pull her behind me swimming toward the sailboat but it was really slow going. I was blowing the whistle for help but the rubber rafts were busy rescuing people nearer the sailboat and could not hear my distant whistle with their outboard motors going. I pulled her against the current for about 150 yards before a rescue rubber raft from another sailboat came to the rescue and helped get her into the raft. I was tired, but had a lifevest so I would not sink so they took her to one of our rescue rafts and then they came back for me and took me to the sailboat.

Our rescue rubber raft drove around picking up other snorkelers with Carolyn breathing from an oxygen mask they had onboard. It was about 30 minutes before Carolyn was actually brought on board the sailboat still sucking oxygen. The captain of the sailboat said he though it was a heart attack, but Carolyn took the mask off and said it was just an asthma attack. At any rate, by the time we got back to the cruise ship Carolyn seemed to be alright. That night she got sick at her stomach, but neither of us had ever had any symptom of sea sickness which I found out later was another symptom of a heart attack. And all because Carolyn had done this just to give me the opportunity to snorkel.

When we got home from the cruise both of her shoulders were hurting, but no chest pain, another symptom of a woman having a heart attack. The doctors she was seeing gave her steroids for both the breathing and the shoulder pain. She kept getting worse. In mid-November they prescribed a nebulizer to atomize albuterol for her breathing and more steroids for her shoulder pain. They called it COPD and arthritis. When we went to visit her sister 120 miles south in Fort Myers Beach, Florida for Thanksgiving, I bought an inverter to run her 120 volt AC nebulizer from the 12 volt DC car power so she could use the nebulizer during the 2 hour car trip. By Christmas she was worse. She had seen 5 different doctors since Thanksgiving and 3 doctors the week after Christmas.

When her feet started swelling, I gave up on the doctors and took her to the hospital ER. They immediately diagnosed it as heart and started treating her until they could arrange for an ambulance to take her to Tampa General hospital and a heart surgeon, which turned out to be another unexplained miracle God gave us.

It turned out to be very serious. Apparently, that incident in trying to snorkel caused a heart attack. The other doctors in Tampa General said there were only two doctors in the United States that could have done the surgery and she had one that had studied under the only other doctor. The most serious issue was that part of her left ventricle had died and was a huge aneurism. The doctor cut out the dead portion of the heart muscle and graphed the heart back together. Was it meant for us to move to the Tampa area where one of only two miracle doctors in the United States could do the operation. Her doctor learned from the other doctor before he moved to Florida. He primarily did heart transplants, but took an exception for Carolyn.

He then replaced all three of the major veins feeding the heart noting that one was very undersized probably from birth and 90% blocked and the other two were 100% blocked. He didn't know how she had survived. Carolyn was tough, in the South Bay Hospital in Sun City Center she was walking the hallways and rearranging furniture in her temporary room while waiting for the ambulance transport. Her blood pressure at that time was 125 over 120 with 120 pulse rate.

I didn't know any of this until after the surgery, but the doctors at the hospital were giving her a 2% chance of surviving the surgery. They did not expect her to breathe on her own, but within an hour of the surgery they removed the intubation tube as she was awake and breathing on her own. Her surgeon was the only one not surprised.

Then she had a hard time breathing and they called it severe COPD. For two weeks they kept giving her breathing treatments and pounding on her back to loosen mucus. Finally, they took her down for an echocardiogram and discovered that her heart was beating against the pericardium. The same surgeon opened her chest back up and cut away part of the pericardium to give her now well fed repaired heart room to beat properly. After 5 and a half weeks she went home from the hospital in February. I promised that I would go to church more to thank God for the miracle of having moved to Tampa and getting one of only two doctors that could fix her heart.

I had been only working part time spending at least half a day and half the night in the hospital. When she came home, I told my boss that I was resigning to spend the rest of my life with Carolyn. He wanted me to continue working part time or even mostly work from home, but I decided I had plenty of retirement money and did not need to work. I came in a few afternoons to train my replacement, but I had pretty much automated my job where all the replacement had to do was put new information into the computer and let the computer do most of the work. Then I really quit for good and strictly answered a few questions from home.

47 Surviving the Heart Attack

Carolyn was a new woman. She no longer needed asthma medicine making me think that it was the undersized heart vein that had caused her breathing problems all along. Over the next few years, Carolyn was back to country line dancing two hours at a time once per week, if we were home, and doing swimming pool exercises at Aquasizers for an hour 2-3 days a week. Those were the only times we were not together. We took several cruises, but no more attempts at physical exertion although we walked many miles. We took a cruise tour of Alaska in 2008 that she really enjoyed and a 2 week cruise around the Hawaiian Islands.

Carolyn really enjoyed the cruise tour to Alaska. We arranged to be on the same ship as our first cruise in 2004 when we took my father on a cruise to see the Panama Canal. We had to walk what seemed to be about three miles in the airport in Vancouver, Canada, past stuffed animals and dioramas of Canada dragging our suitcases with us. Finally we got to large area with several hundred people milling around waiting for their bus trip to downtown Vancouver.

We had arrived a day before the cruise and walked to see the victory gardens with all the rosebushes and downtown Vancouver. There were hundreds of homeless people everywhere begging for handouts. Carolyn wanted to give all of them cash at first and then realized we did not have that much money. If you gave a dollar to one then twenty others wanted their dollar too. The steps on steps to government buildings were covered with homeless people. We wondered what they were going to do about these street bums when the Winter Olympics came there in a few months.

The next morning we checked out of our hotel early and took a shuttle bus to the seaport for our cruise. Again, the wait to board the ship. We had to stand most of the time until the ship was ready to board and wait for all the people that had gotten there earlier than we had.

Carolyn loved the cool temperatures in Alaska except that she only brought dress shoes for the ship and cloth tennis shoes for walking. At the first cruise stop we found a store and purchased warm socks and boots for Carolyn. She had a warm winter coat, but all I had was my leather jacket.

We saw the neat towns along the coast of Alaska with their board sidewalks. We took side trips to see glaciers and the cruise ship went among small chunks of floating ice to watch a glacier caving off into the deep water. We saw one small boat that was too close one time and almost capsized before it got away from the glacier. Our on board forest ranger said that some of the glaciers had been growing while further north they were melting. Is that global warming or cooling or is something else warming the Arctic.

The train ride from Seward was nice in the mostly glass passenger train where we could see the snow and the animals as we went past. We didn't see much of Anchorage when we went through. We spent several days in cruise ship hotels in Alaska going between them by train or bus or both until we arrived in Fairbanks. We took a side trip into Denali National Park where we saw many moose and a few bears. At the hotel, Carolyn wanted something sweet, so I walked up to the little store in the multi-building hotel. As I walked Mount McKinley came out of the clouds at sunset. A perfect photo. I had brought my camera and when I tried to use my cell phone all I got was a "low battery". When I came back the mountain was invisible again.

Carolyn loved the hanging baskets at the hotels that were heavy with flowers. As we left the hotels they were selling off all the perishables so we got sweet rolls and sandwiches almost for free. We were the last cruise of the summer and it would be spring when the next group came.

In Fairbanks we took a bus tour of the town and then a paddlewheel riverboat up the river from Fairbanks. That was really the highlight of the trip. As we were leaving a Piper Super Cub on floats took off beside the boat and then came around for a water landing to show how it was done. At the other end of the river boat ride where the boat had to turn around, that same Piper Super Cub, or one just like it landed with huge tires on a sandbank spanning much of the river and then turned around and did a short takeoff to show how it could land and takeoff about anywhere.

On the way north we stopped at a place where they trained dog sled dogs. The owners of the camp had won the Iditarod several times. Some kids were and puppies were playing in the river water that had to be freezing cold. The owners gave a talk about their dogs explaining that there is no such thing as a breed of sled dogs.

They then started hooking up dogs to an old engineless four wheel ATV like they would be hooked to a sled in winter. The dogs obviously wanted to run with the ATV, but it took some time to get the dogs hooked up. Then as the owner got on the ATV the dogs were going crazy until her released the brakes and gave the command to go. The dogs took off and ran around this small pond and brought the ATV back to the ship obviously wanting to go again.

On the way back to Fairbanks we stopped at a village that was set up to look like a typical village. They had cabbages that were 10 feet wide and fur coats made of the fur of multiple animals that were beautiful and probably wildly expensive that some girls modeled for us.

The flight home was something to remember. We flew had made these reservations late so we were on the last flight out of Fairbanks leaving at 10PM. We changed to a regular airliner at Anchorage and then on to Seattle. When we got to Seattle, our next flight had been cancelled so here we had been up for over 24 hours and we are now looking for another flight back toward Florida. We spent a few hours there and then found another flight going to Houston and then on to Tampa so we arrived home after nearly 40 hours since we had last slept.

That winter we took a totally different cruise. We flew to Hawaii arriving in Honolulu on New Years Eve of 2008. We were booked on a 15 day cruise of the Hawaii Islands leaving on January 2, 2009, and arrived a day arrived a day early to see Honolulu since the last time we were here was winter 1989. We watched New Years Eve fireworks from our hotel balcony and then Carolyn discovered she had run out of one medicine and her Primatene Mist.

I immediately started walking the streets looking for an all night pharmacy. There was not a taxi to be had anywhere and only a few people walking back from the fireworks on the beaches. I asked multiple people and went into hotels who directed me to pharmacies that were closed for the night. I must have walked and run 10 miles before I found an all night CVS pharmacy, I got her prescription and Primatene Mist and while I was waiting I talked to another customer also waiting. Thanks to God, this good Samaritan gave me a ride to the hotel. I don't know whether I could have found it by myself out on the streets at 2AM. I tried to pay him, but I just had to say thank you so much. I could not believe how far from the hotel I had walked and run, and that was not counting all the time I was heading in the wrong directions to find a pharmacy that was closed for the night. It took my Good Samaritan nearly 15 minutes to get to there on deserted streets.

The cruise ship left with the lights of Honolulu disappearing slowly in the distance. We learned that on this cruise, there was one speed, slow. The islands are not that large so to not get there too quickly the ship barely keeps headway or steerage.

We had seen Oahu and Maui before. We had spent days on Oahu sightseeing. We only spent a few days on Maui, but we had rented a car and driven the twisty road to Hana and past Hana until we got past the falls on the back side of the volcano and came to the sign that said "Only 4 wheel drive beyond this point."

It was a shame that the waterfall had very little water. The tourist photos show a big waterfall with people playing in the pools below the falls. The "pools" did not have enough water to get wet in.

Anyway, we walked the street rather than take an expensive land excursion to take us to the volcano top that we had been to in 1989 or go to a beach, etc.

That night we went on to the big island, Hawaii. The ship docked at Hilo, Hawaii. We took a tour bus to the Hawaiian Volcanoes National Park driving through the national forest there and the ranger explaining the flora and fauna of Hawaii plus changes caused by humans. We took photos of the volcano, but could not get too close because the volcano was acting more threatening than normal.

When we returned from our bus trip I attempted to telephone an older cousins who reportedly owned a large bed and breakfast on the big island and to make additional money was a high dollar realtor. I did not find him. The closest I got was the bed and breakfast that said he was in the states.

The next day we took a side trip to Kona Coffee and Macadamia Nut farms including a tour of the Mo

Wouldn't you know it, that night the ship was supposed to pass close to the island where lava was flowing into the ocean. I had been looking forward to taking photos and with the slow speed of the ship I would probably get both daylight and night photos of the lava. The fact that the volcano was abnormally active sounded good to me, however, the ship was directed the other way around the island to stay away from the volcano. I was very disappointed in seeing the lava flow in person . for me, was a major high point of the trip.

Oh well, the next morning we were on the other side of the big island at another port where we took a tour to the Mauna Loa Nut Farm. Love those Macadamia nuts. Got a nice photo of Carolyn by their sign.

The next day, we slowly cruised past the islands of Lanai and Molokai with a talk about each. At this point I should mention the outstanding entertainment. They had a banjo player that did things with various different banjos and mandolins that I had no idea was possible. I should have purchased on of his DVDs, but I did not realize how unique he was. He had this pearl banjo with lots of strings. He talked while he played. First he played the grandfather's banjo tune, then his father's banjo tune, and then his. Then, I have no idea how he played them all together sounding like three banjo's in harmony. The magician presents a show in the big theater and some other shows in the bars during the cruise. He used real people not plants because we had met a couple of his participants who were inches away and could not see the slight of hand. At one point they had a big screen and projected a close-up of some of the tricks. Amazing. Of course the chorus line and solo singers were great. At night one bar played ballroom dance music for hours.

Another highlight of the trip was seeing the island of Kauai, the setting for the Jurassic Park movie. I would love to come back there for a few days sometime, but probably not in this lifetime.

We cruised all over the Gulf of Mexico and the Caribbean not missing many islands with numerous visits to the Bahamas. Aruba, Dominica, St Kitts, Martinique, St. Thomas, Puerto Rico, Antigua, Grenada, Jamaica, St Lucia, Caymans, and more. One thing we found pretty common was that they had free health care, but their housing was primarily worse than any slum in the USA and they were dirty.

Carolyn and I took many island tours and just walking around, especially just walking around on our second and third visit to that island.

We had season tickets to Disney World one year and saw everything. Of course we took Zak and Cory, our grandkids there. We had season tickets for about seven years to Busch Gardens, only 30 minutes from the house in Florida and enjoyed repeating that park over and over. Carolyn never cared for the rides there, but went on many at least once. Our guests went over and over. We went to Universal Studios and Sea World more than once.

Carolyn's favorite was Discovery Cove and swimming with the dolphins which was available on many cruises, but could not compare with Discovery Cove next to Sea World. Carolyn never cared for the rides there, but went on many at least once. Our guests went over and over. We went to Universal Studios and Sea World more than once.

Carolyn's favorite was Discovery Cove and swimming with the dolphins which was available on many cruises, but could not compare with Discovery Cove next to Sea World. You have to schedule that ahead because attendance is limited.

When we were in Europe 1972-1975 we never made it to Greece because terrorists were targeting American military and I was forbidden to go. So, in 2009 we flew to Rome to meet with her sister, Shirley, and her daughter, Missy, at Shirley's son's apartment in Rome. He was a civilian working for the US Navy with split duty between Italy and Djibouti, on the horn of Africa.

In Rome we went to the coliseum and the Roman Forum. It was so different from when we were there in 1974. In 1974 we wandered into the coliseum on our own and wondering if we were somewhere we shouldn't be and conscious of getting locked in like we had in other areas in Europe, but then we found a tour group and followed them close enough to hear part of the lecture and enough to know what the guide was saying if not every word. We went by the Roman Forum, but did not see a single person down in there, so we didn't go because it was a closed in area that we really might get locked in.

This time, in 2009, there were a thousand people waiting to get into the coliseum and I managed to find someone to sell us a ticket without standing in line for hours. There were people everywhere in the coliseum versus being the only ones there in 1974. We did stand in line for over an hour to get tickets to go into the Roman Forum and instead of waiting another two hours for a guided tour, we got a brochure and map and made our own way through it. Again, unlike in 1974 when it had zero people, now it was hard to take a photograph without strangers getting in the way. We still had a great time.

Then we caught a commuter flight over to Athens, Greece, found our hotel not too far from the cruise ship docks and when we went up to the rooftop swimming pool had a great nighttime view of the Parthenon all lit up against the sky. By standing on a low wall, I got some good photos without the swimming pool in them.

The next day we walked miles around and up to the Parthenon and got some more good photos from up there and then back to the hotel after 12 hours of walking.

The next morning we boarded the Norwegian Jade cruise ship that took us down through the Greek Islands to

Alexandria, Egypt. One place we both found entrancing was Santorini Island that might have been the site for Atlantis. There was a steep cliff you had a choice of going up by donkey, walking up around donkey dung or taking the cable car. Carolyn wanted the donkeys but there was a long line and Carolyn's legs (and mine) were already tired from walking around Rome and Athens and the ship. We took the cable car. We walked around the town did some souvenir shopping then found a restaurant hanging out over the cliff where we got some good photos of what looked like tiny cruise ships and the volcano out in the bay. It was easy to imagine that it could have been Atlantis.

When we got to Egypt we took a tour bus from the ship to Cairo and the pyramids. I have some great photos. I got another tourist to take a photo of us with the great pyramid and the Sphinx in the background. When we got home I edited out the hundreds of tourists to make it look like we had a private showing. A camel jockey said that Carolyn could get on his camel for free photo taking. I took several photos of Carolyn and the camel and had him take a photo of us together with the camel kneeling with Carolyn astride and me standing beside her. Then it was time to catch the bus. The camel jockey wanted a hundred dollars for his time and the photos taken with my camera. I gave him a twenty and he threatened to call the police that were everywhere. I was not worried because a few years before I had set up an American military detachment at the air base near Cairo so I figured I could get embassy help and told him so and then walked away. Carolyn did not know any of the argument as she was already headed for the bus. I told her after we were on the bus for the next stop.

When we got to the Sphinx Carolyn did not want to take the long walk from the bus to get close to the Sphinx but told me to go on ahead. Probably half the people did not make the walk. There were hundreds of people that did because there were buses and people everywhere. I walked fast because I wanted to get back to Carolyn even though she was with a crowd of Americans and Europeans that did not take the walk so I passed groups of people. At the ideal spot for taking a close-up near the Sphinx's head there was a large gaggle of people that appeared to be crowding around some older gentleman that was laying down. They did not need the crowd, let alone me adding to it, so I went around, took what photos I could and practically ran back to the buses and Carolyn. That night we discovered that gentleman that was laying down was from our ship and had died right there of a massive heart attack from the exertion of climbing up to see the Sphinx close-up. I hadn't seen much more than his shoes through the crowd so I really didn't know if we had seen him on the ship. His body and his wife were flown back to the states.

After the Sphinx we were taken to the Cairo Museum which was hot and so crowded you could hardly see anything. Many things had no identification and sometimes a little tag with a number on it. We tried to find some form of guidebook that would explain the numbers, but none of the workers knew of such a thing, but said no one had ever made up a book of the exhibits. Management would know what the numbers were.

At any rate, the next day, after an evening on the ship in port, we walked miles again to see the Egyptian Museum of Alexandria and some of King Tuts gold and various artifacts. It was crowded to the point of taking baby steps as you walked through the museum, it was un-air-conditioned and very close. We walked out to where we could see a fort built out on a jut of land that supposedly used stones from the mythical lighthouse of Alexandria and took more photos.

Then it was back through the Greek Islands and more walking seeing Minoan artifacts and ruins. Then we got to Turkey and there was a long bus trip to Ephesus and a long guided tour. Carolyn stayed at the ship supposedly because she did not want to spend the money on another walking tour and just told me to take pictures. This was the second time I had left Carolyn's side. I actually paid for both of us to go thinking she would change her mind, but her legs were giving out and we would be in Istanbul the next morning.

I rushed ahead of the group, took lots of photos and caught an earlier bus going back to the ship. While I was there, a person speaking great English offered to sell me an assortment of coins that supposedly came from stealing from an archaeology site that dated back to Alexander the Great and looked authentic. He started at hundreds of dollars and finally I bought six different coins for twenty dollars total figuring I had close to twenty dollars in silver, even if they were fake. They were solid silver and crudely minted with pictures of Alexander the Great. He didn't come down to that price until I had a foot in the bus and we were leaving. Our daughter was working on a masters in archaeology so I figured she would enjoy them even if they were fake. I have no idea if they were fake but strongly suspect they were made for tourists.

The next day we rode buses and walked miles again through the Hagia Sofia, the Basilica Cistern, the Blue Mosque, the Topkapi Palace and then hours in a picturesque street and a Turkish rug sales barn. We did not buy any rugs. Then they unloaded the buses in the famous market which was closed and it was raining. Everyone from the bus took shelter in a the few stores and restaurants that were open until the bus came to pick us up to go back to the ship. Our flight was scheduled to leave Istanbul at 8:30 in the morning so we were supposed to be there no later than 6AM. The buses were leaving the ship at 2:30AM so we didn't bother trying to sleep, but packed our bags, stood on our balcony looking out over the city and then on to the airport. Our flight was delayed, and delayed until finally we flew out at about 10:30 meaning that we missed our flight in Madrid, Spain. We had to walk miles in the airport in Madrid, Spain, to go through various security checks and get to our flight. This took well over an hour of rushing and walking. Security was not difficult except that Carolyn had two artificial hips that set off the alarm, but they quickly wanded her and sent us on the way.

When we got to Miami International Airport it was going to be a short turn around for our flight to Tampa so we were in a hurry, but we got stopped by security. Carolyn was wearing skin tight slacks, but her hips set off the metal detector. Carolyn had told them before she walked through that she would set it off. Instead of just using the wand to pass over her hips through the skin tight stretchy slacks they took her to a separate glassed in room where she had to sit for over 30 minutes. They disassembled her wheeled walker and lost some of the parts. Finally they passed her and we took our bags and the wobbly partly disassembled walker toward our airplane. As we got about 3 gates away, we saw our airplane for Tampa back out of the gate. It was going to be 3 hours for the next flight. Then that flight got canceled due to mechanical issues and it was going to be another 3 hours. That plane was coming from Denver, but was snowed in so it was going to be another 3 hours. When we finally got into Tampa we had been awake for over 48 hours and were dead tired.

I emailed photos of Carolyn and I by the Sphinx and Pyramids to her heart doctors to show she was doing well.

48 Our Florida Routine

Our typical week was on Mondays, Carolyn would go to a mostly female country line dancing class for two hours. I would take her and pick her up in the golf cart unless it was raining, then I would take her in the car. On Tuesday and Thursday and Saturday I would take her to Aquasizers which consisted of swimming pool exercises while I went to the radio club nearby across the golf cart parking lot. Sunday it was early church. Somewhere in there we would go to movies in Brandon, Florida about 20 miles away. We would take the dogs to the dog park in the golf cart 3-4 days a week. Carolyn had her Red Hat Society meetings and outings. Frequently, to fill the bus, they would allow men to go on their trips. Once a month in the winter we had season tickets to the performing arts Broadway shows in Tampa. We were always going in the golf cart to the grocery stores, Walmart, doctors, dentists, etc.

We took many cruises in the Gulf or Caribbean and saw most of the sites you can see by cruise ship and did lots of walking in the various towns shopping for souvenirs. In the evenings we would watch TV together. In the afternoons Carolyn would watch her soap operas and I would sit on the back porch reading my kindle books. Every 30 minutes or so I would walk in to check on Carolyn. She was always okay, but I wanted to see for myself.

Every fall we would drive to Fort Myers Beach, Florida to move Carolyn's sister Shirley's things out of storage closets and bedrooms to set up her porch and swimming pool for her. Shirley and Carolyn alternated Thanksgiving and Christmas between Shirley's place and ours.

We had season tickets to the Broadway Palm Dinner Theater in Fort Myers, Florida, where we had to drive down to visit Shirley at least 4 times a year, go to a fabulous musical after dinner and then in the Spring, I would pack up all her pool and porch furniture to put it back in storage until the next fall when Shirley would come back from Illinois.

At one time we were members of many dancing clubs that had monthly dances for each group we were members of, Oldies but Goodies that we always were members of and had 14 dances a year, Sun City Center Ball Room Dance Club, Moonglow, and another ball room dance club that I have forgotten the name to. We also took several ball room dance lessons, but always seem to go to the first sessions and learn the basics and then would have scheduling conflicts and miss the last two lessons for each dance step. So we could pretend to do a lot of dances, but were never good at any of them, but we had fun. In addition to those dances we attended the annual Military Ball dance and dinner that was very formal, like a dining out where I would have to wear my Tuxedo and Carolyn a long ballroom gown.

We had two other dance groups that closed down for lack of participation that were smaller groups but fun. One was Foxy Seniors but it became a karaoke club. Instead of a paid performer you could dance to a resident attempting to sing. Some of them were very good.

We probably had 10 chances to dance together in all our years before moving to Florida and then multiple times a month after we moved to Sun City Center, Florida.

I don't know if it would qualify as a miracle, but in the 11 years we lived in Florida, there were no hurricanes that even came close. The closest we had were a couple of tropical storms that dumped lots of rain that helped bust a drought and everyone needed the rain. The year before we moved there, there were multiple hurricanes that had come through parts of Florida. To be honest, there is no record of the area of Sun City Center, Florida ever getting a hurricane, but they didn't even come close while we were there.

In 2009, Carolyn's shoulder started hurting bad and she got steroid shots every 3 months. I always wondered if the shoulder problem was caused by the misdiagnosis for 6 months after her 2006 heart attack. Maybe the shoulder pain in 2006 was from lack of blood due to the heart problem and maybe that caused a permanent joint problem. Finally, in 2011 she got a total shoulder replacement so she now had three metal joints. Did that slow her down? Of course not. Within a couple of months she had full range of motion in her shoulder and was doing well.

49 The FDA and Asthma
(Why I don't like environmentalists)

Everything was roses until fall of 2012. Carolyn had asthma since she was 15. In our early marriage she could get TEDROL tablets and half a tablet would bust up an asthma attack in minutes. Then TEDROL was outlawed by the FDA in the US. For a couple of years we were able to buy it from Canada and have it mailed to us but then that source disappeared too. Carolyn had to resort to Primatene Mist inhalers and Primatene tablets which took much longer and sometimes a day or so to really get over an attack. We did not know what was causing her attacks. Carolyn thought it might be dog hair, then it must be the heating vents in the house, but we could not identify why she would be okay for months and then have an asthma attack.

She did not have all the symptoms of female heart attack like she did in 2006, but they were still bad. Then in 2011 the FDA outlawed Primatene Mist inhalers because they had Freon that might be causing global warming. HAH! What about asthma suffers and taking away a rescue inhaler that they depend on because there might be a miniscule amount of Freon to force the medication into a mist.

I had bought all the inhalers I could find in 2011, but in 2012 she ran out of inhalers, had an asthma attack and I had to take her to the South Bay Hospital Emergency Room. They insisted that she had pneumonia and needed to be hospitalized. She refused and went to a Doctor Hooker a lung specialist the next week and he looked at the XRAYS from the hospital and disagreed. He said she had COPD. That was the misdiagnosis from the hospital when they had to cut away part of the pericardium after her heart surgery. He ignored the fact that she was very active and never short of breath unless having an asthma attack, but at least he agreed that the hospital was wrong. He gave her several prescriptions for long term treatment of COPD and albuterol for her nebulizer but no fast-acting treatments like Primatene Mist with Epinephrine instead of albuterol, so she had no immediate reacting medications. After several years of seeing him twice a year he gave her a Ventolin inhaler but it was not even close to being as effective as Primatene Mist because it basically was Albuterol instead of Epinephrine. With an Epinephrine inhaler and maybe an emergency EPIPEN I think she would have lived much longer.

Every six months starting in the fall of 2012 I had to take her to the ER for an asthma treatment. They insisted it was COPD, but it was an allergic reaction. Not a single doctor looked for an allergen that might be causing the attacks. She would be her usual dynamo of energy with no shortness of breath until these occasional attacks.

We cut our cruises back to one per year because we were simply repeating previous cruises. After our bad flight returning from Turkey, and the previous year's bad flight returning from Alaska and that same year's bad flight returning from Hawaii, we gave up flying outside the USA so it was cruising out of Florida. We even started limiting our cruises to being out of Tampa so we could eliminate the day long drive to Miami for a cruise.

50 The Downhill Slope

Carolyn developed a back pain. Her primary care doctor thought it might be kidney but the tests did not indicate that. He sent her to a gastroenterologist and he thought that back pain was gallbladder so he scheduled her for gallbladder surgery. After the surgery he admitted to me that he did not find stones in her gallbladder, but she could live just fine without a gallbladder. I could have sued, but my family does have lawyers in it and we just aren't the kind to sue anyone.

She went to the doctor that had replaced her shoulder and he recommended a back surgeon in his office. That doctor used another CT scan with contrast and then followed that with an injection of cortisone steroids like she had had in her shoulder for a couple of years into the iliac which totally cured the back pain. Why did the doctors say gallbladder? It was arthritis build up in the iliac. She never had a back problem again, but her records indicated it was a serious issue and still going on.

She started seeing an gynecologist for some female problems where sex was too painful. We were only having sex every few months and had basically stopped because of her pain. She was prescribed Osphena for hormone treatment. Because of a genetic disorder she never had normal menstrual periods and we had to adopt. Therefore, the symptoms of menopause were exaggerated. She never told me she was taking it, but she wanted to have sex with me for my sake. That resulted in her having undiagnosed Deep Vein Thrombosis. After she died I found these pills and that she had been taking them for a couple of years. They did not help because we just didn't have sex because I did not want to hurt her even when she claimed it was okay. I looked up Osphena and found that it was likely the cause of her circulation problems in that it has been implicated in deep vein thrombosis (DVT). Either that or the doctors should have been giving her a better blood thinner than a low dose Plavix and a baby aspirin.

In the summer of 2014, Carolyn's lower legs started hurting to where she could not do her two hours of country line dancing and limited it to the first hour of the two hour class. She also cut back on the aquasizer swimming pool exercises for the pain in her lower legs.

In the fall of 2014, Carolyn developed a sore on the top of her foot above the toes. Her regular doctor referred us to a podiatrist who cut it out, packed it with antibiotics and gave her a treatment regimen to follow. It got worse, dug out and repacked several times. Then the podiatrist referred her to a Vascular doctor because he thought it might be related to blood circulation since it would not heal and it wasn't cancer.

The vein doctor gave her some Plavix to take to thin the blood, but it had no effect. The doctor was very brusque and neither of us liked him. We changed to a different vascular doctor, simply because the other was on vacation, and he suggested some tests and determined her veins were blocked in the left leg.

In January 2015 Carolyn got a stent in the lower left leg and some opening of the vein. Within 24 hours the sore on her foot had a scab and a week later it was totally gone with no scar. She went back to line dancing, but now it was mainly her right leg causing the problem. In May 2015, she got two stents in her right leg.

All the CT scans as the result of her blocked leg veins with contrast had caused her kidney function to be subprime. Not serious needing medication but just below normal on blood testing. They also had to do CT scans for the stent surgeries. Now she has added a kidney doctor. For the second leg that doctor ordered minimal radioactive dye for the CT scans. Her kidneys stayed just below what it should be, but not serious and still no special medications or instructions other than to keep radioactive die to the minimum on any future CT scans.

During that fall she seemed to be having more frequent breathing problems but most of the time she was fine. Her legs did not hurt as bad and her night time leg cramps were gone. Why the doctors did not put her on better blood thinners I will never understand. The decreased kidney functions could be poor circulation like in her legs before the stints.

That Christmas her breathing problems got worse when finally in January the ER again said she had pneumonia. This was followed up over the next weeks with her family doctor saying she was fine and her pulmonologist saying she was fine and did not need any prescriptions for steroids or antibiotics.

51 Premonitions

My son and I had premonitions of what was coming. For weeks before our February cruise I had a recurring dream where Carolyn and I were eating on the Lido deck cafeteria. In all of the recurring dreams we had gone to separate parts of the cafeteria because we wanted different foods. We were supposed to meet at a table we had reserved by leaving some fresh glasses of tea there along with jackets or something to show it was taken. When I got to our table, Carolyn was not there. I put my food tray on the table and took a turn around the cafeteria to spot her. In all the dreams I saw her leaving a door with her sister. That put me in a panic because her sister had died in January. One time they went out by the swimming pool, but by the time I got around people between me and the door, they were gone. I went around the pool deck and back into the cafeteria several times but could not find her then I woke up, realized it was a dream, reached over to touch her and make sure she was in our bed, and go back to sleep.

Another time I saw the Carolyn and her sister, Shirley, entering the stair case and wave goodbye, but again, there were too many people for me to get there until they were out of sight. I went to our shipboard room and then searched the ship even down in the crew living areas. Crew members kept telling me I couldn't be there, but got out of my way. I don't know how I seemed to know my way around the crew areas but looked in a lot of the tiny rooms sometimes disturbing people that were upset that I was peeking in. Then I would realize Shirley had died in January, the cruise was in late February, wake up, reach over and touch her, and go back to sleep.

Variations of this dream happened 2-3 times a week for the three weeks before our cruise. Needless to say, I did not let her out of my sight when we actually took the cruise.

Carolyn had been mad at Craig for years. I phoned him from time to time and if he called us, I had to do all the talking. Carolyn refused to talk with him on the phone, she would sometimes listen in and would yell at me to not be so nice to him. Craig could be very talkative to where I didn't get to say much but he wanted some response from me to indicate I was still listening so I would say "uh huh", "I understand" or whatever. Carolyn would tell me to talk and not just say "uh huh" all the time. Frequently, he was needing money and just not coming out and asking for it. Usually when it did come to money Carolyn would say, "Go ahead and send the money, I know you want to."

My son was surprised a week before our cruise when Carolyn phoned him and they had a pleasant phone call for thirty minutes. When she called, Craig thought there must be something wrong with me that she was reporting, but it was just a pleasant conversation asking how he was getting along.

On the cruise, Carolyn seemed to be feeling good, but teared up a few times for no apparent reason. Carolyn was also clingy and wanting to hold my hand or put a hand on my arm. On her birthday, the last night of our cruise, Carolyn would not let me quit dancing with her. We were there before the band came in and never left the dance floor until the band quit. We both tired of fast dancing, but after I tired, we just slow danced to whatever the band was playing. She clung to me like there was no tomorrow. She claimed she was feeling okay, but every so often, even while dancing, there were tears in her eyes. Naturally, if I asked, she said she was just so happy we were together and never wanted to be apart.

Do I need to say we were madly in love for 46 years and 45 years of marriage. I never wanted to be without her and for the last couple of years, she said she could not survive without me being there to help her. Her sister kept saying she needed to be less dependent upon me. I knew Carolyn was smart enough to get along just fine without me. I had paid into survivor benefits to where she would have enough life insurance to pay everything off and $55,000 a year adjusted for inflation to live on.

Although I did not believe she was that dependent upon me I was more than happy for her to feel dependent upon me and I wanted to be there for her for as long as she lived. Other than the occasional injury and a few stitches, I was very healthy and expected to outlive her, but I never imagined I would lose her anytime soon.

I knew that for the last couple of years her health had gone downhill and she was feeling pretty miserable, but she would seldom complain. I wanted to move back to Oklahoma and get away from the poor doctors in Florida. Carolyn would not move as long as her sister, Shirley, was coming to Florida each winter, plus she said it was too much work to pack and move. I told her I was no longer working so I would do all the work.

That summer I had convinced her to take a trip to Oklahoma and at least look at houses. Her sister died in January 2016 solving that problem, but it was too early to go to Oklahoma, or was it.

52 Our Last Cruise

With both doctors saying she was okay we went ahead and took our scheduled cruise out of Tampa going to all the usual places we had cruised before: Cozumel (Mexico); Costa Maya (Mexico); Roatan, Bay Islands (Honduras); Harvest Caye (Belize) and back to Tampa. We had taken this same cruise before plus we had taken the cruise with other cruise lines, but Norwegian was our favorite because of the freestyle dining and entertainment. We did not like being assigned to a table of strangers for meal after meal and having to eat on their schedule. In fact, we always took most of our meals on the top "Lido" deck with the smorgasbord buffet dining where we could pick and choose and not have to spend hours in the formal dining rooms. We were always on the go whether on land or sea and did not want to spend hours waiting for waiters or food.

First stop was Roatan. We took only one excursion and that was a glass bottom boat to see the coral reefs off Roatan. Disappointing in that we could see no color except when fish swam very close to the underwater windows. But no land tours on this trip because we had been there and done that many times. Instead we wandered far away from the crowds and found an American run restaurant on stilts over the water. We were tired from walking for a couple of hours so we got hamburgers, fries and diet cokes. There were a few other customers, but we weren't sure how he managed to stay open. It was all open air under a thatched roof and could have seated 100 people but there was one other family of 8 kids and adults at another large table and us. There was no waiter only the American owner-cook-cashier. Carolyn sat by an outside rail where she could watch the occasional tourist or local walking by on the street and waited while I ordered, went back for the food and drink and then waited again when I paid. We resumed the walk and after a total of about 8 hours souvenir shopping and walking minus 45 minutes for resting and eating, we returned to the ship.

Next stop was Costa Maya where we wandered off the ship, watched some Mayan dancing, Mayans swinging from a large pole, souvenir shopping, picture taking, and watching a dolphin show from a balcony above we went back to the ship.

Next day was Harvest Cay, Belize where we repeated the walking and shopping. We found a phone where we could call our daughter in Oklahoma.

Next was Cozumel, Mexico. We repeated our Cozumel ritual and walked the half mile dock from the ship to the shopping center across the road from the docks, circled the shopping center along the top and then the bottom and then took off walking a couple of miles to downtown to find this little central park near downtown that we had been to before. When we got back to the shopping center, we had our pictures taken with the same parrots we had our pictures taken with years before on a cruise, then back to the ship. We were both tired of walking and just sat on our balcony watching the festivities down on the dock as several cruise ships worth of passengers were returning. We had just beat the crowd returning from land excursions. The land excursion we had been to three other times was to the mainland of the Yucatan peninsula and the Tulum Ruins. We had taken my father there when he was 92, then we went on our own, then we had taken our 30 year old daughter there, but we did not need to do it again. Carolyn had encouraged me to go snorkeling without her or taking a boat ride somewhere, but no way was I going to leave her alone.

We went to the entertainment that night, explored the ship looking for a bar that had good dance music, attended a magician show in one of the bars, played some group games and called it a night around midnight. The next night was her birthday and we ate in one of the formal dining rooms where I had arranged for them to come sing for her and bring her a small cake. We went to the nighttime entertainment in the main theater then went to a bar at the back of the ship. Carolyn wanted to dance and dance. When her legs tired out she insisted we keep on pretending to dance holding each other close, but slow dancing even to fast music. I think she had a premonition that this might be our last time to dance. The band quit at midnight and then they cleared out the room for a game show for the 30 and younger people. We were going to call it a night because we had a big day planned for when we got back to port the next morning but some 30 year olds insisted that we stay at our table next to the dance floor and join them in the game. Carolyn and I got most of the points in the competition and we would have gotten first place for our group, but I refused to take off my trousers and go on stage in my underwear and then we were supposed to dance on stage and when they called out we were supposed to take a sign to the master of ceremonies when he announced. The MC hid at the back of the large bar in the dark and we could not find him from the stage. Another group that was running in second place saw him running to the back of the bar and came on the stage to tell the dancers where he was hiding. This last thing had double points and we missed out entirely. At any rate it was close to 2AM and our group came in second.

53 Our Last Healthy Days Together

The next day on February 28 we got into port at 8AM and we drove to where our dog was in a kennel and brought him home. At 1:00PM we were back in Tampa waiting for a broadway musical we had tickets to. We got home about 4:30, took the dog to the dog park, ate and watched television.

On February 29th, her 62 year old nephew and his 62 year old nurse girlfriend he had met 30 years earlier, and reconnected with on facebook, had flown in from his US Navy civilian assignment in Japan to Sun City Center where they had bought a house to be close to us just before he got his Japan assignment. They had come back to get married where Carolyn and I could be there as best man and bridesmaid on a dock of a neighbor across the street from the house they had purchased. We got dressed up for the wedding and photos. That evening we took the bride and groom out to the coast for dinner where we could watch the sunset over the Gulf. On Wednesday we had them over for dinner and played cards until midnight. On Thursday Carolyn and I had gone to Publix to get some pork roasts for the slow cooker so she could cook them a last dinner in the states before they got on an airplane on March 5th to fly back to Japan where we might not see the again for 3 years.

We just ran in found some pork roasts, took a short cut through the flower isle to the checkouts and came home. An hour of so later she started having some breathing difficulty and it was too late to see her family doctor and did not want to go to a minor emergency clinic in the next town so we went to the ER. She got an XRAY and the doctor said she had some spots on her lower lobes of her lungs that might be pneumonia or the beginning of lung cancer. His recommendation was that the following week she should go see a pulmonologist to investigate further.

She was fine by the next morning and rushing around cleaning house, mopping floors, and starting to cook that meal for her nephew and his new bride. Mid afternoon she asked me to take her to Publix again to pick up some fresh rolls for dinner and some red wine that the new bride would like. I went for the wine at one end of the store and Carolyn rushed to the fresh bread at the other. To meet me at the checkout and get home quick she took the shortcut through the cut flowers to get to the checkout without having to go all the way to the back of the store and then come up an isle when all she had was a package of rolls.

54 I Lost the Love of My Life

I was coming her way when I saw her get trapped in the fresh cut flower isle with other people's shopping carts blocking her egress either back out or on toward the checkout line. I saw her grab hold of one of the fresh cut flower counters and I could tell she was having an immediate asthma attack. I had to almost shove people out of the way to get to her and get her away from the flowers. I dumped the wine and rolls and took her straight out of the store and to the ER. She told me her throat had closed up and she couldn't breathe and needed to get to the ER immediately.

When I got there, I ran inside, grabbed a wheel chair because I had almost had to carry her to the car and thought I would have to carry her into the ER as it was getting worse. I rushed into the ER with the wheel chair and got her in immediately. The ER doctor was free and came in and put a nose cannula in her nose for oxygen because she and I both said she was having an allergic reaction and couldn't breathe. She ripped off the nose cannula and told the doctor, she needed a breathing treatment that nose thing was not working. I said a shot of epinephrine and a breathing treatment was what she needed. He put an oxygen mask on her but no shot and nothing with the oxygen. She took several breaths, ripped off the mask so she could yell at the doctor, "Whoops, I think I broke it (she had broken the strap) but you have to put something with the oxygen and I need a shot for the breathing."

The doctor told me to leave while he did it. In the past, while they were setting up the breathing treatment they had me stand in the hallway to make room and then let me back in for the breathing treatment. As I was standing there, the doctor yelled "Its too big, get me a smaller one, NO a child size".

When I got back into the room she had been intubated with a tube down her throat instead of an oxygen face mask with albuterol, oxygen, and usually something else. Apparently, his yelling I heard was because he had tried to use a standard size tube that would not fit her swollen throat due to the allergic reaction to the flowers.

I asked him why he was not giving her a breathing treatment and a shot for the allergic reaction.

You said she couldn't breathe so I put her on a breathing machine.

I said, "She was able to breathe enough to tell you she needed a breathing treatment. Her living will says no "life support" except during surgery. Take it out and give her an allergy treatment with some Albuterol and a shot of epinephrine."

"I can't do that now and she has something strange about her heart on XRAY and might need surgery. That is not my call. What has she had done to her heart?"

I explained that in 2007 she had a section of left ventricle cut out and graphed back together and the three major veins on her heart replaced, but her heart doctor says she is doing great.

"Well, she needs the breathing support. I'm surprised she lasted this long with just her home oxygen."

"She did NOT have home oxygen. She has asthma, not COPD. She does not need a breathing machine, she needs something for the allergy attack."

He ignored me.

Carolyn had this panicked look on her face. She had told me she never wanted a tube like that again which she had when she had her heart surgery and had left a living will at the hospital the following year to prevent it. Now they had a tube in her throat where she couldn't talk and she was crying. Her blood pressure went up to 225 over 125 and I told the doctor he needed to do something because she had major heart reconstruction and her heart could not take that kind of pressure. Instead of giving her something for it he had her sent to ICU. I went with her of course. Her nephew arrived not too long after getting to the ICU and she was trying to be brave for him, but then her eyes glazed over and she quit breathing. A smaller but powerful male black nurse ordered everyone out of the room and he started CPR immediately. The doctors tried to say she was gone and CPR wouldn't work, he told the other nurses to get the doctors out too.

Ten minutes later I was allowed back in, her blood pressure was down to 140 over 90 and she was breathing but unconscious. I was told she was going to be alright and I should go get something to eat. When I returned, she was conscious and made hand motions for me to pull the tube out of her throat. Then she showed her hands were strapped down and indicated that I would not pull the tube out I should unstrap her hands and she would do it herself.

Carolyn turned her head as much as she could toward me and tears were running out of her eyes. I stupidly said, "I'll get that tube out of your mouth when the doctors get here and we can go home."

She settled down when Bob, her nephew came in early the next morning on his way to the airport to fly back to Japan. She tried to smile around the tube in her mouth and waved at him as much as she could with her arms strapped down.

Shortly thereafter her family doctor came in and she waved and smiled at him then made the motions to remove the tube. He said she needed it to breathe and she shook her head no and then tried to frown around the tube.

I told the doctor that Carolyn did not need the breathing tube and did not want life support in her living will and I wanted him to remove the tube as I knew she could breathe without it. In fact, I thought her allergy attack was over so she really could be fine if they would take the tube out. I also complained that she should have been treated for asthma and not intubated.

The doctor said he had to talk to the other doctors but would be back. He never stepped into her room again as far as I know. I went to him a few days later telling him I wanted her moved to another hospital, but he refused. He acted like she was terminal and he had written her off.

The nurses said the doctors thought she had brain damage because of the way she was pointing at the tube and chewing on it. I said she wanted the tube out.

An hour later Carolyn motioned for me to get a nurse. When the nurse came in Carolyn pointed at her crotch and the nurse said, "If you need to go, you already have a catheter which is hooked to a bag to catch the urine."

Carolyn shook her head no and pointed again. The nurse asked, "You need to do number two?"

Carolyn shook her head yes and the nurse said that they had a pad underneath so just go."

Carolyn strained a little bit and out came mainly blood. The nurse asked if he had blood in her stool before. I replied, "Never, until just now. She must be bleeding internally from the intubation. You need to get that tube out and find out what kind of damage was done to her throat."

"The nurse said, that is up to the doctors."

She was not brain damaged or she would not have had me get a nurse and then used sign language to explain she needed a bowel movement and didn't want to mess up the sheets. The doctors were either idiots or trying to cover up a gross error by killing her.

When I threatened to remove the tube myself, they made me stay away from her bed and keep the curtains open to see me to make sure I didn't remove the tube. They threatened to call security if I tried anything. I should have pulled the tube and the IV, taken her out of that hospital and saved her life, but was afraid to go against the doctors. I killed her by not trusting in myself and going against the doctors and risking being arrested. I should have done it, but I didn't.

Carolyn kept telling in by sign language and pointing that I needed to remove the tube or get her hands loose so she could do it since no one else would. Finally, she just pointed at me, and then pointed to the door and looked mad at me.

"I said, you don't want me to leave do you?"

She violently shook her head yes, and pointed at me then the door. I said, "Okay, but I will be back."

I used the time away to phone Saint Joeseph's Hospital about getting her transferred there, but they said they would not take her unless she was released from South Bay Hospital in Sun City Center. I talked to hospital administration who said it was up to the doctors. I called three law firms in Tampa to see if I could get a court order to get her out of that hospital.

When I went back to her room, she had been put in a coma. I found the doctor that had ordered it and said to wake her up right now. "She can't take long term anesthesia, it would kill her. She has had anesthesia for just a few hours during surgeries and had a hard time recovering from it."

"She was fighting the breathing machine and it wasn't fair to her to be so upset, we had to calm her down."

"Why didn't you call me? Of course she was upset, her living will states that she does not want a breathing machine or any artificial means of keeping her alive and I told you already to remove that tube. She can breathe just fine without a machine if you wake her up."

The pulmonologist said that she had fluid in her lungs and that they were going to suck the fluid out through that tube and by tomorrow when I came back the tube would be out and she would be better and awake. It was already late afternoon and mistakenly believed him. I had been up for over 30 hours so I went home to feed the dog and give him his shot of insulation for his diabetes.

I came back before daylight after maybe 2 hours of trying to sleep and she still had the tube in and was unconscious. I was ranting mad, the pulmonologist was there and said the intubation tube was too small to vacuum out her lungs so they changed the tube and decided that was hard enough on her. They induced a coma because of brain damage and they would use the new tube to vacuum liquid from her lungs that night.

I said she wasn't brain damaged. He said, she was fighting the intubation tube and it wasn't right to keep her awake. We'll vacuum her lungs tonight and tomorrow when you get here the tube will be out and she will be awake. I said, "You should not have put her in a coma. She is very sensitive to any anesthetic. When she had her shoulder replacement she was only under for about an hour and it took a week of drinking magnesium citrate by the half gallon daily to get her bowels working again. You'll kill her if you don't get her awake and I mean now."

"We can't do that. We have to get that fluid out of her lungs and can't do it without her being asleep. It was traumatic for her to have that small tube removed and the larger tube inserted. She needs the rest."

"You'll be killing her if you don't wake her up now and then if you have to put her to sleep again tonight."

"We're not going to do that. We know what we're doing."

"No, you are killing her. She specifically said in her living will she did not want life support. I am her caregiver, and I want her woken up."

He just walked away, ignoring my plea.

I spent the day and the night there until they told me I had to leave the ICU while they did the procedure which would take 3-4 hours. So, I went home when they ran me out that evening with a feeling of doom. I was pretty sure I would never be able to talk to her again, but I had hope that the doctors knew what they were doing. I came in the next morning to find the tube still in place and she was still being kept unconscious. Now I was really mad.

My son, Craig, and my daughter, Christine both wanted to come see her in the hospital, but I already knew what was going to happen after the doctors would not listen to me and had already made the mistakes they had made by the first full day when they put her in an induced coma. I told them, "NO, I don't want you to see her this way. I may need you more later."

Again, I was forced to leave the hospital and returned before daylight. She still had the tube and was still drugged in her coma.

When I asked, I was told that they had gotten the fluid (blood?) out of her lungs but she had some hard blockages in her passageways and they were going to go back in that next night to try to wash out the blockages. I asked whether they were dried mucus or blood clots.

So another day of induced coma and another night being pushed out for the evening while they washed out her lungs. The next morning when I came in they had 12 bags of medicine flowing through 7 of those machines to regulate fluid flow going into her. They wanted to keep me out after I complained they were trying to kill her. They said she had a massive infection and they needed to clear it up. I sneaked into the room and took a photo of the machines. All the machines were still there but the bags were less than the 12 that had been there before they forced me out.

I went to the doctor on duty and the doctor basically pushed me out of the office and closed the door. Now I was sure that Carolyn was going to die from their treatments, but there was nothing I could do to stop them. The nurses were still nice to me and explained everything they were doing from a nurses standpoint. They had not been allowed in when she was getting her lungs cleaned out so they could not say, but the intubation tube had a small suction device they used every few hours and they showed me how it was clear now and not getting any fluid from her lungs but the suction did not reach all the way to the bottom.

That day was a repeat. I held her hand, talked to her, and cried a lot. I went to the hospital chapel and prayed several times a day like I had in 2007 when she had her heart surgery. I left several times to eat a TV dinner or feed the dog, but I spent most of the time with her. Carolyn was totally unresponsive. They repeated the process that night. When I came in the next morning the doctors said they had cleared out the passageways but that they were keeping the tube in because she couldn't breathe on her own. However, the nurses showed me how they could temporarily turn off the machine and she was breathing on her own. There was nothing they could do either. The doctors were gods.

I went with her when they took her gurney down to the main floor for tests and procedures and the nurse showed me that they did not have to keep squeezing the air bag because she could breathe on her own. "Why can't you just remove the tube and let her breathe on her own then?"

"Because the doctors have to order it. I shouldn't even be showing you she can breathe."

Later that day, a nurse told me that her urine bag was showing no additional liquid. "I think her kidneys quit working."

When they brought her back to the room, I found one of the doctors and told him she could breathe on her own in the elevator, so why can't you remove the breathing machine.   He said she was unresponsive and couldn't breathe on her own. I said that was not true, ask the nurses. The nurses did not acknowledge anything of course or they would probably get fired. The doctor went into her room, thumped her chest hard and got no reaction and said, "See, if she had any brain activity she would have flinched."

"You just don't know how tough she is. That would hardly make her flinch if she were talking right now. Let me show you. I went up close to the head of the bed, leaned over the rail and loudly said in her ear, "Carolyn, open your eyes." I repeated it again and she opened her eyes but was looking somewhere toward the foot of the bed. I loudly said, "Carolyn, look at me I am beside the bed." She could not turn her head because of the tube in her mouth but rolled her eyes, looked at me, a few tears rolled out of her eyes and then she looked away and closed her eyes."

I was nearly crying when I told the doctor, "See, I told you so."

"That was just a motor reaction, she is brain dead."

"Then why did she tear up?"

"That was because she had her eyes open and it is dry in here, that was not conscious."

I know Carolyn is dying, but how can I give up?

I should mention that we had numerous visitors from our church, Saint John the Devine, Episcopal Church of Sun City Center. Especially our associate minister that I think was there several times a day, every day. He prayed with us daily and about the third day suggested that I move her to another hospital where they would listen to me instead of instantly assuming that she was going to die from the moment she walked into that emergency room. I told him I had already tried and was helpless to do anything. They had the wrong records and would not admit their error.

The nurse talked to the doctor and he asked if they could do a kidney dialysis to try to relieve her kidneys. I said, "Sure, but I told you that you were keeping her asleep too long." Then I referred them to an article from a 2012 study that showed that an induced coma can cause the internals to go into a coma and the kidneys and liver can permanently shut down.

The doctor said they had done this plenty of times and it was not going to happen. The dialysis would relieve pressure on the kidneys and allow them to recover. The dialysis was repeated 3 time over the next two days with the operator of the dialysis machine saying she filtered nothing out the 3rd time.

I stayed most of the night there. That morning a nurse came in to take a blood sample and showed me she could get nothing out of an arm vein and then she asked if I minded if she tried to get some arterial blood. I said go ahead, and the nurse only got clear liquid from the artery and with hardly any volume. I tracked down a doctor and told him she has to have some blood. Since her arm and leg veins and arteries were basically empty they had to install a Picc Line in her chest to inject the blood almost directly into her heart that was still beating. They gave her two units, her hands warmed up from room temperature and they were able to once again get blood samples from her arms. Her iron level was only 7 out of the minimum 12 it should have been.

The doctors were now saying they wanted to install a permanent dialysis port in her chest and do a tractotomy and transfer her to a long term care facility in Tampa 40 miles away. I said, "I thought she could not be transported 6 miles to another hospital when she was doing much better than now and you're telling me you can transport her to a long term care facility in Tampa? I have repeated many times that she does not want to be on life support kept artificially alive."

"We have done all we can do for her. She can't breathe on her own, now her kidney's and liver have shut down. She has been brain dead for a week now. They're going to make you leave this hospital."

How can I come to grips with the fact that she will never again look at me or hold my hand, or talk to me? How can I go on living without her. It is not fair to keep her alive on machines in some long term care facility that both of us said we never ever wanted.

55 It Ended With Thunder

I was faced with having her on full life support 40 miles from my house and slowly dying in a long term care facility or letting her die soon. It had been days since I had gotten a response from her except occasionally open her eyes on command, but she was not seeing anything. Even if I moved to where her eyes were pointing there was no reaction. Her kidneys and liver had been destroyed. Since they were not even getting anything with dialysis they had quit feeding her through the tube so she had no nutrition for three days.

The doctors said she was brain dead but I did not believe it. A technician came to the room, made me leave, and did an encephalogram and said she was brain dead. He showed me the printout that was basically a flatlined brain wave chart with just a few waves at the bottom. He said those were motor functions and not much of them.

The doctors came to me and said she was brain dead, could not breathe on her own, she is in total kidney and liver failure, her bowels are not accepting food. There is no hope for her, but if you want we will send her to our long term care facility in Tampa and keep her heart and lungs going for some more time.

I argued that "When they took her for tests she could breathe on her own every single day when she was not hooked to the machines. I told you not to keep her in a coma and have complained every day."

"She was in terminal COPD when she came to the hospital, we have done all we can."

"No, she didn't have COPD, she was having an allergic reaction. I told you over and over that she had asthma since she was 15 years old and we have been married for 45 years and she has allergy attacks."

"Well, we took her off the meds to keep her sedated 3 days ago and she has not woken up, but then with her whole body failing, that is no surprise. We did an encephalogram and she has no brain activity even without the sedatives."

"Do another encephalogram. I don't believe it."

That night I was told to leave while they did another encephalogram. I left, but then found a corner out of sight and waited until the technician was leaving her room and stopped him. "Well?"

"She is still brain dead."

"You come in here and watch this." I had to pull his arm to get him to come back into her room. He then came without me pulling him and I leaned down close to her ear without touching her or the bed and loudly said, "Carolyn, open your eyes now!"

She did for just a moment. "Did you see that? How can you say she is brain dead?"

"I saw that, but I have to go with and report the results of my test that say there is no brain activity."

....

Okay. Now they are demanding that I either send her to this long term care facility for full life support of give up and remove the life support in the hospital.

"I have been telling you to remove that breathing machine from the start. Are you willing to do it now?"

"Yes, do you want to be in the room. She will die within two minutes after we pull that intubation tube and it will be horrible."

"Yes!"

Carolyn did not die immediately. After 10 minutes went by and she was still breathing and her heart rate did not change I said, "I have been telling you that all along, but you would not believe me. She never needed that machine. All she needed was a shot of epinephrine and some albuterol. She never had COPD, she had asthma all her life and now you have killed her."

"She will quit breathing in thirty minutes to an hour. She can't survive without her kidneys and liver."

"You killed those too with your induced coma. I told you to get her off the sedation from the time you started it. She would have been better off if I had taken her home instead of bringing her here."

The doctors left in a huff. The nurses commiserated with me and treated me nice. Carolyn breathed on her own with no change in blood pressure or oxygen level for 38 hours and then a distant thunderstorm could be heard booming distant thunder if you were outside or near a window. If you were not near a window or outside the thunder was too distant. Then the power went out for just a moment and the emergency generator kicked in.

The nurses said that lightning had hit a transformer a few miles away and power was out on that side of town, but the emergency generator is providing power to most of the hospital except for some overhead lights away from the ICU and other important rooms.

I was sitting near the window holding Carolyn's hand and watching her and the monitors hooked to her. Every so often I would stand close to her, tell her I loved her, and ask her to open her eyes or squeeze my hand or give me some sign, but nothing except her slow breathing. I put cream on her cracked lips from having that breathing tube in her mouth for two weeks. Starting at 42 hours after the removal of the intubation tube and every time I heard distant thunder her oxygen level dropped just a few points and her blood pressure dropped a few points.   After 43 hours it started dropping faster with her breathing getting slow and her blood pressure dropping. After a total of 44 hours her oxygen started dropping rapidly to only 60% and her blood pressure was down to 80 over 30. I knew she was about to die any moment. I stood very close to her, kissed her forehead and lips and said, "Carolyn, I am so sorry I brought you to this hospital but I thought I was saving your life. Your kidneys and liver have failed.   Your blood pressure is dropping. I love you. I will follow your wishes and put you in the Fort Smith National Cemetery and put headstones in my parents' and your parents' graveyards. You can go now. I love you."

There was no reaction, but I as I started to sit still holding her hand tightly she took a big lung full of air. I tried to stop the sitting motion and stand back up but I was overbalanced and my weight carried me on into the chair. Then before I could stand she let the air out in a long sigh. At that moment, exactly 3PM on March 19th, 2016 lightning hit the hospital shaking the entire building like an earthquake, knocking out the emergency generator and knocking out all the lights and monitors in the ICU and the entire hospital. I just sat there holding her hand and through tears looked for any sign of breathing, but there was none. After about two and a half minutes her monitors came back on power and they were flatlined with no sign of life. I waited another few seconds and went out to the nurses station and said, "She's gone."

The computers and monitors at the nurses station were still rebooting and when their monitors for her showed flatlined the nurse got up and checked for any sign of life. Her death was officially called at 3:03 PM.

The nurse asked me if I wanted an autopsy and I said, "Of course. The doctors murdered her and I want to prove it to them. They should have listened to me."

I cried my way out of the hospital and went to the funeral home a few blocks away and said my wife had just died.

I was told it would take 10 days to 2 weeks to get state permission for a cremation and then another 5 days to schedule it for a cremation. Our wills both stated that we wanted cremation. While the funeral home was typing up the paperwork, I looked at a flyer on funeral urns. At the top of the list and the same price as all the other brass urns was a green one. There was no picture of it, but the brochure had pictures of basically plain different colored urns. I said, "I will take that green urn. She started liking green as her favorite color these last few years."

"Do you want to see a picture of it? There should be a color photo in the actual catalog."

"Yeah, I guess so, but that is the only green one the brochure had."

It was not just a plain green and brass urn like all the other urns in that catalog, but had a beautiful almost floral design of forest green that she would have liked on a background of shiny brass. It was the only one with a design like that.

Bottom Line: How would Prince Charming feel if Cinderella and he were kidnapped and Cinderella slowly killed while he was made to watch.

56 The Aftermath

After she died, I had my daughter, Christine, fly from Oklahoma the next day. Carolyn packed up all of Carolyn's clothes and we made 4 trips in the car, with the trunk and the large back seat filled to the windows, out to the women's shelter. I hope some of them can wear size 4 clothing and size 5 ½ shoes. I always called her my Cinderella because of her small shoes. How would Prince Charming have felt if his Cinderella was slowly killed in front of him over a two week period and then told to just forget it? Many time when looking for dress shoes she bought the display item which was the only size 5 ½ shoes in that style. Stores like to have a tiny display size so women will see the shoe as dainty. We gave away three garbage bags of just shoes.

I donated her sewing machine to the sewing club, her small organ to the organ club, her paints and art supplies to the art club or the ceramics club. I hope that either the clubs made good use of all the things or at least sold them to help their clubs instead of throwing them away. I took a piled high pickup load of holiday decorations to the women's shelter for them to sell to raise money for the women's shelter. Carolyn had boxes of decorations for every holiday. I didn't know until this Christmas that Christine had gotten carried away and donated Carolyn's multi-year collection of Santa Clauses and Snowmen. She had a large Rubbermaid box of each of those. I had been buying a new Santa each year for many years, dating back to Europe. Some of the carved wooden ones were only a few inches tall with the largest two feet tall. No two were the same. I didn't want to have given those away, but they are gone now.

Carolyn's cremation was supposed to take 2 weeks to just get permission from the state and another 5 days to get it scheduled with the crematorium, but for some reason, it only took a total of 5 days eliminating the possibility of hiring a private autopsy to prove that the doctors killed her unnecessarily. Why only 5 days instead of the three weeks when I could have had a private autopsy I will never know.

Thank God, literally, Saint John the Devine Episcopal Church in Sun City Center, Florida got a marvelous memorial service for her. I had 140 of my and her friends, not just acquaintances attend the memorial service making it a large service for our town. It could not have been better. The regular minister balked at some of my ideas but Father Lee Miller, the assistant minister that had spent so much time with Carolyn and I in the hospital was marvelous. I had given him a paper on the miracles in my marriage to Carolyn and he worked all of them into his talk and then literally read the Signs from God included as the last chapter of this book. I added more signs from God to the end of this book that occurred after Carolyn's death.

Our audiovisual person played a slideshow prior to the service that played our song, "Unchained Melody" while showing a slide show of Carolyn's photos. Every time they played that song we sang it to each other, I nearly cried with happiness when I was singing it to her, now I sing it crying from sadness. I actually got the legal permission from the writer to use that song when putting that slide show on Facebook https://www.facebook.com/albert.l.clark/videos/vb.114803 5324/10210100682770750/?type=2&theater.

Here is my permission to use the song online:

"Unchained Melody"
Written by Hy Zaret and Alex North
Published by HZUM Publishing (SESAC) and North Melody Publishing (SESAC)
Courtesy of Unchained Melody Publishing LLC
Best,
Abby North

The actual memorial service without the song and slideshow are on Youtube
-htttps://www.youtube.com/watch?v=AnXBdK43RA8.

Christine and I packed up some bags and the dog and drove to Fort Smith, Arkansas where I met with Carolyn's brother and his family. I had made phone arrangements in advance and the Fort Smith National Cemetery could not have been nicer. I also used the phone to arrange for the minister of Saint John's Episcopal Church of Fort Smith, Arkansas to say a few words at her service at the cemetery and the Fort Smith chapter of Eastern Stars (a masonic club for women) to give their memorial ceremony. The Fort Smith Eastern Star chapter had to borrow a lot of Eastern Star people from an Oklahoma chapter. It was a nice service with her urn there for all to see. The national cemetery asked us to leave because another service was coming in right after ours and come back the next day.

The next day when we came back, they had dug a spot for the urn, put in in, and put a temporary marker awaiting the official government headstone that had been ordered.

We drove on to Norman and Christine went back to work and I went looking for houses. I drove around our old neighborhood without finding anything so then drove around other neighborhoods that I had been to that were upscale, but affordable on my income. I went with the realtor I had worked for right after my civil service retirement. The only ones I knew there were the managers and one other whose husband had just been killed in a head-on accident so ended up with a woman I did not know. I had looked at many houses on the computer and they were either already sold or something was wrong with them.

An example is one house was cheaper and looked nice until I saw the back of the house where the yard was about a 30 degree slope and I could see where the carpet against that wall had been very wet more than once. Another house at the upper end of affordable had a 30 degree slope in the front yard. Now Norman, Oklahoma doesn't get much snow but they get ice maybe a total of 7 days a year. If you stepped out the front door or moved a car out of the garage you wouldn't stop until you hit the house across the street.

I found one house that came up for sale in my old neighborhood that I really liked, but after seeing the inside I could tell the carpet was the original put in around 1978 and someone had overhauled a car engine in the living area. The woodwork in the house had never been refinished or the walls painted and looked it. As I was about to give up, I was driving around the neighborhood again and caught a realtor just putting a sign in the front yard. I asked if I could see it and he let me in since the family was not there. It was not perfect, but, by far, the best I found. It was $100,000 more than what I expected my house in Florida to sell for but it was within the upper range of the prices I wanted and had a nearly new wood floor, a new 15X25 foot wood deck in the back, an oversize garage with storage over the garage. The house had 2 master bedroom suites and my daughter needed to get out of the very bad 2 bedroom apartment she was living in so she could take the one behind the garage next to the kitchen and I could take the slightly larger master bedroom suite with the other two bedrooms and spare bath at the other end of the house with the greatroom and dining room separating her end from my end of the house. It is the kind of house Carolyn would have liked and made me feel badly we ever bought that house in Florida that was definitely a step down.

Taking out a 30 year loan would make my monthly payment comparable with the 15 year loan on my Florida house.

I bought the house for the asking price if they would leave the matching stainless steel refrigerator. I think they were very surprised that I did not haggle the price, but I didn't want to spend more time and it was a nice house. I thought about knocking on the door of the house I used to have in the neighborhood and asking if they would sell it, but the house I bought was actually probably better. The only thing missing was a porch and I wanted both an open and a glassed in porch area, but I could have those built (and I did).

I then took the dog and drove back to Florida to put that house for sale. I could have qualified for the new loan even if I still had the Florida house, but I just wanted to get out of Florida. I loved Florida while I was there. I had more friends than I ever had anywhere when I was working. The only thing I did not like was the fact that Carolyn had died there. I had to leave and go back to Norman where my kids, grandchildren and many cousins live. I am also closer to my brother-in-law, Gerald Denson who lives in Arkansas and had made it to the national cemetery memorial. Several of Carolyn's cousins from Fort Smith had also attended.

I put the house up for sale using a realtor I knew from Shriners. I put my 1996 Ford F250 pickup for sale on the internet and got it sold cheaply in three weeks. During that time I was packing boxes for the move to Oklahoma and working with the mortgage company back in Oklahoma using phone, email and the fax machine. It only took hours after the for sale sign before I had a buyer for the Florida house. I sold too cheaply for less than I had paid for the house 11 years earlier, but it looked like everything would be good. I had to get inspections on the house done for the sale and a few things fixed. I filled in all the nail holes from pictures we had all over the walls. I got multiple bids on the move and finally got a good deal with a national mover that was a little higher than the fly-by-night movers that claimed they were famous, but I never heard of them. On June 1st the movers arrived and started carrying my furniture and all the boxes I had packed to their truck. I had taken some very important and valuable things I did not trust the mover with and either put them in my old motor home or in the car. My 15 year old rat terrier dog that had been my father's dog for his first 4 years had gone nearly blind and nearly deft before Carolyn died. He could hear a whistle, but didn't know where it came from. He would nearly bump into me in the house because of his eyesight. Around December of 2015 he lost the hearing and eyesight and started to have occasional seizures resulting from diabetes for the last 4 years. Pretty amazing, considering. We had been regulars at the dog park and I did not know of any other dogs that lasted more than a year after starting insulin. Poor Domino had been taking 10 units of insulin morning and night for over 4 years. That is more than most humans take. At any rate, not long before they got the truck loaded, Domino had a major seizure far worse than any previous seizure. His first seizures Carolyn and I were in the kitchen when we heard him screaming. We went into the laundry room and he was beside his water bowl and could only scream and move his eyes. His body was frozen. I patted him and rubbed him and he came out of it ready to play. The seizures had become more frequent, but he was easily brought out of it. This one went on for over 5 minutes before he came out of it and then all he could do was lay there limply and pant with his tongue hanging out. All I could think about with Domino was that he had been getting progressively worse for 3 months and now I was facing a 2-3 day drive with a dog that might have a major seizure while I was driving in traffic and then die with me not knowing what to do with a dead dog in the car. He was my last friend and I had planned on taking him with me. Instead I took him to the vet to have him euthanized. All the way there he just laid where I had put him laying on the front seat limp with his tongue hanging out and breathing heavy. Then I drove back to watch the movers finish up. I had left a few pieces of furniture to include a daybed and trundle my daughter had in her small bedroom in high school and we used in the computer room as an emergency bedroom in Florida. I slept there and took off driving in the morning.

When I left for Oklahoma, Carolyn's headstone had not been placed in the Fort Smith, Arkansas National Cemetery, but they thought it had arrived. I said it would be great if it was there when I came through Fort Smith on Sunday and it was. I found a florist and put flowers there and cried on her headstone and put my arms around it and took photos.

I signed the paperwork taking possession of my house in Norman the day before the mover arrived on June 7th, 2016. I used the phone and internet to arrange design and order headstones for Carolyn and I to be placed in the Clark cemetery in Oklahoma (Muncie officially near Seiling, Oklahoma) and in the Liberty Cemetery near Greenwood Arkansas where Carolyn's parents and grandparents were. Both of those are shiny black granite with engraving on both sides. On the back of both headstones it says, in part, "Our Romance Began with a Flash of Lightning and Ended with Boom of Thunder" They both have my name as well as hers. In the national cemetery my name and dates will be on the backside of the stone that has her name and date.

57 SIGNS FROM GOD
Miracles Still Occur Around Us

- I think I first saw her when we were both 12. It was love at first sight, but I never got to talk to her or know her name or where she was from. She was at California Disney Land at the same time I was. I remember a very blond very small girl arguing with an older brother about him taking her on the Mad Hatter Ride. Years after we were married she mentioned the fight at Disney and I always wondered if I had seen her then.
- Lightening brought us together. We were both 26 years old and the only two people outside watching the lightening when I saw her for the first time and suggested we get married.
- We had a near perfect marriage.
- We adopted two kids, a boy and a girl, both blue eyed like Carolyn with birthdays near Christmas. Carolyn, Craig, and Christine all have the initials CAC. Both were quick free adoptions. Craig, only 3 months after application when we were told it would be 3-5 years. We got Craig when he was only 3 weeks old and had to stop by SEARS as it was getting dark to buy a crib, clothing, everything. The clerks thought we must be really poor planners until we told them and then they pitched in

recommending things or telling us we didn't really need that. Christine came pretty quick after we found the same agency in Ohio.

- We showed up with our van and a tent at the Grand Canyon after it got dark and were told to forget it we needed reservations a year ago. I went into the campground to turn around and a college kid ran out and told us they had reserved several campsites and didn't know they were so big so we could have one of theirs by paying them the standard camping fee. Everywhere we went we had that kind of "luck". Why make reservations when God is watching out for you.

- I retired for a second time in 2004. In early 2005 her brother-in-law died and my father died. She had spent many hours helping my father until I retired in 2004, then it was my job to watch out for him in an assisted living near our house. A few days after he died, I got a job offer to come back to work here in Florida near her newly widowed sister in Fort Myers. Providence?

- A few weeks before her trip to the ER.
  o I had dreams where we were on a cruise ship and went to separate food lines in the cafeteria and then I could not find her and went around the whole ship in a panic until I woke and she was beside me. This was a recurring dream several different nights that made no sense.
  o My son dreamed I pulled up in the motor home this next summer and he didn't see Mom. When he asked where she was I

looked over at the passenger seat and got confused and said to him "I don't know". Then he would wake up. This was his recurring dream about when I had mine.

- About 3 days before she died:
  - ○ Craig was in Oklahoma and spoke to her as if she could hear him in the hospital in Florida and the rain quit just in the spot where he was and the sun came out and then started raining again. As he went across town this happened three times. That evening he was in the house and mentioned this miracle to his friend and the sun came out. The rest of daylight hours were cloud covered with light rain.
  - ○ Carolyn's brother and his wife were admiring the flowers on a redbud tree when a sudden gust of strong wind came from nowhere and stripped off the flowers and deposited almost every one on their balcony. Then the wind died again leaving the tree bare.
  - ○ I had come home for a few minutes and was on my way back to the hospital in my golf cart and a 1 inch white fluffy feather, like from a woman's boa, or an angle's wing blew in from somewhere and hit the bridge of my glasses and then hovered behind the windshield of the golf cart. I immediately thought of Carolyn and reached for the feather, but it suddenly blew on out the right side of the golf cart and disappeared. I stopped and looked, but nothing was

moving anywhere in sight. I think that was her spirit passing. Technically she was still alive, but that feather was from her angel wings. Three days later it was official.

- The day she died:
  - ○ There was distant thunder, but the hospital went to emergency power so most things were working, except for overhead lights, televisions, the public bathrooms and probably some other non-essential areas. The thunder could not be heard unless you were near a window or outside.
  - ○ With each distant thunder her blood pressure dropped 10-15 points. I was holding her hand when it dropped to 25 beats per minute and the end was imminent. I was crying as I leaned down close to her ear and said, "I love you Carolyn, but it is okay to go. I will see you in heaven." Keep in mind that the EEG had said she was gone two days in a row. I sat back down holding her hand. She took in a very large intake of breath and sighed it out. There was a second of silence while I waited for another breath, then a loud boom of thunder that felt like an earthquake and heard throughout the hospital knocking out the hospital emergency generator. It took about 2 and a half minutes for the generator to restart and her monitors showed flat lined. I waited a few seconds waiting for another breath I knew would not come and then

after a couple of seconds staring at the flat-lined monitors, I went to the nursing station just outside her door and said, "She's gone." Their equipment was just then rebooting and they saw the flat line and went into her room to verify.

- o I had repeated several times to her in the hospital how wonderful it was for that lightning storm to bring us together. I had brought in a photo from our cruise the week before coming to the hospital with printing below explaining how we met in a lightning storm. That photo page had been in her room for about the last 10 days, so I know with a certainty that was a sign from God that she was with him now.

- o When I called my son to tell him she had died, a blue jay, highlighted by direct sunlight landed on the windowsill and looked in at him as I was talking then flew away highlighted by the sun. The blue jay is perfect for her, brightly colored, pretty, but feisty. A blue jay will attack a cat getting too close to its nest and they can be very brightly colored, not like the scrub jays we got in Florida.

- Saturday

- o My son was telling me on the phone that I should not blame myself, it was her time and God's will after having a good life with me. What appeared to be the same blue jay he had only seen that one other time landed on a branch ten feet away from him and looked at him for about 20 seconds while he was telling me and then flew away.

- I was telling my daughter about this when a red cardinal landed on a supporting bar for the awning near her and then hopped down onto the little one inch wide outside window sill next to my daughter and looked in at her for about 20 seconds. We both just stared.

God not only spoke to us, he yelled loudly. What more signs do you want?

But the signs continued.

- Only 3 days after she died she came to me in a dream and told me she still loved me but it was the flowers in the Publix Grocery Store that had caused all of her allergy attacks since we moved to Florida. I was holding her tightly when I woke up. I rolled over to touch her thinking the whole hospital episode was just a bad dream, but she wasn't there and the hospital had not been the bad dream, but a true nightmare.

- During her memorial service at Saint John the Devine Episcopal Church in Sun City Center, Florida a red cardinal landed on a tree limb behind the minister and just stayed there. A lot of people saw the bird as it was the only thing besides the tree limbs through the clear two story tall windows behind the alter. It moved a few times, but stayed in sight and seemed to be looking in. There were 140 people at her memorial and I am not sure who saw the bird, but my son, Craig, and her 50 year old niece, Missy both saw it. Several of my friends had also seen it and wondered about it.

- During the memorial service for the interment of her ashes in the Fort Smith, Arkansas National Cemetery, a cardinal again showed up landing inside the shelter on the temporary alter while that Episcopal minister was speaking. During the Eastern Star memorial part of the service they were using the alter, but the cardinal landed on a headstone just outside the shelter.

- When we got to the hotel in Fort Smith after the memorial service at the national cemetery, the parking lot seemed full, but a cardinal landed in the parking lot just feet in front of our car and then hopped and flew and hopped and flew again into the one remaining parking space that happened to be near the back door near our room, then it flew out of sight.

- My son was having a very rough time in his life. He always had a temper, but when back in Norman, Oklahoma, every time his temper flared up a Blue Jay would land within feet of him on a tree limb a piece of yard furniture or whatever was close and screech at him.

- Anytime he was outside and trying to decide something either a red cardinal or the bluejay would land nearby. When he acknowledged it and said mom it would just look at him. This happened over and over. One really good example was when he was sitting with a friend on the back patio in lawn chairs trying to make a decision and he was telling his friend about the birds he kept seeing. The friend said, "Like that one that just landed on the Bar B Que grill 4 feet away?" "Mom, is that you? Where is the blue jay." With that the cardinal flew away and the blue jay actually landed on the small patio table between their lawn chairs and scolded at him as only a blue jay can. "Okay, Mom. I know which decision I need to make."

- Another time he was outside arguing with his girlfriend of 19 years and the blue jay landed on a branch less than 5 feet away and screeched at him. Tonya said, "Listen to your mom and settle down." "Okay, Mom, I'll settle down."

- A few weeks later Tonya was talking to Craig on the telephone. They had made a decision about their oldest son, but Tonya was getting cold feet and was about to backdown. That was why she called Craig. A cardinal landed on the windowsill next to her and pecked at the window. "My God! It's your mom. A cardinal is sitting on the windowsill looking at me. When I didn't pay attention it pecked at the window and is still there. Okay, Mom, I won't back down and I'll do what I agreed to." The cardinal pecked at the window again and flew away.

- When I moved into my house in Norman, Oklahoma I had a cardinal greet me by landing on the railing to the deck behind the house only feet from where I was sitting. I put up a bird feeder, but the squirrels ate the food and chased away the cardinals. Maybe next spring.

- I finally got around to unpacking everything in my master bed room. I looked around and saw all the boxes gone, the drawers closed, the bed made, the lamps on the side tables, the photographs on the walls and was thinking, "I wish Carolyn was here, she would have liked this room." With that I went toward the bathroom to brush my teeth and stepped on something small and hard at the foot of the bed. It was a small white dove label pin. I thought how fitting, picked it up and went into the bathroom where I took off my wedding ring, and placed it next to the wall size mirror behind the left hand sink nearest the door and then placed the label pin in the wedding right where I would be reminded of her. I then brushed my teeth and stepped out of the bathroom and went to the chest of drawers to place my watch there. I stepped on a US flag label pin like the Presidential candidates wore. I placed it next to my wedding ring that held the dove angled to see it.

- She has 3 headstones also engraved with my name. The last one was placed in the Liberty Cemetery near Greenwood, Arkansas in October 2016. The workers had left leaving me alone to grieve over her death. I was standing back from the headstone when I vaguely notice a flock of about 20 geese coming my way and ignored them suddenly I heard the geese honking and looked up, they were coming right for me like they were going to land all around me. They came over low enough that I ducked, at the last minute they climbed to get over the tree I had parked by and then seemed to fly away. Then just as I was about to look away I saw them turning almost out of vision. They flew in a huge circle and were approaching from the original direction. This time they were higher and did not have to climb as they came over the tree. Then they started the huge circle again. This time I got my camera out and they approached from that same original direction again. This time I got a couple of photos of them before they continued out of sight. Three passes for the third headstone set in her honor.

- I had another realistic dream of her where we were together until I realized it couldn't be her because I saw her last breath.

- About the same time Craig, her son, was waiting for his alarm to go off and dreamed he was driving by one of her and her sisters favorite stores when a cardinal dive bombed his windshield. He was afraid he hit it so he pulled into the parking lot of that store to see if there was a hurt cardinal. As he was getting out of his car he thought he saw Mom and Shirley walking into Kohl's so he closed his door and headed for the door to the store. He looked for them, but couldn't find them. As he was giving up because he must have been dreaming he heard Mom talking to Shirley and tried following the voice to find them. He could never catch up, they were always one department over. He then didn't care whether he disturbed other shoppers but started yelling "Mom" but they couldn't hear him. Then he couldn't hear them any longer and couldn't find them so he left. He went out looking for the cardinal he thought might have hit his car, then got in the car and started to drive away. As he was entering the main road he looked back and there was Mom and Shirley at the door to Kohl's waving goodbye. He was going to turn around and go back when his alarm went off waking him up. He was embarrassed telling me his story, but he and I felt that Mom and Shirley were in heaven doing whatever they wanted to do, just as if they were alive and watching us, but could not communicate and vise versa.

- As he told me this story I had to wonder if heaven is where people are young and healthy again and just go about what they enjoyed doing on earth. Shopping in Kohl's with her sister is something she would enjoy. Do they just live here around us seeing what we do and go about their way waiting for us to join them, but cannot speak to us. Surely they can hear us. If heaven is not being married to her again and carefree and healthy like when we first married, I don't have anything else I want in heaven. Was I in heaven for the last 46 years and will never get back to that.

It was my first Christmas without her and I had gotten no signs from her for months, but Christmas night I saw her with the kids and grandkids. She looked at me and smiled. Before I could do anything, she disappeared, the spot where she was standing was empty and no one else had seen her standing between them, then I woke up.

It was a love made by God that started with lightning and ended with thunder. I will miss her until I join her in heaven someday. at least I hope I do.

Every night, several times every evening I look at the stars and say a prayer aimed at Carolyn and God, "Star Light, Star Bright, all the stars I see tonight (there are always more than one star) I wish I may I wish I might get the wish I wish tonight. I wish that Carolyn is healthy, and whole (without her metal joints and repaired heart), and happy, and strong in heaven with her sister, her parents and my parents, and all the people she liked that have gone to heaven, but still loves me and misses me and wishes we could be together and forgives me for all the things I did wrong, or said wrong, and I pray that when I die, we will be together as husband and wife again where I can hug and kiss her, and talk with her, and just be with her, and have our adventures again."

If it is cloudy I change it to "...all the stars I don't see tonight..."

ABOUT THE AUTHOR

The Author spent over 39 years with the United States Air Force in the USA, Asia, and Europe. He had some part in the development of most of the new weapons system in development between 1979 and 1989. Some of those systems are just now being delivered. He taught classes in weapons system research and development and logistics management as a guest lecturer and substitute professor at the Air Force Institute of Technology and various conference rooms around the USA. Over 3000 current and future managers attended his class on R&D scheduling. He served on many brain storming teams to come up with unique solutions to military problems from shooting down space objects to moving "dud" bombs off an active runway.

When think groups got stalled, I was asked to step in. Some of these groups were headed by general officers and the attendees were all full colonels and GS-15's or SES's. I would get a few hours to review the problem they had spent weeks locked in some conference room looking for a solution. In less than 24 hours I had studied the issue and developed some briefing charts on the issue and my recommendation. The think group always took my suggestion and went back to their regular jobs in no more than 2 days.

He is now retired from both active duty and civil service. He is still active in writing, the local amateur radio club, traveling and writing books.

"I don't think I could ever find anyone like Carolyn and don't know if it is worth even trying for female companionship again.

Made in the USA
San Bernardino, CA
27 January 2017